'HEELICOPTER'
PIONEERING WITH
IGOR SIKORSKY

'HEELICOPTER'
PIONEERING WITH
IGOR SIKORSKY

BASED ON A PERSONAL ACCOUNT BY
WILLIAM E. HUNT

Airlife

England

Photo and Illustration Credits
U/T = United Technologies; S/A = Sikorsky Archives;
H/P = Hunt – Personal.
Page Nos.: 8 – H/P; 10 – U/T; 12 – U/T; 14 – S/A; 15 – H/P; 16 – H/P;
19 – S/A; 20 – S/A; 24 – S/A; 25 – U/T; 26 – U/T; 27 – U/T; 28 – U/T;
30 – U/T; 31 – U/T; 32 – U/T; 34 – H/P; 35 – H/P; 36 – H/P; 38 – H/P;
39 – H/P; 41 – U/T, Drwg. – H/P; 43 – H/P; 44 – H/P; 45 – U/T;
46 – H/P; 47 – H/P; 49 – U/T; 51 – H/P; 51 – U/T; 52 – Luscombe;
53 – U/T; 54 – H/P; 55 – H/P; 56 – U/T; 57 – H/P; 58 – H/P; 59 – H/P;
60 – U/T; 61 – U/T; 63 – U/T; 65 – U/T; 66 – U/T; 67 – U/T; 69 – U/T;
70 – U/T; 72 – H/P; 73 – H/P; 76 – H/P; 78 – H/P; 80 – H/P; 81 – H/P;
82 – H/P; 83 – H/P; 85 – H/P; 86 – H/P; 88 – U/T; 89 – U/T; 90 – H/P;
92 – U/T; 94 – H/P; 95 – U/T; 96 – U/T; 97 – H/P; 100 – U/T,
Drwg. – H/P; 103 – U/T; 104 – H/P; 105 – U/T; 107 – H/P; 108 – H/P;
109 – H/P; 112 – H/P; 114 – U/T; 116 – U/T; 118 – H/P; 119 – H/P;
120 – H/P; 121 – H/P; 123 – U/T; 124 – U/T; 126 – U/T; 127 – U/T;
129 – U/T; 131 – U/T; 132 – U/T; 134 – H/P; 138 – U/T; 140 – H/P;
141 – H/P; 142 – H/P; 147 – U/T; 149 – U/T; 150 – H/P; 151 – U/T &
H/P; 153 – U/T & H/P; 155 – U/T; 159 – U/T & H/P; 160 – H/P;
162 – H/P; 163 – U/T; 166 – U/T; 170 – H/P; 172 – U/T; 174 – U/T;
175 – H/P; 177 – Luscombe H/P49; 178 – Luscombe H/P49; 180 – U/T;
185 – U/T; 188 – H/P; 189 – Vertiflite; 192 – U/T; 193 – U/T;
194 – H/P; 195 – H/P; 197 – H/P; 199 – H/P; 200 – U/T; 201 – H/P;
203 – U/T; 204 – U/T; 206 – H/P; 211 – H/P; 215 – U/T; 216 – U/T;
217 – U/T; 218 – U/T; 219 – U/T; 220 – U/T; 222U/T

First published in the UK in 1998
by Airlife Publishing Ltd

British Library Cataloguing-in-Publication Data
A catalogue record for this book is available from
the British Library

ISBN 1 85310 768 9

Typeset by Phoenix Typesetting,
Ilkley, West Yorkshire.
Printed and bound in Great Britain by
The Bath Press, Bath

Airlife Publishing Ltd
101 Longden Road, Shrewsbury,
SY3 9EB, England

Dedicated to everyone else who took part in this account.

Dear Reader,
Should you come to a 'dry area'
Please do not dismay,
There is an 'Oasis' just ahead.

NOTE:-
Igor's pronunciation of helicopter actually
sounded more like 'HEELICOOPTUR'

About
William E. Hunt

It is interesting to note, that there is a growing body of books and articles about the development of Sikorsky helicopters. However, none of them can lay claim to have been written by the engineer who worked with Igor Sikorsky on his experimental VS-300 helicopter, as was the case with Bill Hunt. He lived with the machine in those early days, so aptly described by another member of that pioneering group, as the 'period of crystal ball, and educated guess'.

When they started, the concept of a single-main-lifting rotor helicopter, with a small tail rotor to control torque, was considered to be impractical, if not impossible.

In some two brief – but brilliant – years, that pioneering group had solved, with VS-300, the basic problems associated with the single-main-rotor type helicopter. Those corrections were incorporated into both the XR-4 and XR-5 models. As with VS-300, Bill Hunt was both the designer and Project Engineer for both models. The production R-5 would grow into the S-51, the first Sikorsky commercial, four-place helicopter.

Consequently, there is no doubt in my mind, that Bill Hunt is very well qualified to record the saga of 'Heelicopter' Pioneering with Igor I. Sikorsky.

Sergei Sikorsky
Stratford, Connecticut

22 March 1996

SIKORSKY AIRCRAFT

DIVISION OF UNITED AIRCRAFT CORPORATION

BRIDGEPORT I, CONNECTICUT

May 6, 1947

Mr. William E. Hunt
The Cottage
Brooklyn, Conn.

Dear Bill:

I learned with great interest about your coming trip to the Argentine and the important position which you will occupy there.

Knowing the fine work you did here and the vast experience you have in connection with helicopters, particularly with the design of the R-5, I am sure that you will do a good and successful job in your new position. The S-51, being a commercial version of the original R-5, which was constructed under your direct supervision, will therefore be very familiar to you.

I would indeed be very glad to be of any assistance in furthering your plans and in particular I suggest that you do not hesitate to give my name as reference to any individual or organization who would like to secure more detailed information concerning your qualifications and experience.

With best wishes for success in your new position and with kindest personal regards, I am

Sincerely yours,

I. I. Sikorsky
Engineering Manager

IIS:CB

According to Mr Labensky, at the time that this letter was written, it was the first letter of recommendation that Mr Sikorsky had written in some 25 years.

I was then negotiating with the Argentine Government in regard to my heading up the technical administration team regarding the S-51s they were planning to buy from United Aircraft Corp. for the locust control programme then contemplated. Which, in the event, did not materialize.

Preface

I believe it is fitting, as we read about the successful aerial achievements of others, that we remind ourselves of all those other magnificent attempts and failures, not to mention the lives lost, of those who had the courage and daring to actually teach themselves how to successfully fly their own creations, in what they then believed to be a practical solution for the safe transportation of humans.

Of such was Igor I. Sikorsky, with the extraordinary achievement of not only so doing, during his early efforts with the first fixed-wing aeroplane he had created at the age of 21, but to yet again repeat the same achievement with the rotating-winged helicopter at the age of 52!

In Russia, when only 24 years old, he had designed, piloted and successfully demonstrated in 1914, the first ever large, four-engined civil air transport in the world, on the very eve of the first great World War. When redesigned, it became the first formidable armed bomber of that war. Abhoring war, that success, being of necessity, was not entirely to his liking.

Curiously, 26 years later in 1939, eleven days after the Second World War began, Igor Sikorsky briefly, but successfully, piloted the lift-off of the progenitor of a world-wide successful series of helicopters, that also first saw duty as military aircraft, rather than civil aircraft. They did nevertheless, in the event mercifully, save many lives.

But before all that could happen, the process of getting to recognize and understand the cause of each problem, before being able to solve it, that is the basis for the following account.

Acknowledgements

On the 6th of July 1989, I wrote a letter to Igor Sikorsky Jr., acquainting him with my past association with his father, that I was in the process of gathering material to write a personal account of same, and asking him if he would be willing to help me with it. His prompt reply was most kind and generous. Ever since then, his help and interest has been unfailing. Including his arranging to have Harry Woodman, an acknowledged authority on Igor Sikorsky's aviation career in Russia, to kindly check my account of the same period.

To Mary S. Lovell, the author of the biographies of the aviation careers of Beryl Markham, and Amelia Earhart, both international "best sellers", who took so generously of her time to critically review my first manuscript efforts, in a strictly professional manner, but ending with the unqualified encouragement to continue my efforts, as my story was well worth its telling, and in the style I had chosen.

To David C. Burnham, Headmaster of two-hundred years old Moses Brown School, in Providence, Rhode Island, U.S.A. An ex-Colonel of the United States Marine Corps; John Davies, retired International News Correspondent of the Australian State Consolidated Press, with Headquarters in Sydney, was in charge of their U.S. News Bureau Headquarters in New York, during the 1940s; Paul Amundsen, author and recognized Consultant on Marine Port Management; Edward Katzenberger, Chief Engineer of The Sikorsky Aircraft Division of United Aircraft (United Technologies Corp.); Jack Bornstein, professional aeroplane pilot; and Hilda Perkins, for their much appreciated, and greatly needed, diverse comments and suggestions, as the account progressed; also to E. Brie for constant encouragement and interest from the very beginning. Finally, to the Managing Staff of Airlife Publishing Limited, whose generous patience and encouragement made possible this publication.

Contents

Fig 1
The Sikorsky SH-2 at Sikorsky's home in Kiev.
This last model made several uncontrolled hops
before crashing. (This copy made from original
photo taken by Michael Buivid)

Chapter One
1908 to 1939

From Rotating Wings to Fixed Wings
– to Rotating Wings

While this foreword to my following personal account may seem rather lengthy, I feel it is very necessary, to enable the reader to appreciate what took place in Igor Sikorsky's later life, through the years 1938 to 1946 next to the quiet little New England town of Stratford in the state of Connecticut, USA. That is where the Sikorsky Division of the then United Aircraft Corporation (now United Technologies) was located, and he was Engineering Manager.

In so doing I shall draw together once more, alas almost entirely in spirit, those of us who had the honour and privilege of being directly associated with Igor Sikorsky in helping him create the world's first successful vertical-lifting, single-main-rotor-type helicopter. For him it was to be the culmination of an extraordinarily diverse and creative life. But first let me tell you about the initial failure then and the remarkable successes he had in his native Russia.

Igor's first serious interest in aviation was focused on the potential of the then little-known helicopter. He saw this as the next logical generation of heavier-than-air aircraft because it eliminated the necessity of the long take-off and landing runs at relatively high speeds associated with fixed-wing aircraft.

During 1908, at the age of 19, Igor had designed a co-axial helicopter (with one rotor contrarotating above the other to negate torque), and by so doing had thus decided to make aviation his future career. In January 1909, seeking further information regarding helicopters, he went with parental blessing to Paris, France, which was then considered the most advanced centre of aviation with regard to aircraft engines, structures and aerodynamics. He first sought out a certain Capt. Ferdinand Ferber, who was considered to be one of the top authorities on aeronautical matters. He told the captain that he had come to Paris to study the latest developments in aviation and to purchase a suitable engine to power the helicopter he had designed. Ferber replied that Igor should not waste his time on helicopters, but instead concentrate his energies on designing and building an aeroplane, and added: 'To invent a flying machine is nothing, to build it is little, but to test it is everything'. Igor never forgot this sage remark, as will be noted later on. At the captain's suggestion he enrolled in a course of study at Port-Aviation at Juvisy, where he was able to examine various types of aeroplanes. Witnessing at first hand both successful and unsuccessful attempts to fly forewarned him of the danger of expecting immediate success, without failures.

On his return to Kiev in April, Igor took with him a 25 hp Anzani air-cooled motorcycle engine, various types of metal aircraft fittings, a great many magazines and papers on aviation, and his now first-hand basic knowledge of aircraft structures. However, in spite of Capt. Ferber's suggestion to the contrary, Igor decided to build the helicopter (SH-1) he had already designed, working alone during May and June 1909.

This first machine was unpiloted and lacked any system of remote control. It was unable to lift itself off, due to either inefficient lifting rotors or lack of power, or a combination of both (450 lb/25 hp, a power loading of 18 lb/hp was high).

The second machine, 50 lb lighter with new blades, made only short uncontrolled hops before it crashed. Unable to find sufficient additional information on helicopter design, Igor reluctantly turned his attention to the non-rotating fixed-wing aeroplane, as he felt he had acquired sufficient basic engineering information on his Paris trip to design a well established type of biplane.

Here we find the basic philosophy adopted by Igor, and that was to avoid short-cuts. He was one of the most fearless persons I have known, yet when he decided to teach himself how to fly the first aeroplane he designed, he did so in a series of distinctly progressive steps, still very much resembling her sister the S-3, except that *she* was powered. The very important role played by Igor's older sister, Olga, throughout this early era must be mentioned. Not only did she provide the continual encouragement that was so necessary, but she also gave financial help

The S-1 was the first step. These first homebuilt aircraft of Igor's were built with the aid of his youthful and mechanically skilled neighbour, Michael Buivid, of whom much will be related in due course. This first aeroplane was purposely designed not to fly, for Igor's vivid memory of the many ground-manoeuvring accidents at aerodromes around Paris prompted him first to master the skill required to control the aircraft on the ground, at speeds needed for both take-off and landing. This was accomplished by using a little engine of only 15 hp, mounted behind the pilot and turning a pusher propeller. This arrangement not only prevented the pilot from being thrown forward into the propeller in the event of under-

carriage failure, but also provided him with a clear field of vision, while the insufficient wing area precluded a possible inadvertent take-off.

During this period of partial 'plane destruction, Igor and Michael spent as much time repairing S-1

Fig 3   *S-2, 25 hp, with Igor Sikorsky ready to take off, while V. S Panasiuk holds up the incomplete tail section which lacked proper bracing. Two others who also helped Igor were F.I. Blynkin and V.V. Iodin.*

as did Igor manoeuvring it, until it finally reached the point where the entire structure was in danger of collapsing. So S-1, having accomplished her main purpose, was dismantled.

The S-2 was an entirely new design with a 25 hp engine located on the forward central portion of the lower wing, in front of the pilot, turning a tractor propeller. The wing area had been increased to allow free flight, and a more rugged undercarriage was fitted. The photograph of the S-2 shows Igor seated as though ready to take off, or perhaps in his mind's eye flying into the blue yonder, though Panasiuk, standing towards the end of the tail structure, is helping to hold it up, as it is still incomplete. At this stage, according to Michael, Igor was so anxious to get a feeling of his latest creation that he had to have a picture taken.

With the S-2 Igor was able to make a number of successful and ever longer straight hops. However, it was obvious, from the required length of take-off run, that it was underpowered, which finally resulted in an undercarriage failure. Fortunately Igor was not seriously injured.

Fig 2   *Sikorsky S-1, 15 hp ground trainer. Note Hands are busy, as well as his feet. Right hand to rear elevator (back-and-forth) left hand to lower wing ailerons (side-to-side). Both feet to control rudder at tail. Fuel tank to his right with fuel line to engine. 'Pusher' propeller and engine behind him, used only on S-1.*

The S-3 had a 35 hp engine and increased upper wing span. Igor was now able to make sustained straight forward flights of up to several minutes with greater assurance of control. The take-off distances were also becoming more realistic. Progress was slow, but Igor was gaining increasing confidence in both his engineering and his piloting ability.

Finally, in the spring of 1911, the S-4 was wheeled out for its maiden flight. It very much resembled the S-3, except that she was powered by a new German aircraft engine, a water-cooled Argus developing 50 hp. At last Igor was able to take off in a longer distance, and for the first time he could make a circuit of his flying field, executing shallow banked turns. By now he was attracting the attention of the military, as he was on the verge of piloting a practical flying machine. There was just one more step to take, and that resulted in the final model of the series.

On 17 May 1911 the S-5 was ready for take-off. The only significant change was the addition of ailerons to the lower wingtips to improve the rate and degree of lateral control. After several short test-hops to accustom himself to the new control response, Igor took off for what turned out to be his longest flight to date, demonstrating good control and stability throughout a series of turns with varying degrees of lateral tilting to the left and right with increasing dexterity. He was obviously rejoicing in his final attainment of controlled free flight, and it was also most rewarding for Michael Buivid to witness the S-4 flying safely over 50 mph.

Igor was soon making half-hour cross-country flights in various weather conditions at altitudes up to 1,500 ft, with the 50 hp Argus engine giving troublefree performance. During the succeeding weeks he accumulated the solo flying hours necessary for him to obtain Pilot's Licence No. 64, which he received on 8 August 1911 from L'Aero Club Imperial de Russie. This led to him being invited to take part in the Imperial Army manoeuvres near his home in Kiev, which in turn resulted in the additional honour of being presented to Tsar Nicholas II. Igor was the first Russian to have designed, built, test flown, and developed a practical aeroplane in which he was allowed to obtain his licence, and the quality of his workmanship was such that the Imperial Army had invited him to participate in their manoeuvres. All of this had been accomplished in 18 months, Igor having attained the ripe

old age of 22! By the end of September 1911 he had successfully demonstrated the S-5 at a number of air shows at Kiev and Kharkov, which established his reputation as a capable designer and pilot.

Igor was now eager to enter his next phase of endeavour, aircraft manufacturing. By now he had a number of friends and helpers assisting him, and he felt confident that he could design and build a larger, more modern competitive aircraft, to carry a pilot and two passengers at a reasonable cruising speed over a good range. This he did during the winter of 1911–1912, creating the S-6, powered by a 100 hp water-cooled Argus engine. The initial flight tests showed a need to increase lift, and by adding outer panels to the upper wings the machine became the S-6a. For the first time Igor incorporated a slender, fully-covered fuselage to reduce air resistance, and the S-6a could cruise at 70 mph fully loaded. The further modified S-6b took first prize at a Russian military competition at Moscow in 1912, and Igor's aviation career was officially launched.

Recognition brought almost instant reward. Igor was asked by M. V. Shidlovsky, the director of the Russo-Baltic Wagon Company (BWC), one of the largest industrial firms, to join the company, which manufactured not only railway rolling stock, motorcars and agricultural machinery, but had recently opened up a small aircraft division at St Petersburg. The contract offered to Igor gave the company the exclusive rights to manufacture the S-6b and any subsequent designs. He would be chief engineer and designer of the new division, with the freedom to continue his 'S' series and to create new experimental aircraft, and would receive a substantial salary and royalties from all of his designs that were produced. What was perhaps more important to Igor, however, was that he would be able to bring in and expand his faithful group of engineers, mechanics and skilled shop personnel. One can well understand the eagerness and thrill with which he signed that contract.

No sooner had Igor and his team set up their new facilities in St Petersburg during the spring of 1912 than they produced the first of four monoplanes, the two-seat S-7. It was quickly followed by the S-9, a two-seat trainer powered by a radial engine. Both of these were S-6b variants. There is no record of an S-10, but in the spring of 1913 the S-12, an improved S-11 took first prize at a military competition against similar types of French aircraft,

Fig 4 *St. Petersburg, 13 May 1913. The Grand makes her original debut with Igor Sikorsky pilot, Capt. Alechnovich co-pilot, and V. Panasiuk flight mechanic (seen on front balcony) as she steadily climbs to 600ft after a smooth take-off.*

and the S-11 took second prize. This proved to be the benchmark for Russian military acceptance of Sikorsky-designed aircraft. Incidentally, the S-12 was the first Russian aeroplane to loop.

However, as early as the late summer of 1912 Igor's active and imaginative mind began to formulate his next quantum step towards what he conceived to be the real future of aviation. This was the aerial transportation of both passengers and goods by means of large heavier-than-air aircraft, rather than the vastly more cumbersome lighter-than-air craft being built by Count Zeppelin in Germany for the same purpose. On the fateful evening of the 17 September 1912, Igor presented his carefully prepared thoughts to his host, M. V. Shidlovsky, who by now, as chairman of the

Russo-Baltic Wagon Co, was also Igor's chief backer.

After listening intently for several hours to Igor's detailed proposal, Shidlovsky said without hesitation that he was in complete agreement, and that he would issue orders for the immediate commencement of the new project. This was like sailing in uncharted coastal waters, not knowing what real dangers lay ahead. The two men made the decision with courage and deep respect for each other's integrity; one with the sagacity of much experience, and the other with the eagerness of a youth of 23 facing a new and exciting challenge.

Igor's original data was so complete that *The Grand*, as this seemingly huge aeroplane was dubbed, with a wingspan of 90 ft and a length of 60 ft, was ready for its first test flight within six months. It was cleverly built, as several major subassemblies which could be readily transported and reassembled at the Komendantski airfield near St Petersburg.

The entire fuselage structure was covered with plywood to improve structural rigidity, and there was a unique outside observation balcony just in front of, and accessible from, the main cabin. For the first time ever, the pilot and copilot were located side-by-side in the front of the completely enclosed main passenger cabin, which had exceptionally large windows. Not surprisingly, the cabin interior resembled a Russo-Baltic first-class railway compartment, with electric lighting, curtains, four lounge seats, a table and a small sofa. To the rear of the cabin was a washroom and wardrobe. Such a degree of operational and passenger comfort was completely novel in aviation.

In a characteristic initial step-by-step approach to a first flight test, Igor had carefully calculated that, if he left off two of the four 100 hp Argus engines, and had minimum fuel and just himself aboard to keep the all-up weight of *The Grand* to a minimum, he could safely take off. This he cautiously accomplished, and after making several such take-offs and landings he was able to determine the correct amount of control required and become accustomed to the entirely new and slower rate of response of such a large multi-engined aeroplane.

Having satisfied himself that his creation was airworthy, Igor had the two remaining engines installed with their pusher propellers in their previously prepared positions, behind the two existing forward-facing engines with their tractor propellers, the four engines being in tandem pairs. With full power now available, *The Grand* was readied for its first official take-off on the afternoon of 13 May 1913, before a large gathering including Shidlovsky. (Fig 4)

Accompanying Igor was Capt Alechnovich as copilot, whose other main duty was to move fore or aft as necessary, to adjust the aeroplane's centre of gravity, and his long-time chief flight mechanic, V. Panasiuk, who was positioned in the front balcony. The smooth, straightforward take-off and climb-out astonished the onlookers, and *The Grand* climbed steadily at 60 mph. At an altitude of 400 ft Igor successfully made his very first turn, to the left, and then climbed to 600 ft, where he levelled off and made his second perfect left turn over the hangar and the amazed and now even larger and enthusiastic crowd below. Next, Igor calmly tried the effect of an engine failure by throttling back one of the engines, and found that the required rudder correction was easily managed.

The most difficult manoeuvre, the landing, still remained. However, he then decided to investigate the effect of a total power failure! He cut all four engines during the final approach glide-in, and proceeded to make a perfect power-off landing. *The Grand* rolled to a gentle stop after its 10 min maiden flight, having proved to all the critics and disbelievers that their predictions of failure had been wrong.

Among the first to rush up to the aircraft and congratulate Igor and his crew was Shidlovsky. Many years later, when I asked Igor what he felt was the most significantly rewarding moment during his aviation career, he said it was that moment when *The Grand* rolled safely to a halt, and the especially warm look and strong congratulatory handshake that Shidlovsky gave him. Unfortunately, at the time this significant event remained almost entirely unknown to the rest of the world, though it was one of the most outstanding flights in aviation history.

After further testing Igor decided to move the two rearward facing engines to their final outboard wing positions, as in their rearward positions the pusher propellers were being adversely affected by the propeller wash from the front engines. In this configuration flight testing continued, and on 2 August 1913 a record flight was made that lasted 1 hr 54 min with eight people aboard.

Soon afterwards, at Komendantski aerodrome, in September 1913, where *The Grand* was parked outside her hangar, a Polish pilot was demonstrating a new single-engined military aeroplane when it suddenly lost its rear-mounted engine and propeller. Unfortunately they crashed on to *The Grand* and caused sufficient damage to cause it to be scrapped, since by now it had become redundant. While practical, this action deprived aeronautical history of a priceless example of human endeavour.

Owing to Igor's foresight and Shidlovsky's backing, design and engineering for a new version of *The Grand* had already been in progress for several months, and construction could begin almost immediately. By early December 1913 final assembly was complete.

The *Il'ya Muromets*, as this next Sikorsky design was to be named, was an entirely new design, but followed the basic biplane configuration of *The Grand*, with the four engines positioned on the leading edge of the shorter lower wing. It had a

'HEELICOPTER' – PIONEERING WITH IGOR SIKORSKY

longer, thicker rear fuselage to which the cable-braced tail surfaces were attached. Unlike that of *The Grand*, the cabin did not protrude in front of the wings, nor did it have a balcony. Instead the aircraft had a snub-nosed cabin section, and a light platform was located beneath the nose between the landing skids. It was accessible through a floor hatch in the cabin, later removed.

Because of the heavier, larger and lengthier rear fuselage, Igor was uncertain whether the horizontal tail surfaces, which were already built, had sufficient area to produce the required lift. With that in mind, he added two small wings about halfway back on the fuselage.

The blunt, aluminium-covered nose with its large windows provided the pilot with greatly improved visibility from the control cabin, which for the first time separated the pilot and mechanic from the passenger cabin. Two side doors allowed in-flight emergency maintenance of the four engines. The main cabin had four large windows, four wicker armchairs and a table, aft of which was a toilet and a private cabin with a berth, table and closet. Electric lighting was provided, and two radiators, through which hot engine exhaust gases passed, gave the necessary heating. Directly above the private cabin was a railed-off, stand-up observation platform, reached by a ladder at the rear of the main cabin.

On 11 December 1913 at a fully loaded weight of 11,245 lb, the *Il'ya Muromets* made her first test flight with her creator at the controls. All went well as experienced hands controlled a normal smooth take-off, but upon reaching an altitude of about 200 ft Igor was unable to reduce the exaggerated nose-up attitude that was obviously causing the aeroplane to stall. It landed very heavily, damaging the right outer wing assembly. Apparently Igor had underestimated the extra lift of the added pair of mid-way wings, which, owing to their location, overcame the controlling power of the elevators.

By the end of December IM was airworthy again, and had had her official christening and the Russo-Baltic Wagon Co number R-BVZ model 107 given to her. Usually in January around Kiev the ground is covered with at least a foot or two of snow, so in anticipation Igor had designed a set of skis, which had been fitted. As it happened, that particular January was exceptionally mild, so much of the snow had melted away. Although new, larger tyres had been ordered, they had not been

received, so Igor had the remaining snow piled into two parallel rows. With consummate daring and skill he coaxed the IM into flight with all four 100 hp Argus engines pounding their hearts out, but once airborne Igor found himself fighting to retain control, as this time the aircraft was excessively tail heavy. He was only able to stay up for a few minutes, but it was sufficient to again confound those critics who claimed the aeroplane would never fly.

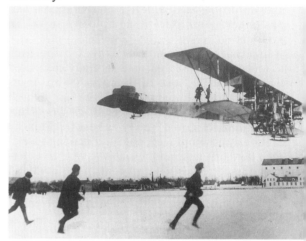

Fig 5 *The Il'ya Muromets is being demonstrated and piloted by Igor Sikorsky, at Kapusnoi aerodrome in 1914. The observation platform is being used by two army officers. One must realize that the cruising speed was 60–65 mph, and the landing speed 40–45 mph, with no wind. Note snow skis.*

Even though this first IM was knowingly underpowered, it proved a great weightlifter. Two adjustments were therefore needed and quickly made. The recent arrival of some new engines made it possible to install two 115 hp Argus inline engines outboard and two 200 hp Salmson radial engines inboard. The other adjustment was to increase the angle of incidence of the horizontal tail surfaces to increase lift and eliminate the tail-heaviness. After several test flights with the extra 230 hp and tail surface adjustments, Igor was so favourably impressed with IM's greatly improved performance that on 12 February, with fresh snow on the ground, he took off with no fewer than 16 persons on board plus his dog. Climbing steadily, IM-1 reached 1,000ft without any difficulty in a flight lasting 16 min. Then, for an encore, Igor carried eight passengers to 3,200ft and cruised around for a record-breaking 2hr 6min.

However, these large aircraft with their great lengths of wire/cable controls (much of it exposed to the airflow) which were subject to considerable slackness, had a generally 'sloppy' control system, much pilot control movement producing far less control surface movement. Another problem was the lateral instability of the aircraft, which made it dangerous to execute anything more than a shallow side-tilting turn owing to the possibility of initiating a rapid loss of altitude, or even complete loss of control due to stalling. Furthermore, the considerable physical strength required simply to move the pilot's control column, let alone the constant necessity to counteract the aircraft's movements, made piloting an endurance contest. Another basic contributory factor to this situation was that none of the moving control surfaces were balanced aerodynamically, other than (possibly) the rudder(s), to make the task easier.

A few weeks later, in April, the BWC was approached by the Imperial Navy regarding the feasibility of an IM-1 version mounted on floats. Igor immediately initiated the design and fabrication of the largest set of floats ever made. So equipped, the IM-1 was delivered in July to the Naval Air Station at Libau. Even by then, Igor was still the only pilot truly qualified enough to test this unique version and made several test flights, though no results are available. On 1 August 1914 the day that war was declared, Libau was expected to be overrun by the Germans. The crew of IM-1 spotted several naval craft approaching which they mistook for those of the enemy, and promptly destroyed the aircraft. Another historical loss.

Earlier, in March/April, the IM-2 was completed. This was a lighter version of the IM-1, with a shorter, lighter fuselage and a reduced-span

Fig 6 *The Il'ya Muromets-1 at Libau, the Imperial Naval Station on the Baltic Coast in July 1914. She was the largest ever float-plane in the world. Igor Sikorsky is seen standing on the starboard float. He did all the test flying.*

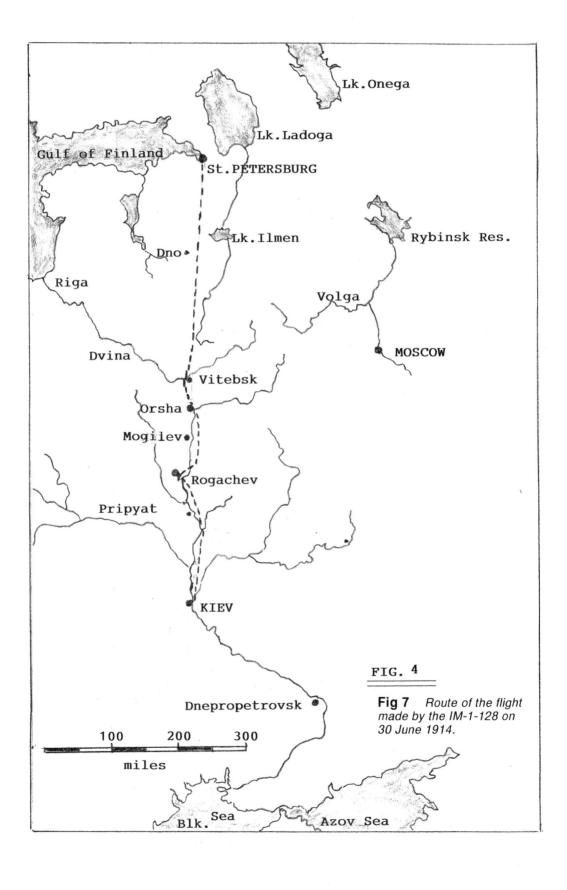

Lk.Onega

Lk.Ladoga

Gulf of Finland

St.PETERSBURG

Lk.Ilmen

Dno

Rybinsk Res.

Riga

Volga

Dvina

MOSCOW

Vitebsk

Orsha

Mogilev

Rogachev

Pripyat

KIEV

Dnepropetrovsk

FIG. 4

Fig 7 *Route of the flight made by the IM-1-128 on 30 June 1914.*

100   200   300

miles

Blk. Sea

Azov Sea

upper wing. Consequently, although the two outboard engines of 125 hp and the two inboard engines of 140 hp totalled 530 hp (100 hp less than IM-1), the overall power loading remained approximately the same. The IM-2 had different engines to the IM-1a because the availability of foreign engines had become acute, and a choice no longer existed. The IM-2 was given the BWC factory number 128 and became the first prototype production model of a practical multi-engined transport aeroplane.

Those who have not traversed the rough road of experimentation in new fields of endeavour might find it difficult to appreciate the amount of dedication and patience (sometimes years) involved in overcoming general scepticism and indifference. So it may seem somewhat repetitious when I state that, despite Igor's remarkable achievements in demonstrating the feasibility of aerial transportation, there still remained many sceptics.

In May, Igor finally had the opportunity to demonstrate an entirely new and more efficient aircraft properly. This particular flight, no doubt due to Shidlovsky's sagacity, included among its 12 passengers important members of both the government and military establishments. The result was the unanimous consensus that direct negotiations should begin immediately between BWC and the War Ministry, and these resulted in an order for ten Army type IM-2s.

Although this recognition of BWC by the War Ministry was of vital importance, there still remained the fact that not a single one of these huge Sikorsky aeroplanes had made a cross-country flight of any significant distance to actually demonstrate their reliability as aerial transports. To remedy this, Igor immediately began preparations for what was to be another world record flight. It was typical of Igor's belief that one can only find the right answer by doing.

The 1,400-mile round trip from St Petersburg to Kiev and back, refuelling approximately midway at Orsha, was both bold and daring, and the stage lengths were such that no one could doubt the practicability of large, multi-engined transport aeroplanes if the flight was successful. (Fig 7)

Having ascertained the hourly rate of fuel consumption, Igor provided extra fuel tanks to assure ample reserves to cover the midway refuelling at Orsha, as there were no other prepared landing areas between Kiev and St Petersburg.

There would be a crew of four: Igor Sikorsky, Chief pilot; Lt G.I. Lavrov, copilot and navigator; Capt. K.F. Prossis, 3rd Pilot; and V.S. Panasiuk, chief mechanic. Prepared food and water were carried. There was no form of wireless contact, and navigation mainly consisted of following familiar railways (the 'iron-compass'), roads, rivers and landscapes. A horizontal bar inside the front window indicated lateral level against the horizon (as used by Igor on his VS-300 experimental helicopter 25 years later).

At the early morning hour of 0100hrs on 30 June 1914 the heavily laden IM-2-128 successfully took off from Komendantski outside St Petersburg on its epic flight and headed south towards Orsha and Kiev. Climbing steadily to the predetermined 5,000 ft cruising altitude and flying at 65 mph airspeed (not groundspeed, which depends entirely upon the direction of the prevailing winds which can either help or hinder) the aeroplane arrived without incident at the prepared halfway point at 0900hr and refuelled. The first leg proved to be the most enjoyable, the crew lazily viewing the beautiful scenery with little or no air disturbance to worry them; truly a pilot's delight. As planned, the three pilots rotated their 30 min turns at the controls to avoid fatigue, for flying an IM-2 was no easy task. This arrangement allowed a 45 min break for each pilot.

In passing over the city of Vitebsk before landing at Orsha, two large tubes with brightly coloured identifying streamers were dropped containing messages of safe progress. One was to be telegraphed to Igor's home, and the other to Shidlovsky.

The sloping field at Orsha demanded much of Igor's skill and cool courage, together with his remarkable gift of co-ordination, to negotiate the uphill landing and the downhill take-off (to help acceleration) over rough terrain. The latter was especially difficult since the pilot had to keep the huge, lumbering and heavily laden accelerating aircraft directionally aligned, the site being 1,200ft ahead of the lip of a cliff which overlooked both a river and Orsha, some 100ft below.

The second part of the flight was an entirely different matter. After taking off from Orsha, the flight path veered south-west before turning southwards towards Kiev, parallel with the river Dneiper, then turned back westwards towards the city of Rogachev. On approaching the river just before that city, fire suddenly broke out in the port inboard engine. Igor immediately stopped the engine and reduced speed sufficiently to allow Lavrov and Panasiuk to climb out on to the wing and use their heavy overcoats to beat out the flames. Nowadays, such a scene would be associated with an old Mack Sennet comedy rather than the dangerous reality that faced Igor as he deftly struggled to keep IM-2 reasonably level. An emergency landing was made near Rogachev, where the broken fuel line that had caused the fire was properly repaired. However, owing to the late start made from Orsha and the fact that it was late afternoon by the time the repair was finished, Igor decided to wait until the next day before continuing on to Kiev.

A gusty, rainy day with low-lying clouds and fog greeted the intrepid aeronauts the next morning. Nevertheless, they decided to proceed regardless, as Kiev was less than 200 miles away. Soon after take-off, rough air was encountered and control became very difficult, being compounded by poor visibility. At times Igor was flying blind, completely enveloped in either dense fog or cloud, and the ordeal severely tested both Igor's skills and endurance and the Il'ya's structural integrity to their limits. At one point the violently pitching IM went into an uncontrollable spiral dive (spin), rapidly losing 1,200ft before Igor suddenly remembered, just in time, the only known recovery, which was to release all the controls and let them neutralise themselves. It was a nerve-wracking moment for all concerned, but was successfully overcome by a cool head.

As Igor took over the controls again, he eased his huge still wind buffeted Il'ya upwards towards a break in the clouds. As it climbed up through them into glorious uninterrupted sunshine in a clear blue sky above a limitless soft blanket of cloud, the great wet wings sparkled in the sun's rays. At that moment Il'ya ceased her trembling and, like her crew, relaxed, levelling out and droning smoothly on to her destination.

Igor's homecoming arrival over Kiev was also quite spectacular, for the cloud cover was such that it was purely a time-speed guess at dead-reckoning navigation when Il'ya nosed down gently through it, to find spread out straight ahead before them, the familiar sight, to Igor, of Kiev, with the golden domes of the Pechersk Monastery glittering from a single ray of sunshine. The total flying time for the entire trip was 12 hrs and 57 min, which amounted to an average cruising speed of 61½ mph. A new world record.

A large enthusiastic crowd headed by the city officials had awaited the arrival of Il'ya Muromets 2, not to mention the joyful Sikorsky family reunion that this remarkable flight had afforded them. This first long-distance flight of a large multi-engined transport, like the very first flight of The Grand, which in both instances he piloted, remained indelible memories in Igor's mind. When he occasionally recalled them, one could sense he was also reliving them emotionally in the enthusiastic and dramatic manner of his speech.

The triumphant return flight to St Petersburg apparently kept the crew just as busy as before, if not more so, handling the more frequent periods of turbulent or stormy weather. It also required a similar open-air engine repair by none other than the gallant ship's captain, as Igor proceeded to battle the elements to fix the carburettor of the port outboard engine, which was streaming fuel. A more genteel occasion came when Prossis was taking his turn piloting, evidently during a relatively calm spell of weather, when the rest of the crew joined Sikorsky for breakfast, comfortably seating themselves in the wicker armchairs around the white-clothed dining table in the rear compartment. What first-class airborne accommodation can boast of such comforts 78 years later?

The landing, refuelling and take-off from Orsha was successfully accomplished without incident, and upon landing at St Petersburg, some 13 flying hours after leaving Kiev, there was great civic response, with awards being given Igor and his crew. Not the least of which was the Tsar's rechristening the aeroplane Il'ya Muromets Kievskiy to honour the carefully planned and splendidly executed epic flight.

In that era telegraphy was the universal means of spreading news via telephone lines, as well as intercontinental underwater cables, and it was through this media that the civilised world finally became aware of what had been accomplished by Russia's Sikorsky-designed record-breaking aircraft. The dawn of the large multi-engined transport had arrived. The Russian press was so enthused that there were even suggestions of using an IMK type for polar exploration.

Writing about the foregoing many years later, it seems almost unreal that, barely four weeks before

Fig 8   *The dining-lounge area in the Il'ya Muromets.*

on 1 August, Germany declared war, the Russian press was talking about polar exploration! Two weeks later Igor was testing the float version of the IM-1 at Libau on the Baltic. Only at the last hour is mention made of the impending German invasion of Russian soil. Like the USA and Pearl Harbor, I presume, the Russian Government was well aware of the closeness of the impending storm, but chose to keep its citizens unaware of it.

Thus began the end of Igor Sikorsky's brilliant aviation career in his native Russia. For although he achieved several outstanding successes with new aircraft embodying his advanced ideas, it was such that with the fall of Tsarist rule and the establishment of subsequent revolutionary governments forced Igor to bear the humility of having to flee upon pain of death (Shidlovsky and son had already been killed trying to escape). He had to go through the heart-rending ordeal of leaving both his family and his beloved Russia, where he had twice been extraordinarily honoured by the Tsar himself for his outstanding pioneering contribu-

tions to Russian aviation. At that time, when he was still only 29, such success would not only have assured Igor's own future, but also that of Russian aviation in the field of transportation.

Igor's successful escape started in early March 1918 from his home in St Petersburg. He travelled some 650 miles north up to the Arctic Ocean port-city of Kola (now Murmansk) on the Kola Peninsula, where he was luckily able to book a passage on the British steamer *Oporto*, bound for Newcastle, in England. One can only surmise the thoughts that ran through his mind as he watched the Russian coastline, that he would never see again, slowly disappearing before him. After an uneventful crossing Igor made his way down to London, arriving there to witness an air raid by German bombers. Then he went on to Paris where he was better known (he spoke French). By June 1918, purely because of his fine reputation, the French Air Service accepted his preliminary proposal for a large bomber he had designed alone in his hotel room. He was then commissioned to prepare with the Aeronautical Technical Section a completely engineered design, and this was finished and approved by August, at which time an official contract was awarded to produce five prototypes.

All necessary production facilities had been approved and were in place by October, and work had started. Then, on 11 November 1918, the Armistice was signed in that famous railway carriage (the official Peace Treaty ending the war was not signed until 1919), halting the totally unnecessary and ghastly human carnage of the Great War, for which Germany had so carefully prepared, and deliberately initiated, on *der Tag*, 1 August 1914. Sikorsky's contract was immediately cancelled.

Although he considered remaining in France and hoping for the best to occur in Russia, so that

Fig 9 *On 14 March 1919 Igor Sikorsky arrived at New York City, U.S.A., determined to bring to America what he had so successfully created and demonstrated in his native Russia, the need for large commercial aircraft.*

he would be able to return, it became increasingly evident that the chaotic condition in his homeland was, to a less violent extent, also gripping postwar Europe. So Igor finally decided that the more normal domestic conditions of the burgeoning postwar economy in the United States of America offered him the best chance of starting a new life. This brings us to the beginning of the next phase in the life-story of Igor Sikorsky. Thus it happened that, on 14 March 1919, almost a year to the day after he had left his home, Igor arrived in New York on the passenger steamer *Lorraine*. He was 30, and was determined to accomplish in America what he had hoped to achieve in Russia. He wanted to produce large commercial aircraft capable of transporting passengers and goods throughout a developing, dynamic country.

Igor arrived with very limited funds, a few letters of recommendation and a rather limited English vocabulary. However, his very first venture was to organise in conjunction with a group of White (not Red) Russian emigrants in New York the Hannevig-Sikorsky Aircraft Company in Wantagh, Long Island, with the idea of constructing a prototype commercial aircraft having a payload of no less than six tons. But this did not materialise.

What most amazed Igor was how much more advanced Europe was in aviation thinking than the USA. There was little interest in investing in the future of commercial air transportation, as suggested by an almost completely unknown Russian emigrant. Undaunted, Igor once again reluctantly decided to turn to the military, as he had a fine letter of recommendation from General Patrick, who had been Commander of the US Army Air Service (USAAS) of the American Expeditionary Forces in Europe. By 27 September Igor was able to submit to the US Army in Washington DC, his design for a huge bomber based on his French-approved Avion Atlas design of the year before. He named it the Sikorsky Battleplane, Type I.S.27.

Lieutenant-Colonel B. Q. Jones was very favourably impressed with the Battleplane design, and wrote a letter of recommendation to the Engineering Division of McCook Field in Dayton, Ohio, the research and development section for the US Army. It read: 'In as much as the Air Service is at present particularly interested in the design of a superbomber, there is no doubt but that the arrival of the most experienced designer of super machines in the world, will be of very great interest to the Engineering Division'. This resulted in a request for Igor to submit a preliminary design proposal, 'showing two types of multi-seater airplane with three 700 hp engines each'. They were to be capable of night bombing.

Igor moved to Dayton, and by mid-December 1919 he had completed and submitted his proposal to the Engineering Division. There it was reviewed, but was turned down, Col Thurman Bane told him, because of a lack of funds. Considering the context of that time, one wonders if the foregoing sequence of events amounted to nothing more than a polite gesture, since so little was known in the USA of either Sikorsky or of Russian aviation technology. Or was it just an easy means of obtaining valuable information? However, there were those in the Engineering Division who genuinely admired his outstanding pioneering contributions to aviation in the field of very large aircraft. At least he had earned $1,500 (in gold) and front-page notoriety in the Dayton Press. Once again it was back to square one.

This also meant back to New York City, and his new-found friends and acquaintances. He was, none the less, as determined as ever to raise enough capital to enter into the business of commercial air transport. He formed another partnership in February 1920, only to be disappointed again by the continuing disinterest and reluctance to invest risk-capital in what was still considered to be an impractical venture, which involved the building of a prototype air transport, his newly designed S-28.

It now became abundantly clear to Igor that he had to make a critical decision regarding his immediate future versus his ultimate goal. The desire of finding a proper position as an aeronautical engineer, he realised, would have to be subordinated in order for him actually to exist. Wisely heeding the advice of a friend, who was a member of a larger Russian community in the city than the one to which he belonged, he started teaching mathematics and astronomy (characteristically his two basic thought-areas, methodology and vision) at the New York City Russian Collegiate Institute, and then proceeded to broaden his scope by lecturing before the Nauka Science Society. There he found audiences who understood his impatience in wanting to initiate aerial transport in the USA as he had in Russia, especially as, geographically,

the USA's centres of population were remotely connected, as in Russia, and there would be an increasing necessity for a means of moving both people and goods rapidly between them. He was thus able to live frugally (according to Igor, mostly on baked beans and bread) throughout 1921–1922. One bright happening befell Igor during that period. He met Elizabeth Simion, who like him had managed to escape from the Revolution (via Siberia) after her parents disappeared.

Finally, on 5 March 1923, the Sikorsky Aero Engineering Corporation was formed, with sufficient financial backing from his now numerous Russian associates. Construction soon started on his latest design, the S-29A (an improved S-28) on the donated ex-chicken farm of friend Victor Utgoff, located in Mineola, Long Island, near Roosevelt Field. Thus, after four frustrating years of failure and personal hardship, his steadfast determination had won through.

Among the émigrés now backing Igor with both financial and physical help were ex-Russian naval and army officers, pilots, engineers and mechanics, all anxious to help their much admired and respected compatriot Igor Sikorsky build his very first commercial aeroplane in their newly adopted country.

Because of the importance of their long-standing close friendship and business association with Igor Sikorsky, it is fitting to introduce four members of Sikorsky's original Aero Engineering Corp. at Mineola, Long Island, in 1923: Michael Buivid, Boris (Bob) Labensky, and the brothers Michael and Serge Gluhareff. Both Michael Buivid and Bob Labensky preceded the Gluhareffs. These two very close friends were probably most influential in sustaining Sikorsky in his desire to vindicate his belief that there must be a solution to making a practical single-main-rotor helicopter.

Of all the associates of Sikorsky's original engineering corporation, none knew him better than Michael Buivid. The Buivid and Sikorsky estates had adjoined each other in Kiev, Russia, and it was young Michael who helped Igor build his first series of homebuilt aeroplanes. He was also to build the first propeller-driven 'snowmobile', using one of Igor's discarded 30 hp aero-engines and its propeller. On its ski-type runners it could skim over the snow at 30 mph. Michael built it in a spare bedroom in his home, and a window had to be removed to take it outside. At that time young gentlemen were not required or expected to perform any manual labour, so Michael would go to a car and motorcyle garage in Kiev and change into a mechanic's overalls, as he was very keen to learn all he could about engines.

In the First World War, as a major in the Imperial Russian Air Force, Michael was put in charge of the ground maintenance of several squadrons of fighter aircraft. Later, during the final stages of the Revolution, he was placed in charge of the anti-revolutionary White Army's mobile paymaster's treasury on the southern front. This consisted of a convoy of two armoured cars and three trucks loaded with coffers of gold or silver coins with which to pay the troops (paper money being worthless). Finally, when orders were received to disband, he had his officers secretly bury the gold coins at night. He then paid off the contingent, including himself, in small-denomination coins so as not to arouse any possible suspicion when among strangers. It was then every man for himself, as it was a sparsely settled area and groups of two or more people might have aroused suspicion.

The first odd job that Michael got was chopping wood. Red agents in civilian clothing could unexpectedly arrive at a farm or a village, looking for White Army escapees, and the first thing they would do was inspect the condition of suspects' hands. If they were soft, the person was immediately arrested on suspicion of being an officer, so labourer's hands were desirable. Michael also acquired secondhand peasant's clothing (washed) to avoid possible suspicion. He hid his small pistol and coins within his clothing, and he would hide the pistol in the inevitable woodpile, so that his host should not be involved if he was arrested. Luckily he passed his hand test without question. It was also wise to pretend to have difficulty reading or writing, and to imitate lower-class manners and speech as much as possible. Most of the time he found that the farming people were anti-Bolshevick, and he had little trouble finding willing help during the weeks he slowly worked his way southward through the famous Pripet Marshes, using the tiny compass which was provided for every officer, hidden inside a special button on his uniform. That part of the escape was a saga by itself.

Michael's intended destination was Savastopol, the Black Sea port on the Crimea Peninsula, where Zina, his wife and little George, their only child, would wait for him to arrive.

Meanwhile, a heart-rending scene had taken place at Michael's parents' home in Kiev, where Zina and George, who was barely a year old, were staying just before they were also to depart for Savastopol. Apparently, the Red Army Command had been issued orders to eliminate imperialist male children. Zina said that she, George and his nurse were in the upstairs nursery when a detachment of Red Army soldiers arrived to ransack the dwelling, looking for victims. After an agonising period of waiting they heard heavy footsteps coming up the stairway. The nursery door opened and a big, heavily-set blonde soldier stepped into the room. Zina and the nurse stood holding their breath next to the play crib, with George between them, fearing the worst. They had been told of terrible incidents in which children had been grabbed by a leg, slammed against a wall and killed. The soldier did not say a word, but stood staring intently at George. He then walked slowly over to the crib with his eyes still fixed on the child. As he stopped at the crib he quietly bent over and, gently patting George's head, softly said: 'My son is just like him'. Without another word, and not looking at Zina or the nurse, he turned and walked out of the door. As he was starting down the stairway a voice from below called: 'Anybody up there?' 'Just two old women,' he replied.

Zina and George arrived safely by train at Savastopol. She had also managed to bring with her two oversized wicker hampers, their contents representing the sum total of all their remaining worldly goods that she could safely bring with her. Another great uncertainty now faced Zina. She bravely refused to think that Michael might not arrive. Instead she concentrated on the problem of obtaining a passage on one of the passenger boats that left for Constantinople, Turkey, for fewer and fewer boats were available as time passed. So as to be sure of having a passage when Michael finally appeared, she kept booking ahead. Only when one boat remained did Zina begin to wonder if it was all in vain, and that she would have to leave without Michael.

Then it happened. A tall, bearded and haggard peasant appeared, so changed that Zina could barely recognise him. They were both so overcome with joy and relief that all they could do was hold each other as tightly as they possibly could. While

Michael was recuperating from his ordeal, Zina, to provide an immediate source of income, started a children's kindergarten and a Russian language lending library, donating what books she had managed to bring with her and what she could collect from other Russian emigrants.

Michael became intrigued by the number of small private ferries, powered by oars or sails, that continually crossed the Bosphoros to and from mainland Turkey. They had to deal with a considerable tidal current, which meant that they had first to give way to the direction of the anti-tidal shore current, then combat the main current in the opposite direction, and upon reaching the opposite shore repeat the same operation. All of this took considerable time. To Michael the obvious answer was to install an engine, so he managed to acquire one of the little ferry boats and installed a used car engine fitted with a propeller and shaft he found in a boatyard. It was an immediate success, as it halved the regular crossing time. However, there was one factor he had failed to consider. He was soon facing irate ferry operators who accused him of stealing their customers, and he an outsider, to boot. So Michael said to them: 'I will build you more conversions like this one. Who will buy this one?' That kept him busy until he had saved enough to allow him and his family to move to Italy. Shortly afterwards they left for New York, where Michael soon joined up with his friend Igor Sikorsky.

Boris Petrovitch Labensky was a graduate of the Imperian Russian Naval Academy. Towards the end of the 1917 Revolution he managed to escape with other officers and ratings by commandeering a destroyer and taking it to France, where they handed it over to the French Navy. He also went to America, landing in New York after 1919, and was among the first to join the Sikorsky Aero Engineering Corp. on Long Island.

Boris (Bob) was always very reticent to talk about his past. He was a sensitive person, and I had the feeling that he never quite got over the ordeal of leaving his home and homeland, and especially of never knowing the fate of the loved ones he left behind. However, he will be very much in evidence as this account proceeds. Certainly one would be hard pressed to find a more understanding and loyal friend than Bob.

Michael Gluhareff and his younger brother, Serge, were born on a family estate near St Petersburg (renamed Leningrad by the communists, but now St Petersburg again) on the shores of Lake Ladoga, bordering Finland. Apparently the Gluhareffs were what were then referred to as 'Merchant Princes', being wealthy, well educated and well travelled. They were a third generation of very successful manufacturers of industrial machinery and tools.

As a young gentleman of considerable leisure, Michael became increasingly interested in aeroplanes. In 1912 he designed and built a man-carrying glider, helped by Serge, and they both taught themselves to fly it. They next incorporated an engine, and similarly learned to fly under power. This very closely paralleled young Sikorsky's beginnings. The advent of the First World War interrupted this, and Michael and Serge became involved in the work of the family business for the duration of the war.

After the war Michael was sent first to England to try and resolve non-payments on some large orders that had been placed with the family firm. He was to travel by train, which meant a stopover in Vienna to board the Orient Express. 'After two and a half weeks of Vienna high living', said Michael, raising his eyebrows quickly several times and adding, 'never-to-be-forgotten', 'I received a very curt telegram from my father to move on or be recalled.' In England he was able to secure a reasonable settlement. Upon his arrival in New York he was able, after considerable difficulty, to locate their consignment in an old warehouse on a little-used New York dock. It was so badly rusted that it was almost useless. However, he managed to secure partial payment.

During his search for the lost consignment in New York, Michael came across some large crates. Upon enquiring about their contents he found out that they contained several US Army training aeroplanes that were due to be sent to France when the shipment was cancelled owing to the Armistice. As they were sitting there unclaimed, he was able to acquire the lot from the shipper for a ridiculously low figure.

In the meantime Serge had arrived, and the upshot was that the brothers approached Igor Sikorsky with the idea of substituting the existing wings on the trainers with new ones incorporating Michael's aerofoil section. This was agreed, and the resulting performance was such an improvement that the rejuvenated trainers were soon sold.

The happy ending to this venture came when Igor asked Michael and Serge to join him, and they accepted. Michael would soon become chief engineer and Serge a general factotum, among other duties seeking out businesses which had materials and/or structural forms (such as steel or iron bedframes) that could be readily adapted to the construction of the aircraft Igor was building.

A seldom recorded fact about Michael is that his intuitive designing of aerofoil sections greatly contributed to the outstanding performances of all subsequent Sikorsky fixed-wing aircraft. This enabled certain models to fly faster, cover greater distances and carry greater payloads than other existing aircraft in similar categories.

An amusing incident involving Labensky, Markoff and Glad occurred during the Utgoff Farm days. Not having sufficient funds to afford buying a car, they decided to assemble one in their spare time using material from nearby junk yards, since they had all become adept at improvising while building the 14-passenger S-29A.

With only the body missing, they joyfully set off to a near-by beach on a trial run, and a swim, using a box as a driver's seat. Surmounting a sand dune, they managed to overturn their creation, smashing the steering wheel, but otherwise suffered no injuries or damage. By wrapping a towel around the jagged remains of the steering wheel hub,

Labensky, by virtue of his extraordinary strength, was able to slowly negotiate a slow and safe but less joyful return. When they finally completed their hybrid conveyance it embodied the components of no fewer than seven makes of car.

Life on the Utgoff farm now included not only Igor, his daughter Tania by his first marriage, sisters Olga and Helen Viner with son Dimitri and daughter Galina, but also Labensky, Glad and George Markoff, not to mention the hens. The latter were wont to devour the rivets scattered around until they were troubled, at which point the poor things were relieved of their suffering, ending up on the dinner table, and the precious rivets retrieved. While living conditions were cramped, spirits remained high as the S-29A (for America) took shape, mostly out in the open. Curious onlookers came to watch the first 14-passenger transport aeroplane being built. Some volunteered their services part-time, others full-time, such was the spirit of adventure engendered by Igor and his associates.

This unique open-air aircraft factory had to bow to the winter elements, and final assembly was moved to an old hangar at nearby Roosevelt Field. This was only made possible by Igor's principal and faithful backer, Sergei Rachmaninoff, defraying the cost of the rental. The aircraft's upper wing spanned 69 ft and the lower wing 62 ft 6 in, its overall fuselage length was 49 ft 10 inches, and it was 13 ft 6 in high. The hangar was still a relatively cold working area, but in January 1924 two warm hearts were forever joined together when Igor and Elizabeth married. Their eventful and happy marriage over the following years was heightened by the safe arrival of four fine sons: Sergei, Nikolai, Igor Jr and George.

The long-awaited maiden flight of S-29A took place on 4 May 1924, with Igor at the controls as usual. Though underpowered, it managed to take off with eight privileged passengers. After climbing to about 100 ft, Igor made a touch-and-go landing and take-off at nearby Mitchell Field. Suddenly one of the engines stopped, but fortunately a golf

Fig 11

(8) Rear   *(3) Rear*   *(4)*   *(5)*   *(6)*   *(7)*

Igor Sikorsky and the associates of his Aero Engineering Corp in 1923.

(1) Viner (nephew), (2) Sikorsky, (3) Solovioff, (4) Labensky, (5) Markoff, (6) Glad, (7) Krapish, (8) Buivid

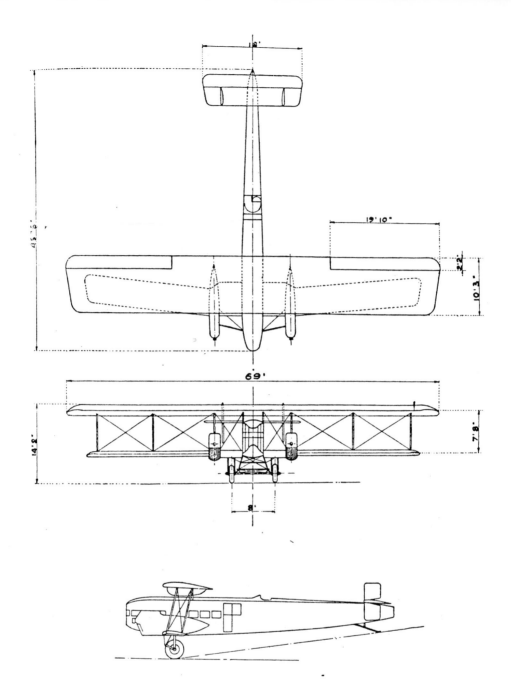

SIKORSKY AERO ENGINEERING CORPORATION

NEW YORK, N.Y.

SIKORSKY TWIN ENGINED TRANSPORT PLANE S-29-A.
ENGINES-LIBERTY "12"; SPEED 116 M.P.H., ON ONE MOTOR 75 M.P.H.
SERVICE CEILING 12500 FEET; CLIMB 5000 FEET IN 7 MIN 10 SEC

Fig 12

course permitted an emergency landing, during which the undercarriage suffered considerable damage. Thanks to skilled piloting and the rugged structure, no one was injured.

The aeroplane was hauled back to her hangar at Roosevelt Field, and repairs began immediately. This event also occasioned the famous crucial emergency meeting of the shareholders, when Igor asked them for additional funds to pay for the necessary repairs. At the start of the meeting, without saying a word, he calmly walked over to the office door, locked it and put the key in his pocket. He then quietly announced to the assembly that no one was to leave the meeting until the required funds had been raised. He got them. Only cool, respected courage could have produced the desired results.

Repaired and re-engined with newly reconditioned Liberty engines providing an extra 200 hp, the S-29A went aloft again on 25 September 1924 on her first truly successful flight, with Igor piloting and only three passengers this time. The next few days were spent taking jubilant stockholders and teammates for joyrides to celebrate not only the first successful Sikorsky design to be built in the USA, but also his first multi-engined, 14-passenger air transport.

Taking full advantage of favourable press reports, Igor started public demonstration flights to include the press as well as the military. Never before had an aeroplane passenger been so comfortably seated, or enjoyed such uninterrupted views of the countryside, especially from the forward section of the cabin. This was because the pilot's open cockpit was located just aft of the main passenger cabin, and was reached by a door at the rear of the cabin, a layout that was gaining popularity on small commercial aircraft such as airmail aeroplanes. The S-29A was also capable of safe single-engine flight at 75 mph, and with both engines running could attain 116 mph and climb to 5000 ft in 7 min 10 sec. Its service ceiling was 12,500 ft.

By the end of 1924 more than 420 passengers had flown with Igor in 45 flights totalling 15 hr and 37 min, averaging of 20.8 min and 9.33 passengers per flight, an unheard-of record at that time. Similar flights continued throughout 1925, gaining in popularity and prestige. Igor was at the controls for about 200 of these flights, Michael Gluhareff or Alex Krapish piloting the rest. Finally the S-29A

was sold to a popular flyer Roscoe Turner, who for two years flew it on numerous charter and advertising flights. In 1928 Turner sold the aeroplane to Howard Hughes, who used it to represent a German 'Gotha bomber' in his famous movie *Hells Angels*, in which it met its final, ignominious demise, ironically so similar to that of IM-1 in 1914.

In spite of the foregoing, the S-29A brought in no orders. But Igor had finally established a reputation in his adopted country as a respected pioneer of practical large transport aircraft, as well as smaller aircraft.

The corporation was re-organised on 4 July 1925 as the Sikorsky Manufacturing Corporation, and a series of smaller aircraft were subsequently designed, built and sold, mainly due to the use of Michael Gruhareff's superior wing profiles. In late 1926 it was decided to move to more modern quarters at College Point, Long Island, as it had water frontage on the Sound. It was to prove a significant move for Igor and his core of faithful associates, marking the beginning of an unexpected era of remarkable successes.

The Wright brothers suddenly placed the USA in the forefront of world aviation when they made the first powered, sustained and controlled flight on 17 December 1903, and then just as suddenly they passed from the scene, leaving it up to Europe to continue the good work. Ten years later young Igor Sikorsky introduced *The Grand* in 1913, the presaging air transport as we see it today. Domestic aviation in the USA suffered from a lack of foresight until Igor Sikorsky appeared there in March 1919, ten years later. Then in 1926, seven years after his arrival in the USA, yet another twist of fate was to occur for him.

Like the limb of a tree, Igor would bend with the wind of circumstance, as he realised that the need for domestic air transport still had to be demonstrated. To that end the huge 101 ft wingspan S-37, long-range twin engine version of the ill-fated S-35 René Fonk transatlantic aeroplane was sold to American Airways International Inc. Christened the *Southern Star*, during 1927–1929 it made a series of outstanding air-route survey flights throughout South and Central America.

Most major cities and industries were sited on large rivers or bodies of water. Igor Sikorsky reasoned that amphibious aircraft could be rolled down a ramp, have their undercarriage retracted, and take off from the water on their boat-type hulls, eliminating the need for costly airports. Consequently a small six-passenger, open-cockpit, twin-engine amphibian, the S-34, was designed by Gluhareff and Debusey (who was responsible for the hull). It was built in 1927 and tested as a scaled-down version of the proposed basic configuration for a commercial amphibian, the eight-passenger, enclosed-cabin 100 mph S-36. With shrewd foresight Igor ordered six to be built.

Another young visionary, Juan Trippe, likewise realised the need and future potential for safe rapid movement of people across large, open stretches of water, as already existed in the Caribbean, where distances between the islands and/or mainland were well within the capabilities of existing aircraft. But this, too, would have to be demonstrated.

As sales soon proved, the S-36 with its rugged boat-type hull was not only the right basic configuration, but, being amphibious, it had a unique operational versatility. The Andean National Corp. replaced its S-32 with the S-36 to enhance the profitability of its operations on the Magdalena River in Columbia, South America, and the US Navy bought one as a utility transport, designated XPS-1, engendering future Navy and Army interest. However, the stepping stone which took the Sikorsky-Gluhareff-Debusey creative design team to greater heights was the purchase of an S-36 on 7 December 1927 by the newly formed Pan American Airways. It was to be used to make a survey of the Caribbean area for possible future air transport routes. The success of the survey did not go unnoticed by Juan Trippe's Aviation Corporation of America, which had recently won an airmail contract serving the Key West to Havana, Cuba, route. Early in 1928 Trippe merged his corporation with Pan American and quickly took advantage of the merger so that Pan American was able eventually to monopolise the entire Caribbean airline system, first pioneered by Charles Lindbergh with his 9,000-mile goodwill

---

Fig 13   *Sikorsky S-35 1926*
Specially built for René Fonk's trans-atlantic attempt, that on take-off, tragically crashed and burned, killing René Fonk.
1 – J. Viner 2 – A. Krapish 3 – M. Gluhareff 4 – I. Sikorsky 5 – M. Buivid 6 – R. Fonk 7 – Solovioff

tour of the Caribbean area in early 1928.

The stage was now set for the joint creation of the S-38 by Trippe, his chief engineer André Priester, Igor Sikorsky and Michael Gluhareff, who now co-signed with Igor all the official design drawings, the number of his wing profile being used for that particular aircraft. This indicated Igor's appreciation of Michael's very important design contributions.

While the first S-38 was conceived, designed and built at College Point, it was obvious that more manufacturing space was needed, at a more suitable site conveniently closer to major suppliers, though still located by water. Such a site was found on an old farm on the mouth of the Housatonic River on Long Island Sound, next to Stratford, Connecticut, and the Sikorsky Aviation Corporation moved into a new modern factory and became the Sikorsky Aircraft Division of the United Aircraft Corporation of Hartford, Connecticut, in July 1929. Eugene E. Wilson from Hamilton Standard Propellers was General Manager and Igor Sikorsky was Engineering Manager, at his request, to allow him greater freedom for concentration on creative work. This also demonstrated his lack of desire for power and his willingness to acknowledge his own limits.

The S-38 was only slightly larger than the six-passenger, two-crew S-36, carrying eight passengers and two crew in a larger and more comfortable cabin, and spanning 2 ft 6 in less, but with another 370 hp and an all-metal hull. It quickly showed its capabilities when piloted by Boris Sergievsky, setting a world altitude record of 19,065 ft with a payload of 4,409 lb, and could maintain safe level flight at gross weight with only one of its two engines operating.

The newly established amicable collaboration between user Pan American Airways and equipment supplier United Aircraft Corporation was soon to blossom into a remarkably successful joint effort. On 4 February 1929 the inaugural pioneering airmail flight between Miami and the Panama Canal was flown in an S-38 by Charles Lindbergh, now the technical adviser for Pan American Airways. This was followed in September 1929 by another spectacular S-38 amphibian goodwill flight. Both the Trippes and the Lindberghs flew over the entire Caribbean area and down to Dutch Guyana, returning via the northern coast of South America to Central America, where arrangements were already being made for further Pan American expansion into South America. Huge enthusiastic crowds and press reporters greeted them everywhere. No fewer than 38 reliable S-38s were sold to Juan Trippe's airline.

Over the succeeding years, an additional 73 S-38 amphibians were sold to a variety of customers including private buyers and commercial airlines. As before, single aircraft were purchased by the US Navy (XPS-2, PS-3) and US Army (C-6). At last Sikorsky transport aircraft had won acceptance in the American aviation market.

Only when an aircraft designer is experienced enough can he interpret and convert the required basic functional and operational needs into the basic elements of a design, so that the minimum possible power required is actually available from the chosen engine(s) at the desired cruising speed. Since wings have to produce the most lift for the least resistance, one can readily understand how important it was for Gluhareff to design just the right wing profile, which he did with such marked success.

The golden age of the amphibious flying boat had dawned for Igor Sikorsky and his associates, and there appeared the small, popular five-place, single-engine S-39 of 1930, of which 29 were sold; the S-40 of 1931, a four-engined luxurious 38–40-passenger transport for Pan American with comfortably upholstered individual chairs, spacious compartments and the first full-course hot meals to be served en route, (three built); and the S-41, an intermediate 14-passenger enlarged version of the S-38 for Pan American's Caribbean services (seven built), also built in 1931.

Then, in 1934, as a result of the close collaboration between Lindbergh and Preister of Pan American and Sikorsky and Gluhareff, plus the engineering teams of Pratt & Whitney engine and Hamilton Standard Propeller the S-42 appeared. The largest, most luxurious and most efficient aircraft produced to date, it carried 32 passengers with a 1,200-mile range, cruising at 150 mph. Though larger than the S-40, it weighed less and had a greater payload capacity, 3,055 lb. Eleven S-42s were built, and the type pioneered the Pacific Ocean routes from California to China for Pan American. Unlike all the previous Sikorsky flying boats, the S-42 was not an amphibian.

Fig 14 *The Sikorsky 40-passenger* American Clipper *S-40, being made ready for her first test flight by Igor Sikorsky, seen sitting at far left.*

When the sleek all-metal, 182 mph, 15–25 passenger, 800-mile range and 6,000 lb-payload S-43 was launched in 1935, little did Sikorsky and his employees realise that it would be the last amphibian they would ever build. The USA was paying scant attention to the warlike rumblings emanating from Germany. Nevertheless, the S-43 proved to be one of the finest and best selling aircraft produced by the Sikorsky team, and by 1939 53 had been sold to domestic and foreign customers, as well as to the US Navy and Army.

The last fixed-wing aircraft design to come from the draughting boards of Sikorsky and Gluhareff Engineering Dept. was launched on 13 August 1937 as the US Navy XPBS-1 (Sikorsky S-44) and named *The Flying Dreadnaught*. It was built in direct competition with the PB2Y from the Consolidated Aircraft Corporation of California to meet a requirement for a coastal patrol bomber. The XPBS-1 had a wingspan of 124 ft, four 1,050 hp Pratt & Whitney engines with 12 ft-diameter Hamilton propellers, a useful load of 22,652 lb, a top speed of 220 mph, could land as slowly as 64 mph (a Gluhareff speciality), remain airborne for 30 hours and had a range of over 4,000 miles.

This contract was a particularly lucrative one, since it called for the costing of no fewer than 250 units, an unheard-of quantity for such a large flying boat. That the contract was awarded to Consolidated was allegedly considered to have been politically motivated at that time, and justified, as the order was cancelled after only 50 had been delivered, apparently because of poor rough-water performance. A bitter pill for Igor to swallow. Had Sikorsky won the contract, the VS-300 experimental helicopter might never have been built.

That this magnificent aircraft was not a total loss was due to the foresight of American Export Airlines, which was looking for just such a long-range aircraft for its recently won right to operate transatlantic services despite Pan American's monopoly of international airline routes. By 1942 three VS-44As (the company had been entitled Vought-Sikorsky since April 1939, when Vought merged with Sikorsky and the S became VS) had been completed and delivered to American Export Airlines. Their hull interiors had been redesigned to accommodate 39 full-size upper and lower berths and a galley. The all-up weight had been increased by 10,166 lb, the total power by 600 hp, the useful load by 7,530 lb, the range by 880 miles, the duration by 14 hr and the top speed by 5 mph; a superb engineering achievement. The three flying boats, named *Excalibur*, *Excambian* and *Exeter*, performed an unfailing transocean service for the remainder of the war.

Before ending the Foreword I am asking you to let me add a few words of a more personal nature regarding Igor Sikorsky. For instance his ability to recognise immediately the possibility of solving a particular problem by basically adapting someone else's successful solution. Thereby the usefulness of an aeroplane could be extended by fitting it for a new role. Such was the case with his amphibious flying boats, especially the S-38 with its wing set high above the boat-like hull, with two parallel booms extending rearwards from its trailing edge and supported by a 'V' strut, attached at its lower apex to the very rear top side of the hull. To the rear ends of the booms were attached the tail surfaces, well clear of the spray during take-off or landing, particularly in rough water. The lower stub wings

supported the outboard stabilising floats, and between the wings, above and to either side of the hull, were the two engines.

This configuration was evolved by Dr Jerome Hunsacker, Professor of Aeronautics at the Massachusetts Institute of Technology, for the US Navy's four Curtiss NC-series special flying boats that attempted the very first crossing west-to-east, by aircraft, of the North Atlantic Ocean in 1919. In the event only one aircraft, the NC-4, completed the crossing as planned. One of the others lost power from one engine, and made a safe water landing. As it was not possible to repair the engine, the aircraft taxied an extraordinary number of miles to safety at the Azores Islands, which would have been impossible in a landplane.

Another of Igor's talents was his ability to 'sell' his ideas to others. As one listened to him and watched him it became increasingly apparent, owing to his sincerity, intelligence and the eloquent enthusiasm of his speech, that he was imbued, but

Fig 15 *S-38-B, 8 passengers – 2 crew.*

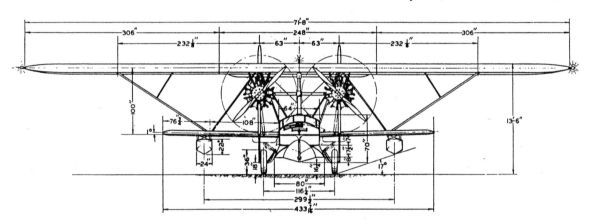

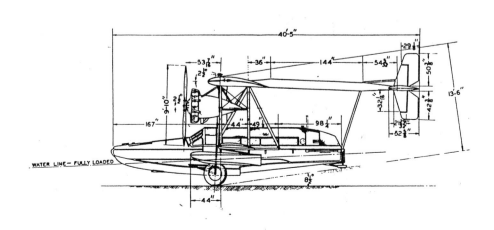

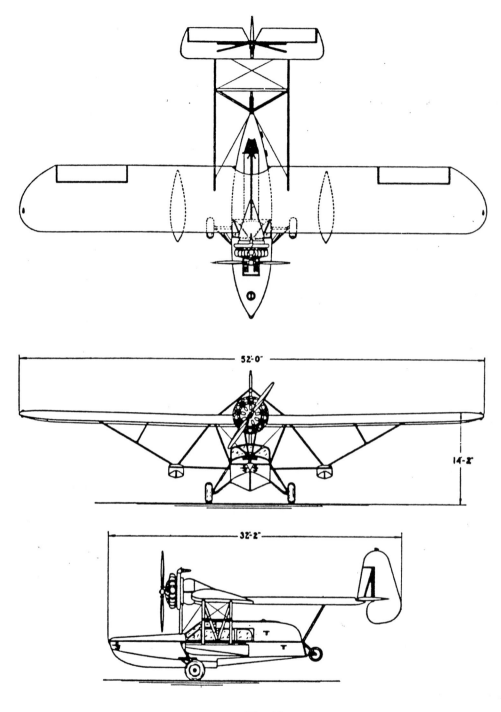

Fig 16

SIKORSKY AVIATION CORPORATION
Bridgeport, Conn.
Amphibian S-39 — 5 Place
Engine: Pratt & Whitney Wasp, Jr.

not obsessed, with his own belief in what he was 'selling', and it was difficult not to agree with him.

An example of this was told to me by his neighbour in Russia, Michael Buivid. In the late 1920s, when the Sikorsky S-38 was rapidly gaining acceptance, Pierre Dupont, a prominent industrialist living near Philadelphia, in Maryland, was interested in acquiring a new aeroplane. He was given a lengthy demonstration of the S-38's excellent land- and waterborne capabilities, as well as its outstanding flying qualities, and was shown its comfortable cabin and attractive interior, with its ease of adaptation to various arrangements.

While Dupont was obviously impressed with the S-38 and its outstanding characteristics, he felt it was more aeroplane than he needed. Igor then suggested that they discuss just what Dupont had in mind. Mr Dupont said he could only give a general description of what he desired as he was leaving for Europe within the next 30 days, but that upon his return he would gladly go into more specific details. Basically, he said, what he had in mind was a singled-engine version of the S-38, with comfortable quarters for the pilot and four passengers.

Barely three weeks later Igor rang up Dupont and asked him if he could spare the time to inspect the preliminary version of the proposed new amphibian. Thinking that Igor was talking about design drawings, Dupont started to decline, whereupon Igor interjected: 'With your permission, Mr Dupont, we could land on your private golf course'. There was dead silence at the other end of the line (while Igor and Michael smiled at each other), then, obviously taken aback, Dupont said: 'But Mr Sikorsky, you told me there is no single-engine version of the S-38'. 'There is now, Mr Dupont,' replied Igor cheerily. (Fig. 16)

The area designated for landing and take-off turned out to be barely adequate, but chief test pilot Sergievsky, with consummate skill, made it look quite routine. A surprised and amazed Dupont enthusiastically inspected this preliminary model especially designed for him, making suggestions here and there. Finally he said that he was eagerly looking forward to his return from Europe, but still found it difficult to believe what Igor and his associates had accomplished, with such excellent detail, in such a short space of time. When properly manufactured and certificated, the S-39 became Pierre Dupont's pride and joy, as well as becoming a popular model.

For those who might have asked themselves, 'How did the author happen to meet Mr Igor I. Sikorsky in the first place'? You might care to read what follows. If not, please turn forward to Chapter 2.

It all began to happen back in 1913 when I had my first sight of an aeroplane near Buenos Aires, Argentina, at the age of four. My parents took me to see a certain Sñr Gataño from Brazil demonstrating his flying prowess at a horse-racing track during an aerial tour of Uruguay and the Argentine Republic. The following episode, particularly its beginning and end, is as clear to me now as when it happened.

We were standing on a raised area beyond the grandstand at one end of the oval dirt race-track, overlooking the entire track. A short distance beyond the other end of the track could be seen the bright orange wings of a monoplane, with people milling around it. Presently the people were being moved away to a safe distance. Then a loud clattering sound erupted, together with much blue smoke, as the engine was started on Sñr Gataño's French Blériot XI monoplane. It was similar to the one in which Louis Blériot himself made the first aeroplane crossing of the English Channel. As the engine speed increased, the dust from the propeller slipstream started to billow up, sending the onlookers scurrying to either side.

My Father lifted me on to his shoulders, and as he stood 6ft 4in tall I had an unobstructed view of the entire track. The Blériot had been positioned for a take-off down the straight. Immediately, with an extra loud clattering roar and ever-increasing clouds of dust, the monoplane gathered speed, bounced upwards several times, and finally bounced into the air, climbing steadily towards us. We could plainly see Gataño when he flew close by, smiling at us as we waved and cheered him on, only orange coloured cloth covering the portion of the structure where he sat. The remaining open framework of the fuselage was painted a bright red.

The monoplane steadily gained altitude as it circled over the area. Then, according to my parents, Gataño made a series of manoeuvres. I remember him circling the tall water tank beyond the far end of the track before making his final landing approach. He came gliding down with the wings wobbling up and down and the engine making odd noises and emitting puffs of blue smoke. Then came the first touchdown, followed by several dusty bounces, and he suddenly swung to his left (ground looping) towards the inner guard rail of the track, the dust completely enveloping the aeroplane. The crowd gasped, the dust settled, and there sat Sñr Gataño, calmly waving to all, with the propeller just inches away from the inner guard railing. Years later I was able to identify it as Santos Dumont's box-like 'plane.

My next sighting was in Switzerland, where the family was visiting Grandmother Hunt in Geneva. This sighting was but a glimpse of an odd looking aeroplane coming in to land on the other side of some tall trees located at various areas.

By the age of ten I had built a four-seat twin-engined biplane (Fig 17). It was a four-seater by virtue of the four ready-made holes in the abandoned red fire-bucket rack, which also served as the major portion of the fuselage. From time to time I would allow my younger brother John, aged 7, the privilege of being the 'pilot', which permitted him to make all the necessary engine and wind noises. This effort was doubtless inspired by the frequent sightings of the twin-engined Navy flying boats operating out of the nearby training station, at Newport, Rhode Island.

This episode took place during the summer of 1919. We had arrived in USA in February 1914 on the *Lusitania* to visit Grandmother Warren in Brooklyn, Connecticut, on our way back to the Argentine, when Germany's Chancellor Bismark, without any consideration for others, started the Great War while Father was visiting his Mater in Switzerland! In 1919 we were awaiting his demobilisation from the Royal Engineers after 2½ years in Palestine under General Allenby.

We arrived at Liverpool in the UK aboard the *Mauretania* in September 1919 and stayed several months in Southampton, where, much to my delight and joy, I learned the whereabouts of a military storage depot for war damaged aeroplanes. They were mostly one- and two-seaters without wings and/or engines. I 'flew' many hazardous 'missions' (making all the necessary sound effects) while my dear Mother patiently awaited my safe return. It was only because she had talked the depot caretaker into letting me 'fly' his disabled birds (my cousin was in the RAF) that I was allowed so to do. Through him I had my first flight in a de-militarised Bristol two-seater fighter at Brooklands in Surrey.

We finally all got back to Argentina in January

Fig 17   *The Height of Imagination, Horseneck Beach, Mass. Summer of 1919.*

1921, to live in Hurlingham, the great polo centre, only a few miles from the Headquarters of the Argentine Army Airfoirce at Palomar. I would often bike over to a road near the airfield and watch the student pilots learning to fly. The take-offs and landings at times could be quite bizarre if not catastrophic.

In 1923 it was back to school in England. However, before being 'accepted' I had to have several months of tutoring to bring me up to acceptable standards. It so happened that Mother, John and I were living in London quite near Hyde Park on the opposite side to the Victoria and Albert Museum. I often used to visit its Science Museum which contained an aviation department and in it, sitting under one of the wings of a huge Vickers Vimy bomber, was the original 1903 Wright brothers biplane, along with some other types of First World War aircraft.

You may recall the British accepted the claim that the Wright aeroplane was indeed the first manned practical self-propelled flying machine, whereas the US Government refused so to do until many years later. Instead, they bestowed the honour on Professor Langley's aborted attempts that took place off a vessel anchored in the Potomac River at the national capital, Washington DC.

Mother returned to Buenos Aires and John and I spent the school holidays with a very dear widowed friend of Father's, a Mrs Tirbutt and her family. There, I built rubber band-powered A-frame type model aeroplanes, trying out all types of wing shapes and sizes, where inherent stability was the desired goal. In February 1926, John and I returned to Argentina for the last time, and a year later, unfortunately, the family became separated, and mother, John and I arrived at New York February 1927.

In July 1929 the three of us, piloted by Capt. Harry Jones, took off from Old Orchard Beach, Maine, on a beautifully clear day in a Stinson Detroiter four-seat cabin biplane for a glorious one-hour flight over the spectacular White Mountain ranges of New Hampshire and Maine.

In 1931, while I was attending a technical school in Washington, DC, taking a two-year course in aircraft design, aerodynamics and draughting, I happened to be passing the back of the White

House when I became aware of an unusually loud aircraft engine noise above and behind me. Quickly turning around, I saw it was an autogyro, and as it passed overhead it aimed directly towards the Rose Garden, which it circled several times. Then I noticed several people standing behind a table on the left side of the garden lawn.

I ran across the street and stood peering over the iron fencing, hedge and flower garden just as the autogyro made its final pass (years later,

Fig 18 *The Plover was 'spin-proof' due to the twin vertical fins mounted on a one-piece rotating elevator; with short-span, wide-chord wings and ailerons. If imitation is the sincerest form of flattery, Prof. Koppen of M.I.T. copied the aileron control system in the design of his 'Skyfarer'.*

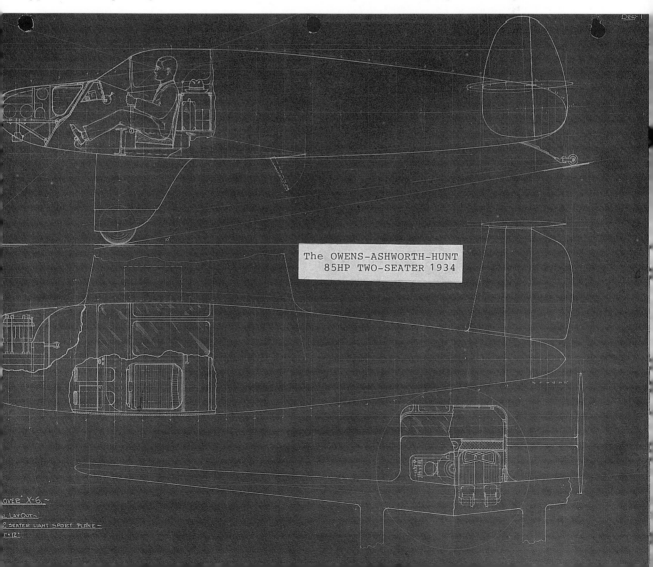

The OWENS-ASHWORTH-HUNT
85HP TWO-SEATER 1934

Fig 19 *The Crouch-Bolas Dragonfly two-seater 1935.*
Powered by two Menasco 125 hp engines derated to 86 hp turning 8ft. 2in. propellers. Wing span 26ft. Wing area 210 sq. ft. Total all-up weight as tested, 2100 lbs.
Minimum 0 wind flying speed – 18/20 mph
Maximum 0 wind flying speed – 130 mph
Minimum 0 wind take-off run – 45/50 ft.
Maximum 0 wind climb angle – 30° (20 wind – 58°)
Minimum 15/20 wind take-off/landing – 0 ft.
with 15/20 wind – vertical descent – ½ throttle.

veteran pilot Jim Ray told me he almost decided not to land) and turned directly towards me, descending at a very steep angle. The aircraft made a quick nose-up 'flare-out', its whirling rotors tilting backwards to provide maximum lift, as Jim Ray with consummate skill made a perfect slow, soft landing on the lawn, the first and last time that

an autogyro would so do. He then turned round and taxied back as far as he could, and turned round again, facing into the wind, keeping the rotor turning with the propeller wash, ready for take-off. As the autogyro came to a stop, a figure walked over to greet Jim, carrying a cloth airmail bag. It was President Hoover. There was a brief meeting, then the President handed the mailbag to Jim with a final handshake. With wheel brakes hard-on, power was increased, causing the rotor blades to whirl faster, then the pilot simultaneously applied full power and released the wheel brakes and the autogyro rapidly gained forward speed into the wind. With another quick nose-up the 'gyro rose as if by magic at a steep angle to clear the tree-encircled lawn, and Jim was safely on his way.

This particular ceremony was to mark the beginning of an express 'roof-top' US Airmail delivery service to downtown city office buildings by autogyro, where specially approved operational areas were provided. Little did I realise at the time that this form of aircraft would lead me to the Sikorsky Division of the United Aircraft Corporation.

In 1932 I joined the engineering department of a machine shop in Providence, Rhode Island, owned by Henry Owens, whose lucrative main business was producing industrial steam traps. He also built experimental mechanical devices, one of which was an exceptionally light 85 hp four-cylinder flat four aircooled aircraft engine. This was designed by a Mr John Ashworth, and my first aviation assignment was to design a light, two-seater aeroplane to take this engine, (Fig 18) using Ashworth moulded structure. In the event, as it turned out, I was also expected to help design rubber-band powered flying models employing a very cleverly conceived patented system, using small thinly gauged aluminium tubing that could be easily connected by special little clips, the invention of a friend of Owens named Rogers. The well-known Lionel Toy Co. had given Mr Rogers a substantial order.

Through these two gentlemen I met, some time later, Shepherd Titcomb, who asked me if I knew of the Crouch-Bolas Aircraft Corporation in Pawtucket, which had recently been established there, very close to Providence. As I did not, he very kindly arranged to introduce me to these two Englishmen, well known in European aviation circles. The company's president was Navy Captain Goodman-Crouch, OBE, and its vice-president and chief engineer was Harold Bolas, MBE. I will not go into any further details except to say that their company was building an experimental aeroplane employing their patented system, whereby the special relative positioning of a propeller in front of a wing, by its induced wash over the wing(s), could dramatically increase the total lift. This permitted safely controlled, greatly reduced take-off runs and/or landings, without sacrificing operational speeds (Fig 19). I joined them as a draughtsman and stayed with the company until the experimental aeroplane was completed and had successfully demonstrated its exceptional qualities. I later acquired an improvement patent on the system.

In 1936 I joined the engineering department of Brown & Sharpe Manufacturing in Providence, an internationally recognised machine and tool manufacturing company. Here I gained valuable experience in mechanical design in their milling machine department, regarding both small-tool jigs and fixtures and gear-type transmission systems. This was to prove of great importance to me later on in my helicopter designing.

Both before and during this period I conducted windtunnel tests at the Worcester Polytechnical Institute in Worcester, Massachusetts, through the generosity of the then Professor Merriam, who was head of the Aeronautical Department. These tests concerned several types of lift-increasing devices, the anti-spinning control of stalled aircraft (a major cause of fatal accidents), and lateral (aileron) wing control systems. The tests also included the scale model of the light aeroplane I had designed for Owens. The results were published in the October 1936 issue of the *Journal of the Institute of Aeronautical Sciences*. (Figs 20, 21 & 22)

Also during this same period I met Alexander Krapish (pronounced Kraypish), one of the original associates who had helped Igor Sikorsky to build his first American transport aeroplane on Long Island, New York, in 1923, and also was a test pilot. Later Alex became chief test pilot of the British subsidiary, the de Havilland Moth Aircraft Co. in Lowell, Massachusetts, where, before his retirement, he designed and built a beautiful two-seat touring monoplane in which he flew with Frank Hawks in the annual Ford Reliability Tour of the USA. As fate would have it, through me Alex was to rejoin Igor Sikorsky, this time on Igor's final venture, his VS-300 experimental helicopter.

Although Harold Bolas was instrumental in my meeting Igor Sikorsky, it was through Alex Krapish that I learned of his almost unknown experimental helicopter programme. Also through Alex, I was able to meet Sikorsky's chief engineer, Michael Gluhareff, for the first time. This brings us up to 1939 and my joining the recently formed Vought-Sikorsky Aircraft Division of the United Aircraft Corporation of East Hartford Connecticut. That is how it happened.

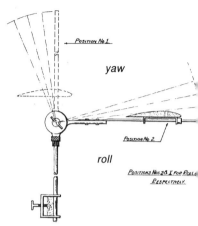

Fig 20 *Worcester Polytechnic Institute Open Throat Wind Tunnel. Wind Velocity 30 to 120 ft/sec.*

Fig 21

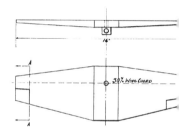

Fig 22

Fig 23 *Mr. Sikorsky poses by VS-300. This photo was taken on the day of her first 'Roll-out', about two months prior to her momentary first free 'Flight'.*
Note single right foot pedal, * also the interconnecting cable in between rotor blades, and lack of coning restricters. (See Fig 24)

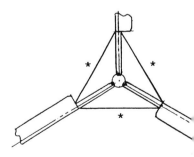

Fig 24

The Basic Difference Between an Autogyro and a Helicopter

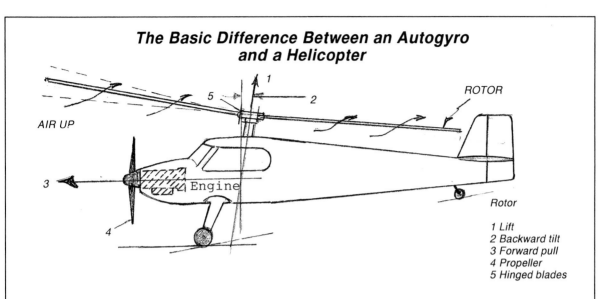

ROTOR

AIR UP

Engine

Rotor

1 Lift
2 Backward tilt
3 Forward pull
4 Propeller
5 Hinged blades

Fig 25 The Autogyro

The autogyro is so called because its lifting rotor automatically gyrates (turns like a windmill) when it is tilted backwards and pulled fast enough through the air, by an engine-driven propeller. More tilt increases lift, for taking-off, climbing, or landing, and less tilt is required for gliding. Note that the oncoming air always passes up through the rotor blades (rotating wings).

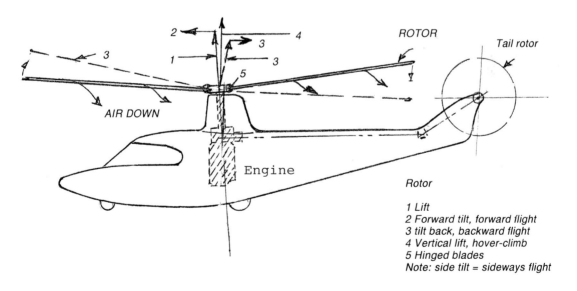

ROTOR

Tail rotor

AIR DOWN

Engine

Rotor

1 Lift
2 Forward tilt, forward flight
3 tilt back, backward flight
4 Vertical lift, hover-climb
5 Hinged blades
Note: side tilt = sideways flight

Fig 26 The Helicopter

The helicopter engine directly turns its rotor (rotating wings), not the wind. Thus the air is pulled down through the rotor and is used for both vertical lift for take-off, climb and hover, and to propel, by tilting the rotor to the desired direction of flight. In the event of a power failure, the helicopter automatically becomes an autogyro, for a safe soft landing. In other words, the whirling wings also now replace the aeroplane propeller.

Chapter Two
1939

The Ultimate Goal

There are those who fortunately have been endowed with certain inherited creative talents and have had the added privilege and ability to successfully and gainfully exercise them in the realm of experimentation, research and development, and so it was with Igor Sikorsky.

It is my feeling that all too often in writing accounts regarding a famous central figure, too little emphasis is placed on the reasoning and or, description of the events that took place leading up to the final decision to change course. In many cases ignoring the person, or persons, other than the central figure himself, that suggested the change in the first place.

I shall therefore endeavour to rectify those omissions in such a manner as to maintain the interest of the reader by using non-technical common terms, and knowledge, for descriptive comparisons. This should in no way diminish the genius of the central figure, but instead should extol his innate ability in recognising the importance of, and willingness to listen to others. Of such was Igor Sikorsky. It was also characteristic of him to deal with great patience with many reversals, and whose gentle but firm leadership with humility, drew to him from those around him, their best performance, unquestionable loyalty and respect.

On 27 June 1931 Igor Sikorsky filed patent application number 547343, comprising 23 claims relating to a direct-lift aircraft, with the United States Patent Office.

On 19 March 1935 he was granted Patent Number 1,994,488 with 23 allowed claims regarding a direct-lift type aircraft. In part it reads:

> The present invention relates to aircraft, and more especially to the direct-lift type. The object of my invention is to solve successfully such direct-lift

aircraft problems as torque compensation, directional steering, and the application of power to a vertical lift producing propeller, either by a power-plant, or means by air through which the vehicle navigates [i.e. he thus included "autorotation"].

> A further object of the invention is the creation of a cheap, simple, and easily operated mechanism for controlling the lateral and longitudinal stability of the aircraft in its various directions of flight.

Thus was heralded, unobstrusively and unbeknown to the world at large, yet another and final success story in his long and creative life.

On 14 September 1939 a 30-year-old dream came true for Igor Sikorsky when he successfully piloted his experimental VS-300 helicopter on its first 'lift-off'. When he did so, a new era in direct-lift aircraft was successfully born: the advent of the single main lifting rotor helicopter, with but a single anti-torque tail rotor.

It so happened that, the week before that famous lift-off, I had, through Alex Krapish, my first meeting with Michael Gluhareff, Igor Sikorsky's chief engineer, about the possibility of my joining their Engineering Department on the helicopter project. I had already sent him my background material, including the drawing and calculations for the light aeroplane I had designed, powered by the Owens-Ashworth engine, the results of the windtunnel tests published in the *Journal of the Institute of Aeronautical Sciences*, and letters of recommendation from Mr Bolas and Mr Owens. All of these he went over very carefully with me, and I was very much impressed with his genuine interest in my work, his thoughtful comments and friendly attitude. At the end of the meeting he said he would like to keep my material and go over it with Mr Sikorsky, and that he would contact me as soon as a decision had been reached.

Fig 27 ORIGINAL IDEA OF CYCLIC BLADE CONTROL VIA AILERON

March 19, 1935.   I. I. SIKORSKY   1,994,488

DIRECT LIFT AIRCRAFT

Filed June 27, 1931   9 Sheets—Sheet 1

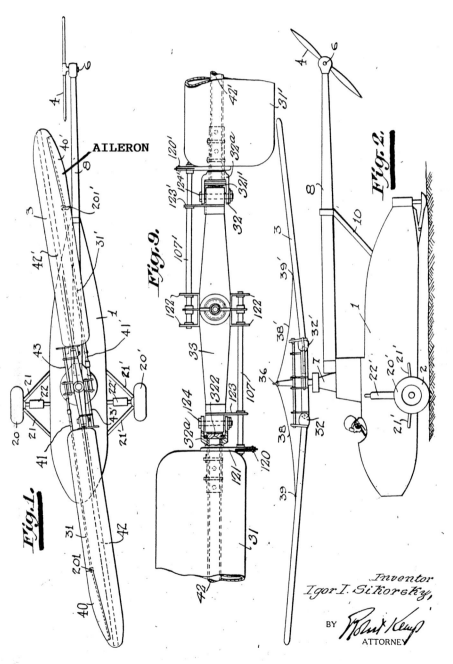

AILERON

Inventor
Igor I. Sikorsky,

BY

ATTORNEY

Notice similarity of Fig 2 in the above plan to the design of the S-38-B on page 31 (Fig 15).

'HEELICOPTER' – PIONEERING WITH IGOR SIKORSKY

On 22 October 1939 I received a telephone call from Michael Gluhareff. He said that both Mr Sikorsky and himself had been favourably impressed by my material, and that as a result they were offering me a position in the Engineering Department with a starting salary of $140 per month, starting the first week in November. I would receive a formal notice as to the exact date. Since the call came on my birthday, I considered it a good omen, not to mention the extra joy caused at home in the midst of the celebrations then ongoing.

The day finally arrived, and to my surprise and great pleasure I was assigned to the Design Office, where the preliminary design work was done for the combined Sikorsky and Vought Engineering Department. It was right next to the engineering managers' offices of Mr Sikorsky and Mr Rexford Beisel of Vought.

There were five other engineers in the office. Two of them, Henry Muther and George Ellis, worked directly under Michael Gluhareff, as I would. The other three worked for Mr Beisel. One of them, Charles Zimmerman, was a project engineer and the inventor-designer of a radical type of observation aircraft for the US Navy, being built in the experimental shop. It was an attempt to circumvent the Crouch-Bolas system of using the propeller slipstream to augment wing lift. He was awaiting the completion of his own office, so he spent much of his 'cloud nine' thoughtful time pacing up and down the office. His aeroplane flew, but did not come up to expectations and was finally cancelled.

The day after my enrolment I was formally introduced to Igor Sikorsky in his office by Michael Gluhareff, and to Michael's brother Serge, who was his assistant. Like so many others before me, I was immediately impressed by Igor's quiet dignity and his ability to make one feel at ease. The meeting was brief but cordial, mainly punctuated by questions from Sikorsky, and I was instructed to report directly to Michael for the time being.

After the meeting Serge took me on a complete tour of the factory, a gesture usually reserved for members of the staff, I was later told. At the time the company was still predominantly completing Sikorsky-related aircraft orders before Vought's move from East Hartford. The work mainly concerned the construction of S-43s for the Dutch, and the converting of three S-44s from their original US Navy coastal patrol bomber role to commercial passenger transports. These four-engined flying boats were the largest such aircraft that Sikorsky had ever built. The experimental shop was mainly occupied with Vought activities, and they were busy building several experimental models for the US Navy, including Zimmerman's creation. There tucked away in an obscure corner, I had my first view of the diminutive first experimental version of the VS-300 helicopter, under the able care of Adolf Plenefisch.

The five other engineers in the Design Office soon proved most helpful and friendly, and my acceptance into their ranks was both pleasing and reassuring. This was also the case with both Michael and Serge Gluhareff, especially Michael, who became a good friend as time passed on.

My first trial assignments from Michael occupied the next few weeks, and included designing the installation of a navigation drift indicator on an S-43 destined for delivery to the Dutch East Indies in spite of Germany's declaration of war on 1st September, and the designing of a retactable nose landing gear for a proposed Sikorsky amphibian for the US Navy. The latter apparently pleased Michael quite a bit, for my next assignment was to design the wheeled ground handling and beaching gear for the S-44. It had to be capable of being manually handled for quick attachment/detachent from the hull while the aircraft was afloat at a beaching ramp. That also won Michael's approval.

I found working for Michael both pleasant and instructive, any criticisms he made being gentle but constructive. He was always prepared to listen to a question or suggestion, and would praise a good one. I could not have been more happily assured of a promising relationship and future.

On 9 December, from the upper-floor window of the office where I was working at my draughting table, I had seen glimpses of VS-300 as it made short forward hops piloted by Serge Gluhareff. Igor had been asked to have somebody else help with the flight testing, so that he did not expose himself to unnecessary danger. The wisdom of that suggestion was soon to be proved. I had not noticed any activity for a while, then all at once I saw a rather battered VS-300 being moved into the Experimental Shop. Serge had been doing some slow forward flights close to the pavement, since that direction was causing the pilot the most difficulty. At that time little was really understood of the main rotor reaction versus the pilot's control input, or even of the proper geometrics of the control system itself, so for protection from the gusty wind Serge was flying in the lee of the hangars. Inadvertently, being engrossed with piloting, he had passed beyond their protection, and a sudden side gust caught him unawares from the right, causing VS-300 to tilt over to the left more than usual.

Serge immediately applied full opposite control, but there was no response and the helicopter started to drift rapidly sideways and lose altitude. He dumped lift and power but the left main wheel struck the pavement, and, completely out of control, VS-300 flipped over, causing the rotor blades to hit the pavement, and the machine finished upsidedown. All of this happened in a matter of seconds. To the onlookers it was a miracle that Serge, now head down, was only shaken. He quickly unfastened his seat belt, dropped safely to the pavement and scrambled from beneath the wreckage. The very next day, 10 December, I joined the original VS-300 team and started to work with Russel Clark, the VS-300 Project Engineer. I immediately thanked Sikorsky and Michael Gluhareff for so unexpectedly affording me this great privilege, and this evidently pleased them both.

It is perhaps fitting at this point to tell how VS-300 came into being before I appeared upon the scene, as told to me by Michael Buivid and Bob Labensky. Perhaps initially, no other in United Aircraft Corporation was more directly responsible for getting the VS-300 started, and subsequently more supportive, than Charles McCarthy, the newly appointed General Manager of the Vought-Sikorsky Aircraft Division. The story begins in 1937, when the Sikorsky Division had lost the big flying boat contract to the California based Consolidated Aircraft Corporation.

What initially gave Sikorsky the confidence in 1930 that he could design and successfully build a safe single-main-rotor helicopter, as described and illustrated in the patent application he submitted at that time? Spanish mathematician and aviation pioneer Sñr Juan de la Cierva, the inventor of the Autogiro (Cierva's own autogyros were spelt with an 'i'), had solved the basic dynamic problem of overcoming the gyroscopic overturning moment associated with main lifting rotor blades rigidly attached to their supporting shaft. Such as was the

case with Cierva's first autogyro in 1920, which he was unable to control. Cierva had so named his freely rotating wing (rotor) type aircraft an autogiro, because its purely wind-driven rotor automatically gyrated. Just like the modern wind-driven rotors used in generating electricity, or the old-fashioned windmills.

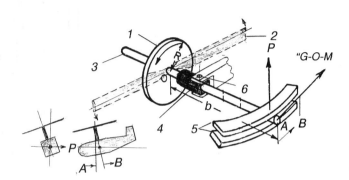

Fig 27A *The Gyroscopic overturning moment (G-O-M).*

What is this 'gyroscopic overturning moment', or force? Referring to Figure 27A, the basic elements are depicted associated with a gyro: 1 is the gyro, a balanced, fast-spinning solid disc that is, at its centre, rigidly mounted at right angles (90°) to its shaft 3, which in turn is rotating inside a bearing 4, also rigidly held but allowed to pivot horizontally 6, but restrained vertically at 5. Any movement of shaft 3 about pivot 6, such as from A to B will immediately cause a reaction vertically at P. That is the 'gyroscopic overturning moment'.

If it is presumed that, instead of a disc, there is a two-bladed rotor 2 spinning around horizontally, rigidly mounted on vertical shaft 3 on top of an aircraft fuselage (See Fig 27A, bottom left), any pivoting movement of the fuselage such as A-B would immediately cause the rotor, together with the fuselage, quickly to tilt over sideways under force P. This is what happened with Sñr Cierva.

Cierva's solution for this problem was remarkably simple: let the gyroscopic overturning moment-force dissipate itself by leaving each blade free to flap up or down about a horizontal hinge located close to the centre of rotation of the supporting shaft.

Having thus been assured of rotor blade rotational stability, Igor next considered the control method by which to tilt the rotor in any desired direction. He chose aerodynamic cyclic rotor blade pitch control.

To understand the full meaning of what is meant by cyclic blade pitch control as a means of tilting the main lifting rotor to the desired direction of flight, refer to Figure 28. The upper roller-coaster-like diagram depicts the desired path which the outer tip of each rotor blade must take in order to tilt the rotor's propelling thrust in the desired direction. It also shows that, in order to achieve the desired forward rotor tilt, the initial rotor blade pitch plus input angle (by the pilot – stick forward) has to begin at a precise point. In this example, for direct forward flight, it is at 0° as indicated, as each blade starts to turn through a single full cycle of 360°.

Actually, the input point would depend upon the weight and the air resistance of any given blade. Thus the 0° plus input angle could be either before or after the indicated 0°, in order to achieve either its maximum upward or downward movement at 90° and 270°. This is indicated as time lag on the

Fig 28
Cyclic rotor blade tilt control.

lower diagram, which is the vertical view looking down on top of the two separated halves of the main rotor, rear and front.

Each full half circle depicts the area of the tip path directly above it, and corresponds to the required direction of tilt to propel the helicopter forwards, as indicated by the side view diagram in between the two circles. The rear half of the rotor 'disc' (circle) has tip up, the front lower half circle tip down, and the forward (FWD) tilted rotor arrow indicates forward propulsion. So that the rotor-blade cyclic system would respond as precisely as the pilot wished, it was necessary to incorporate a mechanical linkage system below the rotor hub. The linkage system devised by Igor in 1930–31, as shown in Figure 29, consisted of a gimballed plate 2, the upper surface of which it was contacted by rollers on the ends of vertical spring-loaded, push-rod-type links 3. The upper ends of these links activated the ailerons through torque tubes 1 on the outer ends of the hinged rotor blades 7 to produce an increased/decreased lift on each blade through each 360° cycle, and a rotor tilting tip path similar to that shown in Figure 28. The plate 2 could be tilted in any desired direction by means of the pilot's control stick 5 through cables

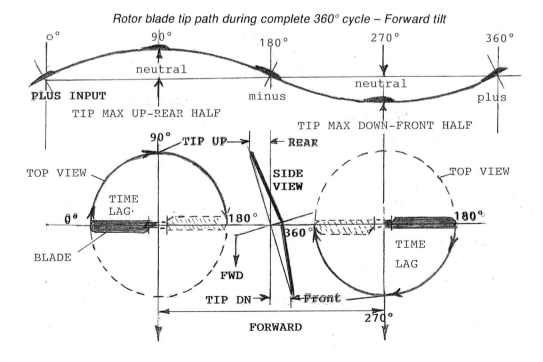

Rotor blade tip path during complete 360° cycle – Forward tilt

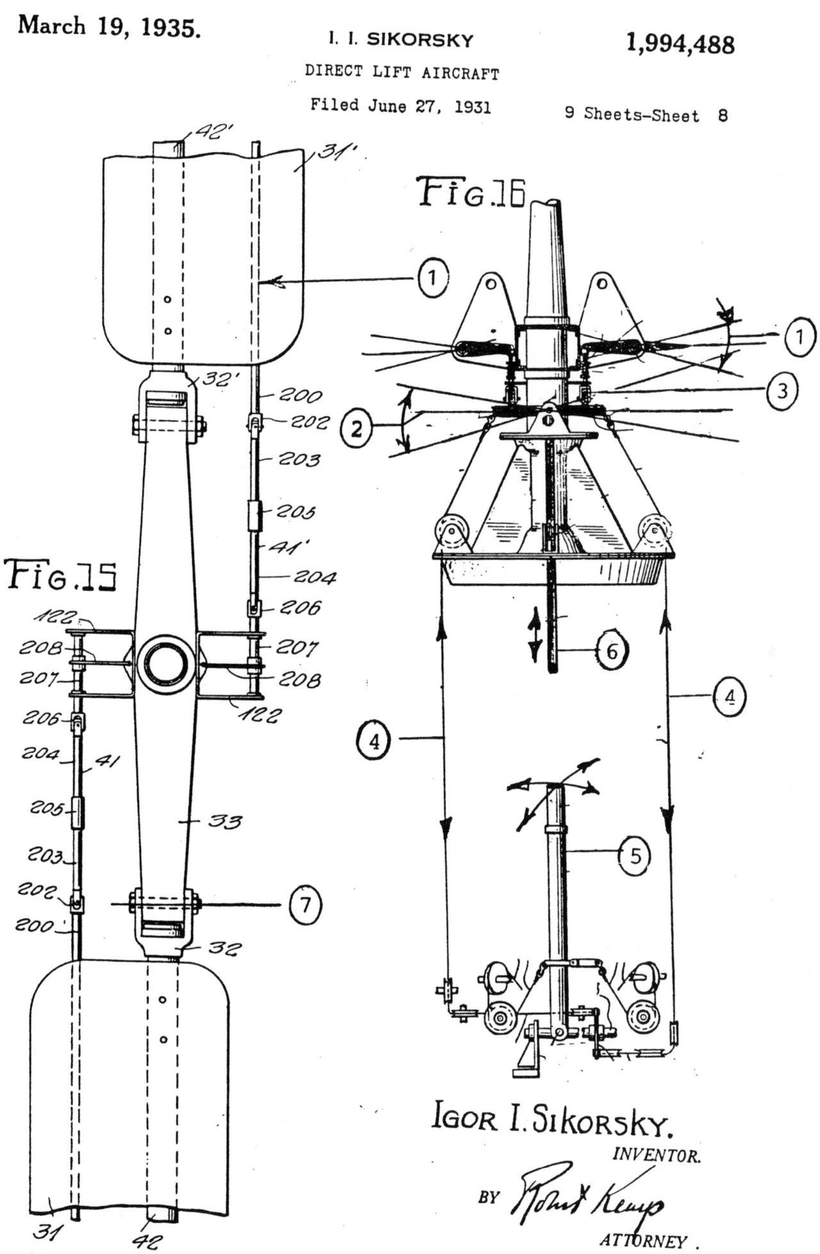

Fig.16

Fig.15

Fig 29

IGOR I. SIKORSKY.
INVENTOR.
BY
ATTORNEY.

4 (lateral), and rod 6 (fore-and-aft) as indicated.

Finally, there was the need to provide not only an equal and opposite force (anti-torque) to counteract the torque required to drive the main lifting rotor, but also a powerful enough force to overcome that torque in order to steer the helicopter in that particular direction. That anti-torque force was to be provided by a single vertical tail rotor, the pilot varying its thrust posi-tively or negatively by means of a right and a left foot pedal.

The only other control not mentioned was the so-called 'collective pitch' control, the system which changed the total thrust or lift of the main rotor. Again, as originally conceived, this was to be controlled by a wheel operated by the pilot's right hand, which caused a control rod to move up or down inside the rotor shaft and collectively

45

increase or decrease the blade angles from on top of the hub.

In other words, the collective pitch would be preset (and/or readjusted), but take-off, landing and all other flight manoeuvres requiring an increase or decrease of total rotor lift would be a function of more or less power, dictated by the pilot operating the engine throttle lever.

All of the foregoing was, of course, purely conceptual. Furthermore, Sikorsky realised that, if he was seriously to consider embarking on an entirely new helicopter venture, it was imperative that he brought himself up-to-date on all matters concerning rotary-wing aircraft.

By the mid-1930s Europe was more advanced in helicopter development than the USA. However, the European models that enjoyed initial success were all multi-rotor types: *coaxial* (one rotor above the other rotating in opposite directions on a common axis); *biaxial* (side-by-side, the rotors turning in opposite directions and mounted on outriggers; *Intermeshing* (1939) (side-by-side, with their hubs close together, but tilted away from each other, so that their driveshafts formed a vertical 'V', and also turning in opposite directions). In each case the configuration was chosen to nullify the effect of torque. Not one successful single-main-rotor helicopter existed anywhere. It was just the type of challenge that Igor Sikorsky needed to reactivate his thoughts regarding aircraft that did not need running take-offs or landings.

Both France and Germany were successfully demonstrating their experimental helicopters, the French with their Breguet-Dorand using a co-axial rotor powered by a 350 hp engine and capable of forward speeds of up to 60 mph, and the Germans with the Focke-Achgelis Fa 61 with its biaxial, non-overlapping rotor configuration powered by 160 hp engine, which was successfully flying at speeds of up to 76 mph. In both aircraft the designers used a similar type of control to move forwards, sideways or backwards; a form of cyclic blade control. For this basic reason Sikorsky decided to visit and inspect these two successful models in Europe, with Corporate blessing, before he proceeded any further with his own untried concepts.

Since he was going to be away on an extended visit, Michael Buivid and Bob Labensky decided to surprise him upon his return with an experimental small-scale helicopter rotor test stand. (Fig 30) They would fabricate this in the Test Laboratory,

of which they were in charge, as an 'under-the-bench' operation. The stand was to consist of a 28 hp aircooled Henderson motorcycle engine and half of a Ford Model A rear end drive, belt-driven by the engine and up-ended to act as the geared-down rotor shaft. On top of this was fastened the rotor hub and the counterbalanced single-bladed rotor, provided with a means of adjusting the blade angle when static.

Fig 30 *The Buivid-Labensky test stand in 1938 that provided information for VS-300. Its shaft was the rear axle of an automobile. The transmission was the automobile's differential. V belts carried the power from a motorcycle engine to the single-bladed rotor.*

A tubular welded frame held the stand together, and was mounted on wheels for transportation. For test purposes the stand could swivel horizontally on a single vertical pedestal when raised as shown in Figure 30. With this arrangement it was possible to measure the rotor torque in foot-pounds on a spring scale, 1, located on a boom at exactly so many feet from the centre of the rotor hub. Using a mathematical formula, that data could be translated into the exact amount of horse-power needed to produce the measured lift of the rotor at any particular angle of rotor blade pitch

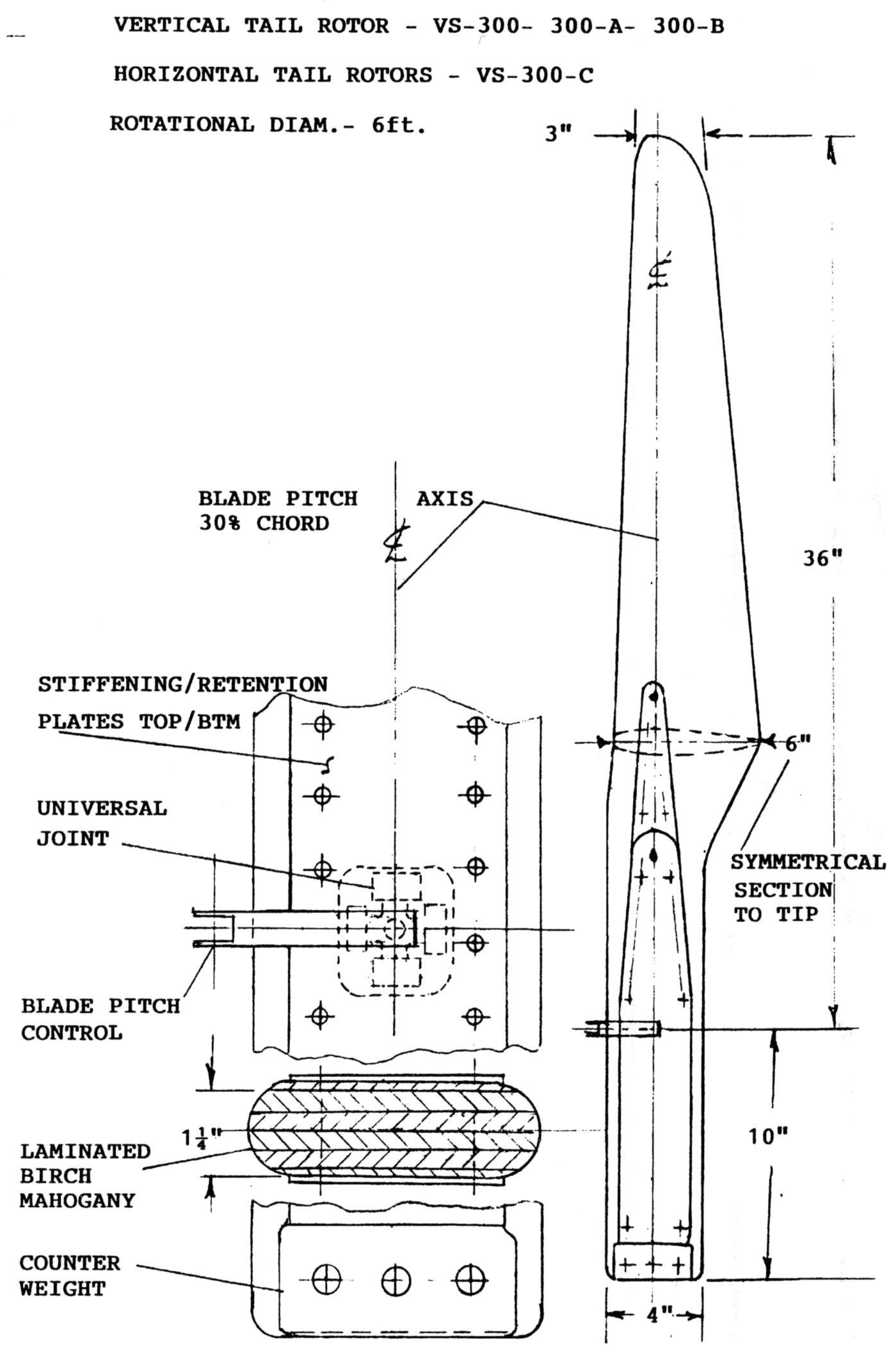

VERTICAL TAIL ROTOR - VS-300- 300-A- 300-B

HORIZONTAL TAIL ROTORS - VS-300-C

ROTATIONAL DIAM.- 6ft.

3"

36"

BLADE PITCH   AXIS
30% CHORD

STIFFENING/RETENTION
PLATES TOP/BTM

6"

UNIVERSAL
JOINT

SYMMETRICAL
SECTION
TO TIP

BLADE PITCH
CONTROL

10"

LAMINATED
BIRCH
MAHOGANY

$1\frac{1}{4}$"

COUNTER
WEIGHT

4"

Fig 31   *Vertical tail rotor. VS-300.*

setting. It would also indicate the amount of thrust needed by an anti-torque tail rotor. At the top of the pedestal an hydraulic piston sensed any change in vertical pressure, which was immediately registered on a pressure gauge that indicated the amount of lift. A careful record of the test results were maintained for Igor to evaluate upon his return.

Igor's surprise and appreciation of what Michael and Bob had accomplished in so short a time, together with the promising results from the test stand, when added to Igor's enthusiastic report on his findings during his trip in Europe, was sufficient to convince Corporate Headquarters in East Hartford that further work should be done. It was also greatly helped by the backing Igor received from Charles McCarthy, the recently elected General Manager of the new Vought-Sikorsky Division. The original preliminary design was therefore started on a proposed one-man, experimental single-main-rotor helicopter, using cyclic blade control and an anti-torque tail rotor. It was given the designation VS-300.

A senior Design Engineer on loan from the Vought Section, Russel (Rus) Clark, was placed in charge of the project (he was awaiting his new assignment, which was to be the Project Engineer on what was to become the famous US Navy F–4U Corsair fighter-bomber of the Second World War and would do the stress analysis. Henry Muther, formerly Chief Engineer of Mooney Aircraft was responsible for the design layouts; Carrol Aumont, formerly Mechanical Design Engineer for the Mack Truck Company, would do all the gear transmission designing; 'Prof' Sikorsky (Igor's nephew) was in charge of the aerodynamics; and Nick Nickolsky was responsible for the rotor dynamics.

The initial and most immediate problem facing Rus Clark in his first aquaintance with a helicopter was estimating the entire weight of the helicopter structure, including the rotor blades, to ensure that the estimated power required was feasible after allowing for the added weights of the pilot, fuel and engine oil.

At this time there was very little information available regarding the forces acting on helicopter main rotor blades, especially during flight or due to sudden control inputs, let alone the formulae required to calculate them. This was where Nick Nickolsky was of great help.

The blades of a wind-driven autogyro, the closest example available, did not have to absorb the additional driving forces imparted to a helicopter rotor blade, but at the same time it was necessary to design the lightest blade possible. In this instance there were to be three blades, each blade having to lift one third of the total weight of the fully loaded helicopter without causing the tips of the blades to rise (cone) upwards appreciably above the horizon, this is called the 'coning angle'. This angle is controlled by the weight of the blade, which generates its own centrifugal force (CF). By its very nature, any horizontally hinged rotor blade that is made to whirl around will, due to its own weight, try to pull itself outwards away from its hub. That is its centrifugal force, and the faster the rotor whirls around, the greater that force. The next trick is to balance the CF against the required lift of the blade to keep the coning angle to a minimum. That is why the careful balancing of all of the different forces is so very important when designing a helicopter rotor blade.

Apart from the power required in turning the main rotor, there are other power absorbing elements such as the engine cooling fan, the main rotor gearbox together with its cooling system, the tail rotor gearbox and its driveshaft, the tail rotor itself, and control of the helicopter. To all of these must be added the estimated power required to overcome the total air resistance of the complete helicopter at various speeds and, uniquely, in various directions of flight. Once all of these items have been added together, a margin for error is provided by the designer, dictated from experience and called the 'fudge factor'.

Experimental shop drawings were soon being released to Mr Reickert, who was in charge of the Experimental Shop, where an able, experienced shop and aircraft mechanic, Adolf Plenefisch, was placed in charge of assembly of VS-300. He was also in charge of its maintenance, both in the shop and in the field during flight testing, being ably assisted by George ('Red') Lubben. They were to continue in these roles for the next two historically famous experimental Sikorsky helicopters, the XR-4 and XR-5. Adolf and Red made a great and loyal team.

When VS-300 was rolled out for the first time for an engine run-up, she closely resembled Igor's original patent concept (Fig 32) as well as being a flying skeleton in order to eliminate any

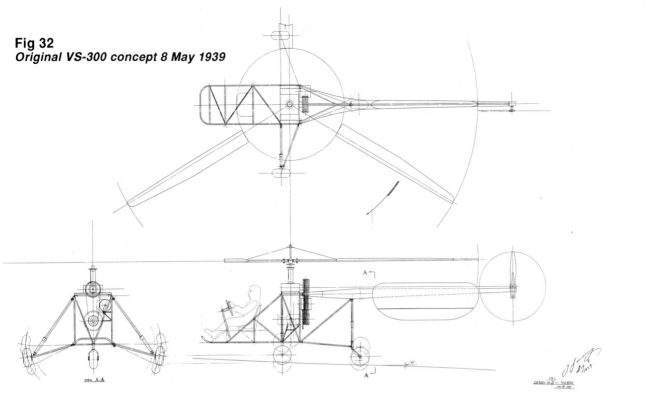

Fig 32
Original VS-300 concept 8 May 1939

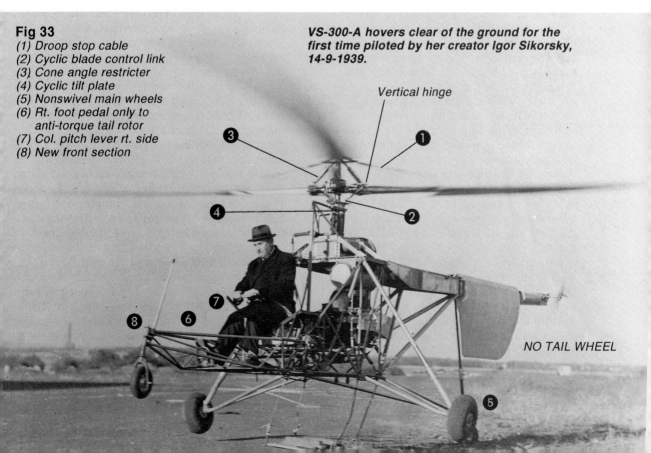

Fig 33
(1) Droop stop cable
(2) Cyclic blade control link
(3) Cone angle restricter
(4) Cyclic tilt plate
(5) Nonswivel main wheels
(6) Rt. foot pedal only to
anti-torque tail rotor
(7) Col. pitch lever rt. side
(8) New front section

VS-300-A hovers clear of the ground for the
first time piloted by her creator Igor Sikorsky,
14-9-1939.

Vertical hinge

NO TAIL WHEEL

unnecessary weight for the 75 hp Lycoming engine to lift off of the ground. **NB. Compare VS-300 with VS-300A on page 49.** The new front section, supporting a swivelling front wheel, the pilot, his flight controls and an instrument panel, was a welded tubular steel structure permanently attached to the similarly constructed centre section. That section supported the main rotor, its controls, the driveshaft, a belt-driven gearbox, the complete powerplant and fuel system and the main wheels. Interestingly, these two sections, except for minor changes, remained intact throughout the entire three years of the machine's active service, including three accidents.

The so-called 'tailboom' was a sheet aluminium riveted box structure attached to the two outer top ends of the centre section by means of two Y-shaped arms, at the apex of which (underneath) was attached an inverted 'V' supporting strut whose lower two ends were attached to the two outer bottom ends of the centre section. (Fig 32) The shaft-driven anti-torque rotor with its gearbox and blade pitch changing control was located at the tail end of the boom.

Just ahead of the tail rotor a vertical fin projected downwards below the tailboom, designed to help provide directional stability both during hovering and in forward flight. The former condition, by virtue of using a high-lift wing section on the fin, was designed to use the downwash from the main rotor to produce lift to counter the main rotor torque. A vertical strut attached to the tailboom originally supported the swivelling tailwheel.

Three cables radiated from a vertical tube on top of the rotor hub to support the three blades when at rest. There were also three cylindrical spring-loaded hydraulic dampers attached to the top inner sections of the blades to prevent the blades from inadvertently folding upwards. This was an early concern of Igor's, and one can hardly blame him from imagining the dire consequences. These dampers were due to play an important part in the development of the proper control of VS-300.

Igor's early attempts to fly VS-300 were bedevilled by vibrations and instabilities accentuated by his own complete lack of helicopter piloting experience. That it took steady nerves plus remarkable co-ordination goes without saying, but it was not long before he was able to persuade VS-300A to lift all four of her wheels off the pavement simultaneously for a few seconds. As already mentioned,

that happened on 14 September 1939. He later told me that his anxieties were greatly relieved at that moment, as he was reassured, as he had been in 1910 when he became airborne on the first short hop with his homebuilt S-2, that he was going to succeed.

During the next two months tethered flights, first by Igor and then by Serge Gluhareff, could be maintained in calm weather as they accustomed themselves to control reactions. The next step was untethered flight. While the helicopter in its VS-300B form could be sustained directionally both sideways and backwards, which was thrilling for the two pilots, any attempts at forward flight immediately brought increased vibration from the main rotor. It became very obvious that this 'leetle problem', as Igor characterised it, had to be solved before any further progress could be made. Another problem was the linkage ratio of the collective pitch lever and engine throttle (See Fig 34).

Other than the proper control of the helicopter, the most outstanding challenge for the helicopter designer was coping with vibration. Anything that rotates must be balanced in order to avoid it, the chief offender being the main rotor. Simple vibration would be caused by one blade being heavier than the others. Induced vibration can occur even when all the blades are perfectly in balance with each other, if they are not properly restrained individually from moving horizontally back and forth towards each other (out of phase) about their vertical hinge.

Another form of induced vibration can be caused by what is called 'natural frequency'. For instance, a helicopter tailboom that has a natural frequency of X number of shakes per minute can start to shake if the tail rotor is out of balance and produces the same number of shakes per minute. The combined frequencies, working together, could cause the helicopter to shake itself to pieces. Only by isolating the cause of the vibration, or changing the natural frequency of the affected structure, can the situation be remedied.

To try and keep rotor-induced vibration to a minimum, the blades of VS-300 were aerodynamically balanced or matched so that all three blades had the same tip path plane, as near as possible. That is, they would all cone upwards to the same level. Initially this was tried by checking each blade angle at the same radius when turned to

Fig 34   ***VS-300-B. First free flight November 1939***
Igor Sikorsky pilot

(1) – (3) Serge & Michael Gluhareff
(2) Mr. Wilson
(4) Russ Clark
(5) Adolf Plenefisch
(6) Counterweight

(7) Swiveling main wheels
(8) Further aft rear wheel
(9) Both feet tail rotor
(10) Collective pitch lever right side

the same checkpoint with the helicopter level. (Fig 36)

Later, as flight testing progressed, we came up with a device which became known as the 'blade tracking flag'. It consisted of a long pole, to which was attached to its top, and parallel to it, a strip of canvas (Fig 35) held in place top and bottom by elastic cords. The strip was high enough to contact the whirling blade tips at its vertical mid-point. First of all VS-300 would be levelled off and the control system checked and locked in neutral position. Next, the flagpole was positioned so that engagement with the whirling blade tips was made when the flag was vertical. This was done with the rotor static, by positioning the flag so that the blade tip overlapped the edge of the flag by two or three inches. Each blade tip was painted a different colour (black, yellow and red). The pole was then pivoted away from the blade tip about its butt end. As soon as the rotor had reached its required test speed, the pole was slowly pivoted forwards and at the instant it engaged the rotor tips it was quickly withdrawn. The resulting colour pattern on the flag showed the necessary adjustments. Blade angle adjustment was made by lengthening or shortening the (pitch) angle control link (Fig 33), but first the blade angle of the correct blade was compared with that of the out-of-track blade(s). Sometimes it took

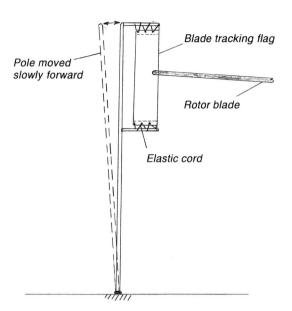

Fig 35   Blade tracking flag.

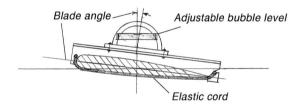

Fig 36   Blade coning angle indicator.

more than one effort to obtain an acceptable pattern. Strict manufacturing control of rotor blade production was to become another special requirement for rotary-wing aircraft, especially with regard to calculating the probable life of all of its rotating parts.

It will be recalled that the first few hops of VS-300 were made with the machine tethered to a large lead disc, the tether being lengthened as pilot proficiency increased. Igor now decided to alter the main wheels from non-swivelling to fully swivelling, to avoid sideways wheel scuffing. He also decided to change the pilot's tail-rotor foot pedal control system. At the time of the original flight attempts only one right foot pedal was provided. Since the rotor torque was always in the same direc-

tion, trying to turn the helicopter to the left, the thrust from the anti-torque rotor at the end of the tailboom was always in the opposite direction. So to turn to the right, more thrust was added by pressing the pedal down, and to turn to the left the pilot simply raised his right foot and let the torque take over. However, this proved to be too sloppy, so a left pedal was installed. At this point, a fourth swivelling wheel was added under the fin. In this form VS-300A became VS-300B.

With these changes the helicopter was given more freedom of action by replacing the lead disc with a lead ball and a 6 ft (Fig 37) flexible cable attached to the underside of the centre section, directly under the main rotor. This allowed hovering practice well off the pavement, as well as restricted horizontal movement.

The next phase of free flight brought us up to December 1939, at which point VS-300B could be flown (Fig 34) in any direction with minimum vibration, except forward. It ended up with Serge being flipped over by a sudden side gust while flying very slowly forwards on 9 December 1939.

Cyclic Blade Control was going to be the first main stumbling block for the single-main-rotor helicopter. It was, and still is, the very source of success or failure (as well as vibration) for any type of helicopter and/or rotary-wing aircraft which incorporates this type of control for both lateral and longitudinal (forwards/backwards/sideways) movement. In other words, an all-in-one type of main rotor control, except for directional (steering) and anti-torque control, which is achieved using the tail rotor.

To the prospective helicopter designer, what was so obviously lacking at this time was the knowledge of what really happened to the rotor blade in response to the commands given to it throughout its 360° cycle, or the actual behaviour of the blade as it reacted to those commands. Curiously enough, this question was not directly addressed until well into the XR-4 programme, and will be dealt with later. The actual mechanical control system itself for cyclic rotor blade control, to tilt the vertical rotor thrust angle aerodynamically, is simple geometrics, and has already been explained. (Fig 29).

In December 1939 the designer knew that the centrifugal outward pull of the rotating blade could be used to help tilt the entire helicopter in any desired direction of flight (Fig 38). This was

Fig 37 *By November, 1939, short "captive" flights (note the ball and chain) were becoming a regular procedure. Serge Gluhareff as pilot. VS-300-B.*

accomplished by placing the horizontal flapping hinge A a certain distance F away from the centre of the rotor hub, so that when the blade was commanded by the pilot to flap up an upwards force H was created at the offset hinge A, while an equal and opposite downward force was created by the opposite blade at the hinge H–1. This caused the rotor shaft B, and consequently the whole aircraft, to tilt in the desired direction.

The problem requires the amount of offset relative to the amount of outward pull (CF) of the blade to be positioned so that it will cause the helicopter to tilt smoothly, without placing too much bending stress on the driveshaft.

Referring back to Fig. 29, it can be seen that only a flapping hinge 7 is indicated, and there is no vertical lead/lag hinge to relieve the fore-and-aft stresses on the blade root attachment to the hub. The vertical hinge was added as a result of Igor's visit to Europe. Thus on VS-300A the interconnecting blade cables were removed and were replaced by spring-loaded stops at the vertical hinge.

The significance of the interplay between cyclic blade control input and its relationship to the direc-

tion of flight, especially forward flight, was evidently not realised, or appreciated, at that time. Nor was its direct influence on the horizontal movement of the rotor blade about its vertical lead/lag hinge.

Although he did not have that knowledge, Igor was fully aware right after Serge's accident that unless prompt action was taken to remedy this sudden reversal, it could well endanger his ability to convince Corporate East Hartford that VS-300 programme should continue. With his calm courage he announced that he had a 'positive alternative to cyclic blade control'. He was accorded permission to proceed with it. That meant it would not appear until after the beginning of 1940. Most of the main basic technical requirements and problems associated with achieving proper control of a single-main-rotor helicopter have now been covered. Hopefully, lay readers will have by now begun to understand and appreciate why, when one sees something that obviously works well, it has taken a long time to reach that stage. Because, until the basic problem is understood, the solution is evasive.

The following is a summary of the changes made

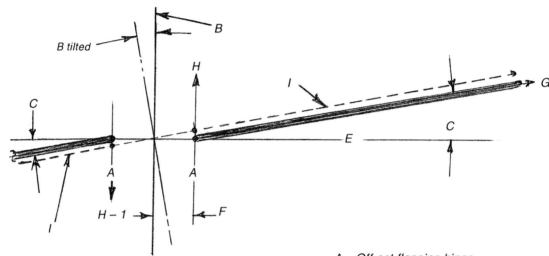

Fig 38 *Using the leverage of the off-set flap-ping hinge, plus the cyclic blade control to gain direct positive directional tilting of the main rotor.*

NB. Combined leverage H + H-1 tilts rotor shaft B

A – Off-set flapping hinge
B – Centre of rotor shaft
C – Input cyclic blade control angle
F – Hinge off-set
G – Centrifugal force – CF
H – Upward leverage
H-1 Downward leverage
I – Final tilted position of rotor blade.

on VS-300 during her first series of trial tests starting in May 1939 and ending with her first accident, on 9 December 1939.

VS-300 (Fig 32)
May–August Originally as pictured, with:
Collective pitch lever on right side
Non-swivelling main undercarriage wheels
Swivelling rear wheel
Interconnecting cables on main rotor
Single right rudder foot pedal only
No vertical rear fin.

VS-300-A (Fig 33)
September New front structure plus swivel nosewheel
Rear wheel eliminated
Vertical rear fin added
Vertical main rotor hinge snubbers added
Interconnecting blade cables eliminated
Main rotor coning restricters added.

VS-300-B (Fig 34)
December Swivelling rear wheel added
New vertical fin
New main swivelling undercarriage wheels
Left rudder pedal added
Front counterweight added
Improved linkage between collective pitch lever and engine.

Chapter Three
1940

A positive alternative to cyclic blade control

This now brings us to a dramatic stage in the developing life of what will now become VS-300C, for Sikorsky had now decided to switch from cyclic blade control to non-cyclic blade control. Ironically, he was so near, yet so far, from achieving his ultimate goal. Analysis by 'feel', vision, or innate senses can be slow and arduous, as each avenue of approach is patiently tried out until 'the light is seen at the end of the tunnel'. That is what the VS-300 team now faced.

The change from cyclic to non-cyclic control was made possible by Igor's many years of experimental aircraft design experience, in his not 'putting all his eggs in one basket', so to speak. As early as February 1939 he had suggested to Bob Labensky and Michael Buivid that perhaps it

might be wise to have an alternative control system other than cyclic blade control.

Their solution was a simple, static, full-scale demonstration model (this still exists) (Fig 39). It consisted of a vertical pedestal, from the top of which, mounted on a universal joint, was a forward structure containing a pilot's seat and flight controls. Counterbalanced by a rear structure supporting two small, hinged, single-bladed laterally disposed horizontal tail rotors, to the rear of which was a similar vertical tail rotor.

Each of the three hinged single-bladed tail rotors was identical to the original vertical tail rotor (Fig 41) and they were powered independently by an electric motor. The basic mixing control system which was similar to that shown in Fig 42, permitted Igor and Serge to get an initial 'feel' of the alternative non-cyclic control system. Both pilots agreed it was a practical method.

Fig 39 *The non-cyclic control system – Buivid/Labensky. VS-300-C.*

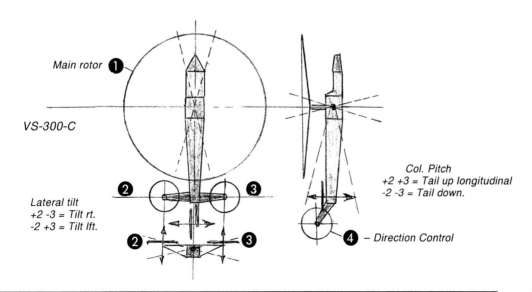

Main rotor ❶

VS-300-C

Lateral tilt
+2 -3 = Tilt rt.
-2 +3 = Tilt lft.

❷ ❸

❷ ❸

Col. Pitch
+2 +3 = Tail up longitudinal
-2 -3 = Tail down.

❹ – Direction Control

Of course, the model could only demonstrate hovering flight, but the actual situation basically only requires the simultaneous exercising of the three control movements of tail up or down and tilting to left or right, using the pilot's 'stick' control, and directional control using the left-right foot pedals. Both pilots felt that the new system would actually enhance the additional required manoeuvres of take-off, landing, and directional flight.

VS-300's flight controls had undergone changes as recorded in Chapter 2, but with the vertically positioned collective pitch lever always on the right side of the pilot and the engine ignition switch and throttle lever on his left. There was a mechanical linkage between the CPL and the engine, wherein more-or-less collective pitch would automatically equally demand the same in power from the engine.

It was rather difficult for the pilot to control three widely separated levers quickly without having three hands, so the CPL was moved from his right to his left side on VS-300C, but still mounted vertically with a friction device to maintain the lever in any desired position. This device consisted of two lengths of wood, one on each side of the lower end of the lever, which pressed against each side of the lever. The pressure and friction was adjusted by turning a thumbscrew and compressing a coiled spring. Pulling the CPL back increased lift and *vice versa*, not only of the main rotor, but also of the horizontal tail rotors, so the helicopter would ascend or descend in a level manner.

What had now been achieved was the total simultaneous movement of the entire helicopter for a given control input. Whereas before, with cyclic blade control, first the main rotor was tilted and then the rest of the helicopter followed suit, the pilot, of a non-cyclic control will have a response more like that of a fixed-wing aircraft.

From a mechanical standpoint, non-cyclic control (Fig 40) simplifies the main rotor hub, as the only mechanical requirement was that of collectively changing the angle of the blades to increase or decrease lift. This was also the case with the two horizontal and single vertical tail rotors.

However, when it came to the matter of operating the main rotor plus the three tail rotors harmoniously together, the complexity of the former cyclic blade controlled rotor hub was now shifted to a central 'mixing control'. In VS-300 it

Fig 40
A – Actuated by pilot's pitch control lever – non-rotating
B – Blade pitch control link
C – Horizontal flapping hinge
D – Blade drag link – horizontal blade movement
E – Blade flapping restrainer/damper
F – Blade horizontal restraint buffer
G – Rotating plate – cyclic blade tilting control removed
H – Upper support mast
I – Vertical Lead-lag hinge for horizontal movement of rotor blades in flight.
J – Rotor shaft

was located just to the rear of the pilot's seat. This was a product of a combined team effort.

Basically, the 'mixing control' permits three interrelated control systems, vertical, longitudinal and lateral, to function in unison and/or independently of each other so that the pilot can monitor any system independently of the other two at any time.

The shaded elements of Figure 42 communicate purely simultaneous collective pitch changes in unison to the main rotor and to the two horizontal tail rotors. Thus by moving the CPL 1 backwards, the entire helicopter will ascend vertically on an even plane (or *vice versa*). This is because mixing link 3 is connected to the CPL torque tube 10 which moves the top end of lever 7 that has its lower end held steady by link 4, causing the unshaded elements 8 to pivot about fulcrum 9, thereby moving the four cables 6 connected to the two horizontal tail rotors, while the unshaded lever 5 and cable 5C are held steady by the control column 2.

Longitudinal (up-down) independent horizontal tail-rotor control is achieved by moving control column 2 forward or backward, and since it is connected to lever 8 by link 4 it causes lever 7 to pivot about its upper end, it being held steady by mixing link 3, thus causing the unshaded elements 8 to pivot about fulcrum 9, thereby moving the four cables 6 connected to the two horizontal tail rotors that are working in unison, to move the tail end of the helicopter up or down.

Lateral (tilting from side to side) independent control is achieved by moving the control column 2 from side to side, causing cables 5C to move unshaded lever 5, which in turn moves elements 8 and control cables 6 so that, simultaneously, one horizontal tail rotor increases its lift and the other decreases its lift, causing the helicopter tilt to one side. Q.E.D. . . . (?) Never mind, it did actually work!

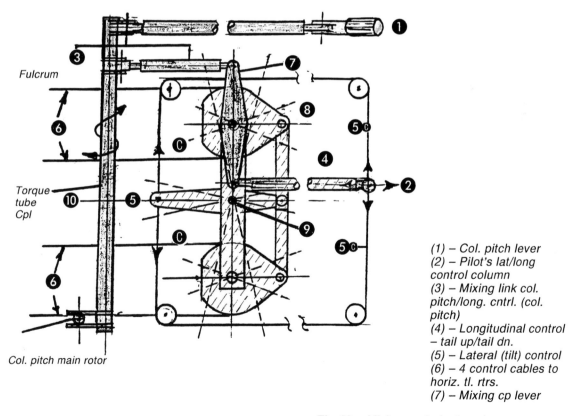

Fulcrum

Torque
tube
Cpl

Col. pitch main rotor

(1) – Col. pitch lever
(2) – Pilot's lat/long control column
(3) – Mixing link col. pitch/long. cntrl. (col. pitch)
(4) – Longitudinal control – tail up/tail dn.
(5) – Lateral (tilt) control
(6) – 4 control cables to horiz. tl. rtrs.
(7) – Mixing cp lever

Fig 42 *Mixing control – top view.*

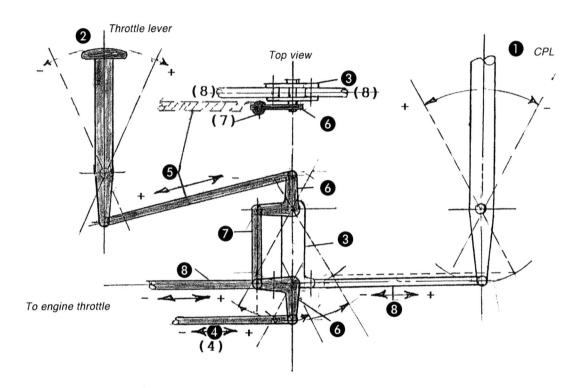

Fig 43 *Mixing control engine throttle-collective-pitch lever. (CPL)*

Figure 43 depicts the simple system that provides the pilot with an automatic increase or decrease in engine power when demanding an increase or decrease in total lift, while using the collective pitch lever, while at the same time providing the pilot with instant independent monitoring of the engine power at all times.

The throttle lever 2, to link 5 – to upper crank 6 – to parallel link 7 and Idler Link 3 – to lower crank 6 – to link 4 (shaded elements) goes directly to the engine throttle. And, as shown in the top view, the throttle system can be moved independently of the CPL 1 and links 8 at any time by the pilot, regardless of any particular position of the CPL. Also, because of parallel links 7 – 3, cranks 6 remain vertical except when moved by throttle lever 2.

The foregoing two control systems were my immediate concern at the outset of the necessary control changes for VS-300C. The main under-carriage and front wheel were to remain unchanged, as were the front and central structure. Since Russ was taking care of the design of the new rear section of the fuselage, I was given the task of incorporating changes in the new set of main rotor blades.

The original design layout of the main rotor blade was missing. In its stead was found a barely legible print. As there were the new changes to be incorporated, I quickly had to make a new drawing, and in my haste I failed to notice that the view shown on the old print was a bottom view of the blade. So my drawing, being the opposite, would have the blade turning in the wrong direction! Serge saved the day by suggesting: 'Do not worry, the printing machine can print it upside down'. Those who might be interested in helicopter main rotor blade design of half a century ago should refer to Figure 44.

At least it can be truthfully said that, during the entire experimental helicopter period of this account, not a single main rotor blade failure occurred. . . . lucky?

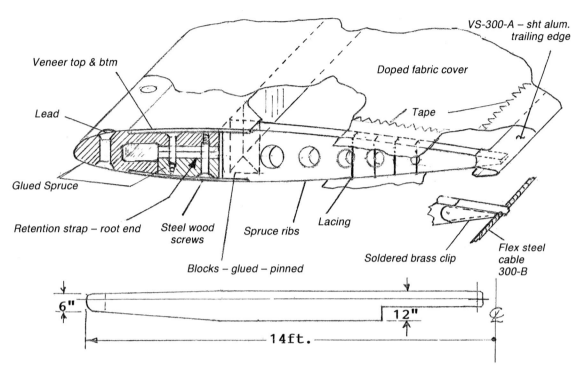

Fig 44 *VS-300 – 300-A – 300-B.*

The new horizontal tail rotor drive, like the main rotor, would consist of Gates 'V' belts; in this case a pair to each rotor, powered off the tail driveshaft. An extention to the rear of that shaft powered the existing vertical tail rotor with its right-angle drive. Again the Gates company insisted on supplying their drive belts gratis. The two single-bladed horizontal tail rotors were duplicates of the vertical tail rotor (Fig 41).

By early March 1940 the initial powered run-ups of VS-300C were successfully made. The helicopter (minus main rotor) was gimbal mounted on top of a specially designed pedestal that allowed Igor to conduct full-scale pre-flight test of the new tail control system.

This time Igor, with Serge's accident in mind, said there would be thorough pre-flight testing, especially because not only were two extra tail rotors involved, but the collective pitch lever was now on the left side. A completely new type of co-ordination had to be learned between the throttle lever and the collective pitch lever, using the left arm and hand. Both Igor and Serge spent quite

some time practising.

Then, on 16 March 1940, complete with its new set of main rotor blades, VS-300C made its debut with the Buivid/Labensky non-cyclic control system. Beginning with tethered hovering flights before attempting free forward flight, the most important flight direction. For these tests, light flexible steel cables were attached to the tops of the main undercarriage structures on each side of -300C, and were held by Russ Clark and Adolf Plenefisch as a 'safety measure' to steady the machine if it appeared to be tilting too far over to one side. While this evidently gave some measure of comfort to Igor Sikorsky, both Russ and Adolf later remarked that they mentally pictured a somewhat less reassuring episode.

Igor first satisfactorily hover-tested all directions of flight. Russ and Adolf then positioned themselves well forward and to either side of VS-300C in readiness for an attempted slow-speed running take-off. As prearranged, as soon as Igor started the ground roll Russ and Adolf also started running forward. He then gradually increased

Fig 45 *Igor Sikorsky tries out the Buivid/Labensky non-cyclic system on VS-300-C mounted on a gimballed pedestal, minus main rotor, in early March 1940. * Artificial horizon*

rotor lift and -300C responded by gently rising from the pavement up to two or three feet. By that time the 'safety crew' were running flat out, and as he came abreast of them he made a true 'running' landing.

I witnessed all of this from the office window. Several more 'flights' were made, each one a little higher and longer than the preceding one, until the safety crew were completely exhausted, but Igor wore a broad satisfied grin. For in each flight there was no indication of apparent increase in vibration! These hops were made on pavement between hangars.

With cables removed another running take-off was made, Igor gradually increasing forward speed until he was well beyond the limits attained by cyclic -300B. At that point he was beyond the S-44 flying-boat hangar and flying some 15–20 ft up in apparently complete control. He then made a broad turn and returned to the now equally jubilant ground crew, making a slow and precise landing. Before any further testing it was decided to have -300C returned to the shop for a thorough checkup; also the throttle linkage needed adjusting.

The next several test flights were made from the meadow (Fig 46), next to the S-44 hangar, and at first were concerned with lateral control response

in all directions of flight. This was evidently causing Igor some concern, as he finally said that there was not enough differential thrust available from the two horizontal tail rotors to create an acceptable rate of roll under gusty/windy conditions, especially during sideways flight. In other words, the rotors would have to be moved further apart.

It was the first time that Igor had to use the new left-hand CPL, and apparently it was an improvement over the old right-hand system. But it still required considerable concentration by the pilot before reactions became automatic. The left hand had to move down some 15 in. to move the throttle lever, then quickly back up to the CPL handle. Eventually these movements were a sight to behold, as Igor's remarkable co-ordination would be demonstrated, such as if he had forgotten to secure his necktie, in the final few feet before making a vertical touchdown the rotor wash, rebounding up off the ground, would keep blowing it up over his face, requiring the added rapid movement of brushing aside the necktie. However, the throttle now needed less attention owing to the improved interconnection with the CPL.

Also of concern was the possibility of driving belt slippage with the proposed increase of its length, as the horizontal tail rotors were to be moved 4 ft further apart. The Gates people assured us that that would not be the case.

The final tests before the -300C went into the shop for changes were further investigations of the transition from hovering flight into forward flight, and *vice versa*. Here there was unquestionable improvement, as in the final test flight the machine accelerated without an additional tremor from zero to 30 mph to zero, as paced by a car. This positive progress was quickly transmitted to East Hartford by a much relieved Igor Sikorsky.

Early on, when Sikorsky was creating in his mind what was eventually to become the first version of VS-300 experimental helicopter, stability was one of his chief concerns, and he evidently gave considerable thought to the practicability of a lightweight automatic stabilising gyro. It would have to produce a stabilising force sufficient to move the main-rotor cyclic blade control mechanism, yet be light enough not to become a weight penalty. A standard full-size bicycle wheel complete with tyre was chosen because of its light weight and availability. It was gimbal mounted so that any

Fig 46 *VS-300-C is flight tested in the meadow for its ability to cope with gust wind conditions. * note safety precautions.*

disturbing force could be measured. Michael Buivid and Bob Labensky produced the rig in the Test Laboratory. To produce the estimated necessary stabilising force, the tyre was filled with water. Rotational speed and its equivalent stabilising force was noted down with each increment of the rotational speed. It began to look fairly promising, when all of a sudden the centrifugal force generated by the water in the tyre pulled the tyre free of its air valve, treating the entire area to a free shower. Sufficient force had not been generated, and a heavier gyro was unacceptable.

Later on, Arthur Young, the designer-inventor of the Bell helicopter, ingeniously solved the gyro problem by the patented method of using a gyro stabilising bar interconnected with the cyclic blade control system. In fact, when first tested it was so powerful that it nullified control inputs, but when modified it became a significant contribution to the success of the Bell helicopter. Then along came young Stanley Hiller with his servo system, similarly interconnected with the cyclic blade control system. Both methods successfully provided auto-stabilisation.

The decision to increase the span of the outriggers, even though it meant an added delay while new outriggers were designed and fabricated, and the tail control cables and driving belts were replaced, proved to be well worthwhile. On 13 May

1940, -300C-1 successfully demonstrated its new 'tail feathers', and for the first time Igor was able to fly smooth figure eights with increasing zeal, making the banked turns with considerable aplomb and ending up at the highest forward speeds so far achieved.

Forward flight was apparently no longer resented by the main rotor. In fact, vibration was now at such a reduced level at 25/30 mph that a new feeling of confidence inspired the -300 team. On the other hand, while lateral control was considerably improved, sideways flight was not quite as good as had been hoped. Nevertheless, at that time it seemed to be not too serious a matter. The euphoria over forward flight was dominant.

Understandably, Igor's renewed enthusiasm was generating an equal desire to demonstrate the cause. I shall not forget the private show he put on for Mr Charles McCarthy, the Division's General Manager, who had so faithfully encouraged and backed him from the very beginning. Upon ending the demonstration with a perfectly executed landing, he stopped the engine, alighted from his creation, then proudly walked over, with just a hint of a swagger, to meet Mr McCarthy, who in turn was eagerly advancing with a broad smile and outstretched hand to congratulate Igor warmly. The -300 was now back on track.

During the foregoing, I noticed that Igor was wearing a navy blue knitted sleeveless pullover under his suit jacket, and sometime earlier, when his jacket was unbuttoned, I had seen several distinct holes in it. I happened to mention this to Nick Nickolsky, as it did not match Igor's usual neat attire. Obviously amused, Nick related why this particular pullover was of such importance. The story went back to the early Long Island period, when times were harder and winter weather dictated warm clothing around the Sikorsky plant. Mrs Sikorsky, as her first introduction to knitting in wool, chose to make a sleeveless pullover for her beloved new husband as a special surprise present. Owing to her inexperience, a series of inadvertently dropped stitches developed into some obvious voids, much to her embarrassment. But Igor was so proud of his bride's loving work of art that he insisted on wearing it just as it was. He had continued so to do during cool weather ever since.

Due to the improved flight and ground manoeuvring control made possible by the non-cyclic control system, -300C-1 had reverted to a non-

swivelling main undercarriage, but with increased lateral distance between the tyres.

A day or so after the private demonstration to McCarthy, on 20 May 1940, Igor gave his first public demonstration at Bridgeport Airport, just across the road from the Vought-Sikorsky plant, before a specially invited gathering which included personnel associated with producing his creation. He had pre-flown -300 over to the demonstration area so as not to discomfort the audience, and could start off with the aircraft as a static display.

First he gave a walk-round explanation of the various functions performed by the basic elements of -300 with its new non-cyclic control system. Then followed a lively question period that provided Igor the opportunity he so enjoyed, providing a polite, quick and precise response to the various questions asked of him. The aircraft was then moved a safe distance away from the spectators by Adolf and his ground crew and the pre-flight engine start was demonstrated.

First, because there was no engine/rotor clutch, the main and tail rotors were set in motion by a separate, removable electric motor that rotated them up to a speed above engine starting speed. Then the engine was started and gradually accelerated to engage at the same speed of the rotors. The electric rotor starter was removed, the collective pitch lever eased back, and -300C-1 gently rose vertically to about 20 ft. Igor began by demonstrating the ease with which the helicopter now responded to flight in all four directions, and the assurance with which he piloted and manoeuvred said as much for the Buivid/Labensky non-cyclic control system as it did for the pilot's skill. But it was his innate sense of showmanship that was a delight to behold.

A bicycle-type wire basket was attached to the front end of -300C-2, and on a mound of earth some 50 yards away Serge was standing, holding a parcel out in front of him. Flying sideways until he was directly opposite to Serge, Igor stopped, then, gradually losing altitude, he slowly approached and deftly manoeuvred the basket directly under the parcel so that Serge only needed to drop it in. He then returned to the starting point, still flying sideways, and delivered the parcel. A small valise was then placed in the basket and the exercise repeated, this time with the valise being delivered to Serge. However, instead of -300C-1 stopping after slowly approaching Serge on his earthen mound, a puff of wind kept it moving gently forwards, and Serge backwards, until he almost fell over, much to the amusement of the spectators. All went well on the second try.

With the next vertical take-off -300C-1 went rapidly up to about 50 ft, hovered a few moments, then turned through 180° and flew off in the opposite direction. It was obvious that the pilot was enjoying the show as much as the audience, especially when he ended up doing his favourite figure eights. Upon landing, the then Commissioner for Aeronautics, Lester Morris, stepped forward and, much to Igor's surprise and delight, presented him with Connecticut State Helicopter Pilot's Licence N° 1 (Fig 47).

At this point in time, another matter of significance to the future development of -300C-1 had already taken place. Earlier in the year Sikorsky had been given a Corporate 'go-ahead' to respond to the US Army's request to bid on a proposed observation helicopter, designated the XR-1, to carry a pilot and observer. This was the very first time the Army had requested an open bid for any type of helicopter. It was the result of a visit to Germany by Messers Platt and Lawence LePage,

where they obtained the manufacturing rights to produce the Focke-Wulf Fw-61 helicopter, one of the only two successful helicopters operating at that time. It was considered by the US military as the logical next step in providing the Army with the most sophisticated form of 'eyes in the sky', being even better than the autogyro, the recently approved rotating-wing aircraft that was being tested at Wright Field, Dayton, Ohio, by the US Army Air Materiel Command under then Lt Frank Gregory. In fact, Lt Gregory and LePage generated sufficient interest in the US Congress to appropriate $300,000 for helicopter development in the Dorsey Bill, $250,000 of which was to be given to the winner of an 'open' competition for an observation helicopter. It was generally conceded that the winner would be the Platt-LePage entry, the XR-1

The Sikorsky proposal was to be based on the

Fig 47   *VS-300-C, After her first successful public demonstration by her creator Igor Sikorsky, he is presented with helicopter licence No. 1 by State Aviation Commissioner Lester Morris, 20 May 1940.*

successful Buivid/Labensky non-cyclic control system version of -300C-1. According to the Army specification, the helicopter was to accommodate a pilot and observer seated in tandem, with the observer in front, affording both him and the pilot the best possible visibility. The single engine had to be of an approved aircraft type. There was no mention of any specific engine type, the number of main lifting rotors, or the rotor configuration. The helicopter was to be capable of flying backwards and sideways out of 'ground effect', under full control. That referred to the ground 'cushion' that occurred under the main rotor(s) as a result of the rotor downwash rebounding upwards directly under the rotor(s), up to a height of approximately one half rotor diameter above the ground. It also had to be capable of flying sideways at not less than 25 mph, since flying out of ground effect requires more power. The helicopter was to be land based and ground manoeuvrable under its own power.

Here we were blithely submitting a proposal, No. VS-311, for a helicopter almost five times heavier and requiring five times more horsepower than VS-300C-1, which itself had but a few hours of total flying time, and not all of them particularly successful. Moreover, it was designed by engineers who, before VS-300, had had no previous experience with any form of rotating-wing aircraft! On top of that, the two pilots had between them barely a few hours of very brief individual 'flights' to their credit. Actually, it was not quite as bad as it might sound, as Sikorsky's only real competitor, Platt-LePage, had autogyro experience but had no helicopter experience at all. The company was relying entirely on somewhat limited foreign knowledge and experience, with a configuration which was still having limited success.

However, of the utmost importance and significance was the formal recognition by both the military and the corporation of the practicability of the Sikorsky-type single-main-rotor helicopter. The VS-300 demonstrated the ability of Vought-Sikorsky Division's helicopter engineering team to produce a creditable design, based on the promisingly demonstrated new configuration of the -300C-1 under the supervision of Project Engineer Russ Clark. Very little data remains of this important proposal.

It was all too obvious that, while the improved control and reduced vibration were most welcome improvements, -300C-1 was suffering from lack of

power. That was the extra price it had to pay for improved control, caused by the extra weight and air resistance of the two outriggers, the tail rotors and their driving systems. So in mid-July Igor agreed to instal a more powerful engine. The next lightest aircraft engine available was the 100hp aircooled opposed flat-four Franklin. With the aid of an extra (sixth) Gates drive belt, the rotor driving system would be able to absorb the extra power needed to drive the two horizontal tail rotors. In fact we found out the new engine produced somewhere between 90 and 95hp.

It was to be late August before -300C-2 was rolled out again, incorporating the following changes. A new, lighter engine air cooling system was required, which Russ asked me to design. The blower was placed directly over the engine cylinders, driven by a new belt and pulley mounted on the engine driveshaft. This proved to be superior to the old system (fortunately!).

Up to that time all three tail rotors had been the same as the original vertical tail rotor; single-bladed (Fig 41) counterweighted and single-hinged, but because of their diameter (6 ft) they were still not capable of producing sufficient thrust to achieve brisk manoeuvring. Igor therefore suggested using larger-diameter rotors. Designed by Russ Clark, the new tail rotors were two-bladed, individually hinged, of 18in greater diameter (7 ft 8 in) and had new hubs, but were almost the same weight as the old ones! The vertical tail rotor was also replaced (Fig 48). I had the pleasure of donating one of these blades to the Helicopter Museum at Weston-super-Mare in England. It had two inches or so broken off of its tip, as a result of Igor's accident, recounted later. The Museum's curator, Elfan ap Rees, had never expected to possess such a rare item, and was delighted with it.

After Serge's accident on 9 December 1939, the new main rotor blades were strengthened in anticipation of a power increase. The new tail rotor, when driven by a 5 hp electric motor, produced over 80 lb of thrust, which was more than anticipated.

Whether the changes were relatively small or major, like those just described, it was not uncommon for Adolf Plenefisch and his loyal crew to work overnight, or stay late, to make changes so that -300C-1 would be ready for Igor to try out the next morning. This was done because we soon found out that, with Igor's active mind, unless an

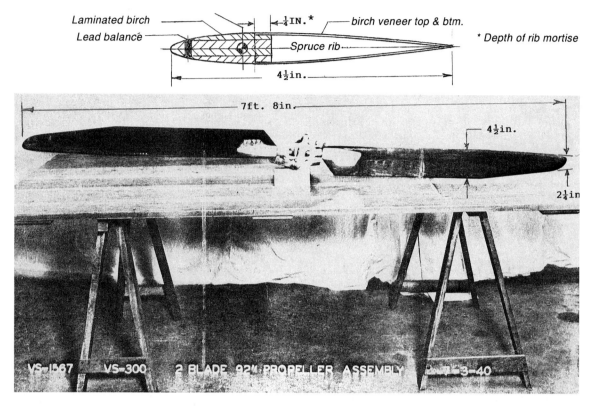

Fig 48 *VS-300-C tail rotor.*

idea of his was not acted upon immediately, it would quickly be succeeded by another one. It was greatly satisfying to Adolf, his crew and myself when, after an all-night stint, Igor would greet us the next morning with 'I think perhaps . . .', and I could chime in with: 'The change is ready for you to test'. He would turn and look at us momentarily and then give us his delightful smile.

After a day or so of ground run-ups and adjustments to -300C-2 before her initial test flight, its creator was soon happily demonstrating its greater manoeuvring precision, faster response, and higher speeds in all directions. Later, on a windy day, sideways flying was also found to be better controlled. Of particular pleasure to Igor was the additional interconnection between collective pitch and engine throttle, with the installation of the throttle mixing control. Readjusting the power required was easier and less frequently needed than before.

When the sounds of enthusiasm came to the attention of Lt Frank Gregory and his second-in-command, Lt Haugen, they decided to see at first hand what was taking place. So in mid-June 1940

they stopped by on their way back to Wright Field after visiting Platt-LePage in Philadelphia; a most pleasant surprise for Igor. After a walk-around explanatory question-and-answer tour, they had all five directions of flight demonstrated. Then came figure eights, and finally Igor's favoured precision parcel deliveries. Both officers were genuinely amazed at the pilot's skill in executing the various manoeuvres and the precise response of the helicopter to the controls. It was soon obvious that both were very keen to try their hands with this strange-looking mechanical bird, which pleased Igor no end.

First they were given the benefit of the unique, slow-motion Sikorsky explanatory helicopter flying lesson. The 'students' stood either side of him and listened intently, watched (heads nodding enthusiastically), and moved when -300 moved, as Igor simultaneously explained and executed each manoeuvre in free flight, only a foot or so off the ground.

'HEELICOPTER' – PIONEERING WITH IGOR SIKORSKY

With that masterful introduction fresh in his mind, Lt Gregory carefully repeated Igor's demonstration before slowly gaining forward speed and circling the famous 'Snivens meadow' next to the S-44 hangar. It was soon obvious that he was enjoying his first piloting of a helicopter, as he carefully executed a figure eight before reluctantly making his first well executed vertical landing. Hearty congratulations followed, especially from Igor.

With Lt Haugen it was an entirely different story. Being younger and full of beans, and no doubt encouraged by his boss's performance, he sort of 'leaped into the saddle and dashed off', as it were, much to the amusement of those of us watching him. I thought I caught fleeting expressions of concern by Igor, for example when Haugen

---

Fig 49 *Igor Sikorsky proudly stands by his first pupil, Lt. Frank Gregory, who successfully pilots a helicopter for the first time, that happens to be the first ever successful single-main-rotor helicopter in the world, the VS-300-C.*

made a rather abrupt stop that was somewhat over-controlled. Nevertheless, neither officer left any doubt as to their very favourable impressions, requesting another similar event the next morning before they left.

Over the next few weeks -300C-2 continued to be tested to establish her limits and possible improvements, and Serge began to learn once again how to fly a helicopter. This time it was a far cry from the struggles he originally had with the VS-300A. Both he and Igor had encountered a curious 'tail twitch' every now and again, and Igor believed it was due to some sort of inexplicable pilot error, especially as otherwise the aircraft was performing well, except perhaps under fairly high wind conditions, when lateral control would become somewhat marginal.

We will now leave -300C-2 to record a significant turn of events, especially for Russ Clark and myself. Russ had been appointed Project Engineer (at that time meaning he was in complete charge) for a design proposal to be submitted to the US Navy for a carrier-based, light-bomber-fighter to be designated Vought F-4U, and later to become known as the 'Corsair'. It was destined to become one of the most outstanding naval aircraft in the Pacific military operations of the Second World War. Later, Russ ended up as Vice-President and Chief Engineer of the Ling-Temco-Vought Corporation at Dallas, Texas (where Vought relocated shortly after 1945) and became an internationally acclaimed designer of fighter aircraft. While I was indeed happy to see Russ so rewarded, I was sorry to lose his helpful companionship. Sadly, he recently made his 'last flight'.

I shall never forget that morning in August 1940 when Russ's appointment was formally announced. I was called into Igor Sikorsky's office, where he, Michael and Serge were waiting for me. I was asked to be seated, then all three silently looked at me and then at each other, with rather solemn expressions. Finally, after a suitable pause, they looked at me again. Michael, who stuttered slightly, said: 'B-B-Beel, since Russ is no longer with us, we do not know who to take his place'. He paused, still with that solemn expression and added: 'except you'. At that they smiled, probably because of my expression, before I realised that the procedure had been prearranged. Igor added that he was sure I would be able to fill the vacancy, and

Fig 50 *Lt. Frank Gregory successfully flies VS-300-C-2 after his first lesson.*

Michael and Serge then left us alone.

Igor then stepped over to his bookcase and showed me his personal library of design notebooks, full of his sketches, data and calculations relative to the various aircraft he had designed. Then, turning to me, he said: 'Please do not hesitate to use any of this information at any time, or ask me if you need help'. It was all I could do to find suitable words to thank him and later Michael and Serge, who assured me he had been favourably impressed with both my work and behaviour since my arrival.

From then on Igor's attitude towards me took on more of a paternal nature. He would call me to his office and ask me pertinent questions regarding my work, or my personal reaction to a change to VS-300 which he had in mind. I recall his suggestion regarding the use of a smaller, multi-bladed fan-type tail rotor, perhaps located in a vertical fin in the tail. He thought it would be less dangerous, as well as better protected from hitting nearby objects, during take-off or landing in restricted areas. After some thought I replied: 'How about

the extra cost of the additional parts, more complicated blade pitch control, and the additional power required due to the considerably reduced diameter, also possibly more maintenance time?' After a few moments' thought, during which he twiddled a chain of paperclips, he smiled and said, in his quiet and precise way: 'Perhaps you are right . . . they would say, "Why did he did it?"'. Only rarely did he slip grammatically, but, as in this instance, it lent an unforgettable charm to his statement.

Both Michael and Serge would also cause me later to realise that I was being tested. For instance, in all fixed-wing aeroplanes, if forward speed is lost and the wings reach too steep an angle of attack they will stall and fall off to one side or the other and begin descending in a spiral. If this is not properly controlled, a fatal crash could result.

Michael was an excellent pilot, and the first time he took me up he announced that he always liked to practise a 'leetle speen', which he did, apparently to watch my reactions, as I was seated beside him. Fortunately I had been through that manoeuvre several times before with Alex Krapish, when from time to time he would ask me to go flying with him in a single-engined, open-cockpit, tandem-seat biplane. He would also let me handle the controls.

Michael then asked me if I would like to take over the controls and fly back to Bridgeport, which I eagerly did. We were then almost over the mainland coast of Long Island Sound, just east of New Haven, at the regulation altitude of 1,200 ft and heading away from Bridgeport. The return flight clearly involved a degree of both piloting and navigational skill, requiring that I make a 180° banked turn. I accomplished this with some loss of altitude, but it was accepted by Michael because he knew I had but a few hours of piloting to my credit over the preceding years.

I found, however, that in true and level flight the engine operated in a noticeably rougher manner, so I trimmed in a slightly nose-up attitude, which immediately smoothed out the engine. Michael smiled, but never said a word, as I happily and correctly navigated our way back to the Bridgeport Airport, admiring the Connecticut scenery below. He did not say another word until we reached the airport, when he kindly remarked: 'A leetle beet too high for landing Beel?', pointing to the altimeter, which read well over 2,000 ft. That was so typical of Michael's gentle sense of humour. With his help I managed a somewhat sloppy landing. Michael continued to keep his hand in by flying well into his seventies, mostly in single-seater sports aeroplanes.

Serge also invited me to fly with him, usually in a side-by-side, two-seat, enclosed cabin single-engine monoplane mounted on floats. On our first time up, he tested my reactions by cutting the engine and alighting among a forest of tidal-net-fishing poles, remarking: 'Emergency landing practice'.

From the time I took over from Russ Clark, I became the only full-time engineer on VS-300, and Igor would smilingly refer to me as 'my engineering department'.

On the 9 October 1940, the now wartime Col Charles Lindbergh, a long-standing friend of Igor's from Pan American flying-boat days who was now an important consultant with the Pratt & Whitney Engine Division of United Aircraft at East Hartford, Connecticut, came down to visit Igor, anxious to see him fly his improved VS-300C-2 'heelicopter'.

After he had finished his demonstration, Igor realised that Lindbergh was not only genuinely amazed and appreciative, but obviously wished to experience the thrill of flying the world's first successful single-main-rotor helicopter. Like Gregory and Haugen, Lindbergh was given an explanatory walk-around. Igor then got back into the pilot's seat, and had Lindbergh stand next to him as he started the engine. Then he gently lifted VS-300 off vertically, hovering just clear of the ground and at the same time explaining his actions as he slowly nudged VS-300 forwards, sideways and backwards, with Lindbergh enthusiastically walking closely beside him. After Igor had landed at the take-off spot, Lindbergh laughed as he said (like his two predecessors) that it was the first time in his life that he had been given a flying lesson from an aircraft actually in flight while he was still standing on the ground.

Lindbergh strapped himself into the pilot's seat and was soon cautiously going through the same demonstrated manoeuvres several times while hovering, and he was soon able to keep the aircraft on a level plane. With a satisfied smile and congratulations from Igor, he was asked if he would like to try a slow, low circuit of the meadow. Needless to say, the offer was quickly accepted. We watched as VS-300 obediently answered the demands of strange hands (and feet) at her controls and successfully turned her passenger towards the starting point as Igor, smiling, waved him on. With a big smile after his second circuit, Lindbergh started to make a landing. He nudged the control stick back correctly, but when the machine stopped moving forward he instinctively reverted to his aeroplane tail-down landing reactions and kept holding the control stick back, instead of moving it forward to its central, neutral position. Of course VS-300 dutifully proceeded to move backwards, and also to increase speed and gain altitude.

Immediately sensing what was happening, Igor started running after the retreating machine just as Lindbergh shouted: 'How do I stop this damn thing?' Igor shouted back: 'Stick forward'. Lindbergh promptly responded and then brought 'collective pitch forward', ending in a rather rough but safe landing. He got his helicopter licence a year later on the XR-4, with Les Morris as his instructor.

On 14 October 1940, Igor having spent as much

Fig 51 *Igor's second pupil was Col. Charles Lindbergh, who also for a few brief moments experienced the privilege of flying the first successful single-main-rotor helicopter.*

'HEELICOPTER' – PIONEERING WITH IGOR SIKORSKY

time as possible improving his piloting proficiency with VS-300C-2, as well as demonstrating its capabilities to important corporate members from East Hartford, it occurred to him that very little of the work to date had been properly documented for technical and historical purposes. This was especially so now that his helicopter was performing so well. (Fig 52). So on this particular day Bob Labensky was detailed to take moving pictures of Igor as he put VS-300C-2 through its paces. In the event this produced one of the most critical personal moments for Igor's future, not to mention his helicopters. While I was not present when the following took place, Bob vividly described it to me directly afterwards.

Igor had been demonstrating VS-300C-2's improved non-cyclic manoeuvrability with stops, starts, hovering turns, flight in all directions, and

with forward speeds paced by a car up to 40 mph. He then started performing his favourite figure eights, alternating direction from time to time, at ever-increasing speeds and with wider turns, at some 10 to 20 ft altitude. This was taking place at a little used, remote area of the airport, but near to the plant.

Bob noticed that on the last few turns nearest to him, when turning to the left, the helicopter was not banking as steeply as when turning to the right. Just at that moment the camera ran out of film. He quickly removed the spent film and was inserting the new one when he happened to glance up as VS-300 passed him and started to make another left-hand banking turn. He watched as the right-hand outrigger started to rise upwards as it should, but instead of continuing to do so it dropped back down momentarily, then, pivoting about its upper connections to the tail structure, suddenly folded right up. The helicopter lurched wildly to the right, then amid clouds of dust came the sounds of breaking main rotor blades as they hit the ground. Igor was momentarily hidden from view as both

---

Fig 52   *Sikorsky – Hunt – Gluhareff – Mackeller – Plenefish – Lubben.   Early October 1940, shortly before accident with VS-300-C-2.*

helicopter and engine stopped simultaneously. With a cry of dismay Bob dashed forward, 'with my heart in my mouth', as he later said.

He found Igor still strapped to his seat, with VS-300 leaning over on its right side on its partly collapsed main landing gear. He was endeavouring to unfasten the safety belt, and was apparently unhurt as Bob helped him stand up. Then, in his usual calm, precise manner, he turned to Adolf Plenefisch who had just arrived white-faced, out of breath from running as fast as he could. 'I do not believe we will be doing any more flying to-day Adolf. Please return her to the shop right away.'

The first indication that something untoward had happened came when Igor returned to his office looking rather dishevelled, with a noticeable scratch on his nose, and advised us he would not be in for the rest of the day. Shortly afterwards Bob appeared and apprised us of what had happened. I then followed him as we went down to the shop to view the extent of the damage, and try to discover the cause of the accident.

Apparently the lower single-bolted attachment fitting of the right-hand outrigger had developed a slowly propagating fatigue crack on the hidden male fitting for quite some time, where it had easily escaped visual inspection. The crack had slowly lengthened and widened from repeated upward control thrusts of the tail rotor and when Igor suddenly demanded maximum thrust when trying to regain control, it was all that was needed finally to pull the male fitting apart. This caused the unsupported outrigger to fold upwards.

At the next meeting, several days later, Igor, now quite recovered from his accident, decided to take this opportunity to increase the diameter of the rotor from 28 ft to 30 ft, since new main rotor blades were needed. The object was to reduce the disc loading, the 'disc' being the total swept area of the rotor diameter, which for VS-300C-2 was 615 sq ft. The all-up weight was 1,253 lb, divided by 615 = 2.03 lb/sq ft. With the 30 ft diameter rotor it would become 1.78 lb/sq ft, so the extra 92 sq ft of disc area x 1.78 in, would net an extra lifting capacity of at least 150 lb for the same 90 hp engine. In other words, this would hopefully yield even better control at 1,270 lb all-up weight.

It was also decided to increase the span between the two horizontal tail rotors yet again, to improve lateral control. The vertical tail rotor was raised, and a new shock absorbing tailskid was fitted to eliminate damage from a possible tail-down landing.

The three new main rotor blades for what now became VS-300C-3 would again be using the new symmetrical (NACA-0012) 12% aerofoil section. A symmetrical section was chosen because the centre of pressure of the air passing over it remains almost the same distance back from the leading edge of the blade throughout the range of angles it assumes while controlling the helicopter. This greatly facilitated tooling, manufacturing and stress calculations in designing the various elements of the blade, especially the main spar (Figure 53-3). In this case the spar comprised a series of steel tubes, each fitting inside the preceding tube as they progressed to the blade tip, in effect tapering the spar. Each section was welded to the next by an especially experienced welder, like Mr Fusco in our shop. Each collar (12) was silver-soldered to the appropriate section of spar (3). Each rib 1 was mortised to a laminated wooden leading edge (2) and blocked (13) to the rear of another spanwise wooden spar (4), the whole forming a box-like structure when covered top and bottom with a three-ply veneer (5) which extended rearwards to support the rear section of the ribs (1). At the rear end of each rib was attached a soldered brass clip to hold the flexible steel cable trailing edge (7). The elliptical blade tips were made solid with glued-in balsa wood.

Silver-doped fabric completely covered the whole blade (8) and was through-laced (9) on the rear section of the ribs (1), the stitching being covered with doped fabric tape (10).

The approximate outer third of each blade had lead slugs (11) added to its leading edge, and each complete blade's width (chord) balancing point was carefully checked as being at the centre of its metal spar (3). Then a final layer of leading-edge doped fabric was added. Similarly, the mid-span balancing point of each blade was checked, and lead added to a blade tip to match up each of the new untapered blades.

For the first time I was doing the necessary design, draughting and strength calculations on all the changes, since Russ was no longer with us, as well as keeping an eye on the resulting assembly in the shop. I was happily very busy.

Regarding the aforementioned meeting, unless otherwise noted such gatherings comprised Igor, Michael, Serge and myself. Usually Igor would

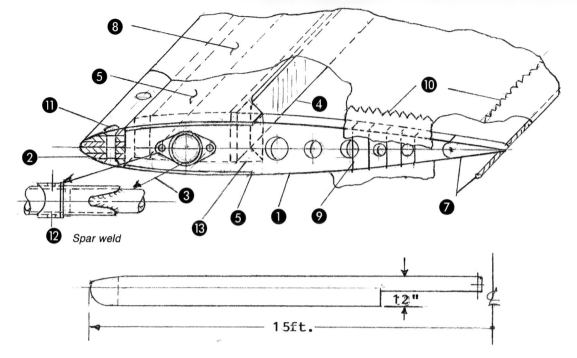

Spar weld

Fig 53 *VS-300-C3. Main rotor blade construction.*

have called the meeting, and would have with him a personal sketch (Fig 54) of a suggestion he had in mind, usually an alteration or an addition, for he was that rare kind of person who would not curtly hand over an outlined order. Instead, he always expected to receive genuine, constructive criticism before any unanimous consent occurred, rather than obedient acceptance. However, once a proposal was agreed upon, he would allow complete freedom of interpretation in its execution, knowing I would first contact Michael (the correct 'pecking order' if he was available) should I suggest a deviation. Nor would I have anyone constantly 'looking over my shoulder' to check on progress. I recently gave a number of Igor's original sketches to his son, Sergei, to place in the family archive he is assembling.

In order to get -300C-3 back in the air as soon as possible (and because our work was non-military) Mr Carboni, the shop foreman, allowed me to make a single design layout assembly drawing of any new assembly (such as a new blade). This included full-scale detail drawings (readily cut out) of all the various parts to be made, together with all the necessary information for shop fabrication, material requirements, and assembly information. This considerably reduced engineering man-hours, shop procurement procedures, etc., that would otherwise have been necessary using standard government procedures.

It was to be two months before -300C-3 would be ready to be rolled out again for testing. Meanwhile, in late June 1940, word filtered back from Headquarters Air Materiel Command at Wright Field, Dayton, Ohio, that there was a possibility of our receiving a helicopter contract for an experimental two-seat trainer.

Several days after Igor's accident, United Aircraft was formally notified that a request to bid on an informal proposal was coming from Air Materiel Command. This was apparently a result of both our 15 April VS-311 non-cyclic configuration proposal and, more recently, the enthusiastic reports from Lts Gregory and Haugen after their visit in June, when they tested the same configuration on VS-300C-2.

The proposal was to be for an observation training helicopter based on VS-300C-2 configuration. The training role was significant, as the only military helicopter appropriation available at that time was primarily for the observation helicopter contract with Platt-LePage. So in order to secure funding readily, an observation training helicopter with an already proven configuration was accepted as a logical next step. It was to be partly financed by the remaining $50,000 in the original Dorsey Appropriation, and anything over that was to be the responsibility of United Aircraft. At last a contract was on the horizon! It now became apparent why (now) Capt Gregory, had split the original $300,000 appropriation.

On the way to lunch, Serge casually remarked to

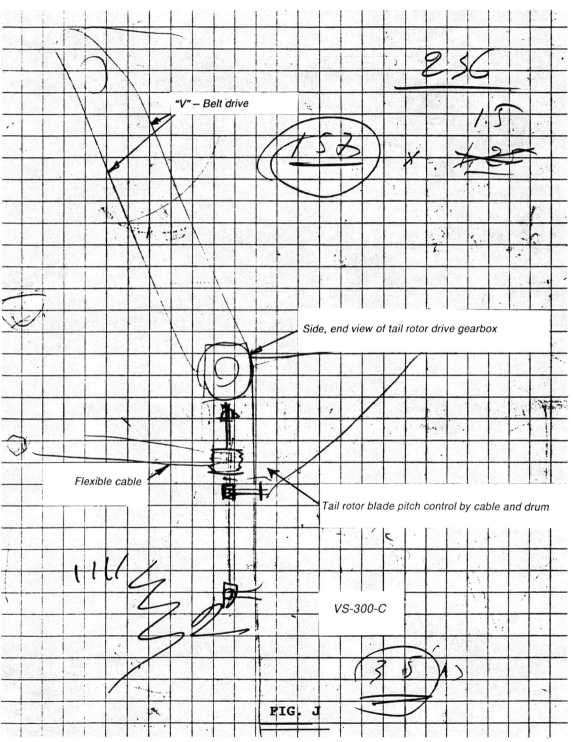

Fig 54   VS-300-C Tail rotor drive and blade pitch control.

me: 'Do you think we can design and build the heeli for $50,000 in eight months?' 'Of course', I replied. Serge chuckled as he repeated 'Of course'. After lunch, Igor called a meeting. Present were Jack Harkness (in charge of Sikorsky divisional contracts with the military), Prof Sikorsky and myself. Jack then outlined what Prof and I were to prepare for an informal proposal (by making it an informal proposal, Capt Gregory automatically excluded any bidding) with a target date of mid-August and a final submittal date before 1st January 1941. This was the first inkling I had that I might possibly be being considered as the Project Engineer.

The Proposal was to include a three-view drawing (side, front and top elevations), an inboard profile (a longitudinal, sectional side view showing all the principle items in their proposed locations), and suitable cross-sectional views for clarity, such as the powerplant installation, mechanical drive systems, and types of construction, with a written description of the same. Also included was a weight-and-balance diagram to identify the expected location of the CG of the fully-loaded aircraft. Prof would take care of all of the performance calculations. A basic 'mock-up' of the control cabin and powerplant section, including the power transmission system, was to be constructed. The Divisional Model designation was to be VS-316, and the military designation was XR-4.

Apparently what Capt Frank Gregory had in mind was a two-seater version of VS-300C configuration, which he had already satisfactorily flown, which would be a good trainer, relatively inexpensive to build and maintain. Furthermore, the XR-4 would not be in direct competition with XR-1.

Since VS-300C-2 was performing well, I was able to start on a preliminary outline on the XR-4. Because of the timeframe it was decided that, like VS-300C-2, it would have a welded tubular steel structure comprising two basic sections. The enclosed control cabin plus powerplant and drive system would form the front section, and the rest of the fuselage with its outriggers, tail drive and tail rotors would comprise the rear section. It would be bolted to the front section, which would be skinned with aluminium sheeting, the rear fuselage being covered with doped fabric, ensuring ease of maintenance.

When checking into all the Army Requirements,

however, it soon became apparent that it was not going to be as simple a design as we thought, if we were to meet the original desired gross weight of 1,700 lb using a 150 hp opposed aircooled flat six-cylinder Franklin engine. Being non-cyclic, the original main rotor hub design was very simple, since it was only necessary to change the pitch of the three blades collectively. The same was true of the three tail control rotors.

The engine was to be mounted horizontally with the engine driveshaft offset forward of the main rotor gearbox, using constant speed universal couplings on the driven shaft in between them. This offset would allow the collective pitch rod to move up or down inside the main rotor shaft. A three-pronged horizontal star at the top end of the collective-pitch rod was linked to each control horn at the root end of each of the three main rotor blades by three vertical, adjustable, ball-jointed control rods. The blades were attached to the hubs in the same way as on VS-300C-2, by an inner, horizontal, flapping hinge and an outer, vertical, lead-lag hinge (all Sikorsky main rotor blades have remained so attached). This free horizontal blade movement was limited by spring-loaded snubbers.

Construction of the 34 ft-diameter main rotor blades would be similar to those of VS-300C-3, but their planform would resemble VS-300C-2 blades, being constant chord out to one-third of the radius, then tapered to the tip.

The three horizontally hinged tail rotors would be identical, with a diameter of 8 ft 2¼ in, and would be tapered from root to tip, using a new method of construction. They would be driven from the main gearbox via a tail driveshaft to a central gearbox and then by shafting to each tail-rotor gearbox. The tail rotors would have the same symmetrical 0012 aerofoil section.

The main undercarriage would be similar to that of VS-300A, but non-swivelling, and was designed to take the rough usage expected from a trainee. A fully swivelling tailwheel was located below the vertical tail rotor.

As originally conceived, the control cabin had the trainee seated on the right-hand side, so that the centrally located and vertically mounted collective pitch lever would be in his left hand, with the throttle lever at the same level, and the flight control stick would be in his right hand, as in VS-300C-2, except that the throttle lever location would be conveniently higher up instead of 14 in lower, incorporating a throttle/CPL mixing control. (Fig 43)

The horizontal instrument panel ran the full width of the cabin, and was placed at a level affording the pilot excellent forward and downward vision while at the same time acting as an artificial horizon reference. Additional downward-forward vision was provided by a lower clear plastic panel in front of the steering foot pedals. All other controls and/or control cabin items were located as per Army standard requirements. Flight manoeuvring via the three tail rotors was to be accomplished by a similar mixing control to that of VS-300C.

Prof's efforts brought forth the following data to be sent to Wright Field in the formal 'Informal' Proposal.

Summary of Anticipated Performance (XR-4) Based on Calculations

Gross weight	1,700 lb
High speed at sea level	102 mph
Operating speed at sea level	85 mph
Endurance at operating speed	1.62 hrs
Endurance at operating speed (pilot only)	5.50 hrs
Service ceiling at zero forward speed	6,000 ft
Absolute ceiling at zero forward speed	7,000 ft
Service ceiling with forward motion	14,000 ft
Minimum speed	0 mph
Rate-of-climb at sea level, zero forward speed	600 ft/min
Best rate of climb at sea level	1,200 ft/min
Free rate of descent, vertical	1,650 ft/min
Take-off over 50 ft obstacle	0 ft
Landing over 50 ft obstacle	0 ft

The main reason for my reproducing the estimated performance of the XR-4 from the original proposal, in addition to the rest of the details of the proposal, is to show how performance estimation from information available at the time could be misinterpreted, not to mention my own accuracy in estimating the weights. To be fair to Prof, however, I must admit that several important estimates were 'improved' upon by others for political reasons.

Later on we shall see how unrewarding that turned out to be.

We met both the August and 1st January dates (Fig 55) with our fifteen-page proposal! In today's bureaucratic governmental labyrinths such an achievement would hardly be noticed.

It was now the autumn of 1940, and preparations were underway in the large S-44 flying-boat hangar to relocate the Sikorsky engineering personnel, including the managerial offices of the Sikorsky Division, next to their centres of interest. Another reason was that Vought was hiring additional help and needed all the available space. This must have been an emotionally trying time for Igor Sikorsky, for, in effect, he was being shoved off into a corner of the domain he had created by dint of the great success of his flying boats he had shared with Michael Gluhareff. Yet withal, he stoically never never showed it.

The remodelling of the three Sikorsky S-44s (Navy XPBS-1s) into commercial S-44As under the able direction of Ed Dudek, and the tiny VS-300 effort, was all that remained under direct Sikorsky control, apart from whatever flying-boat business remained to be completed in the main assembly shop. By this time quite a few of the original Sikorsky engineers had transferred to the Vought side.

Those of us Sikorsky engineers who were engaged with either the flying boats or the helicopter were temporarily located on the ground floor of the attached Vought-Sikorsky Experimental Shop. The site was actually a cleared area at the end of the sheet-metal department, without the benefit of even a partition, and noise was the order of the day.

In mid-December we got word that the Air Materiel Command had approved our XR-4 (VS-316) Informal Proposal, and that a formal contract was on the way. At this point Igor and Michael informed me that I was to be the Project Engineer on the XR-4, as well as on VS-300. While I had hoped this would be the case, I had not dared to set my heart on it. So it was with a very grateful heart that I received the joyful news, expressing my great appreciation of the privilege.

Word got around that I was to be made Project Engineer, and one morning I found what purported to be a helicopter model, made from a child's 'tinker-toy' set, suspended over my desk. Hanging below it was a card with

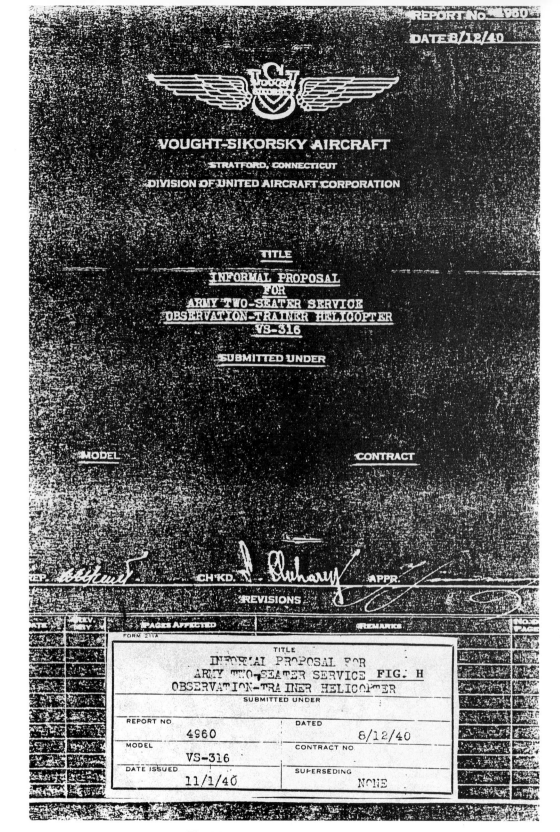

Fig 55 *Our fifteen-page proposal!*

'Congratulations' in large letters. It was one of those sincere gestures of friendly appreciation, freely given by others, that one never forgets. Several of the Sikorsky 'old-timers' separately asked that I keep them in mind, one of them going so far as to say that he had been watching me and believed I knew what I was doing!

The 'Test Lab' run by Michael Buivid and Boris Labensky was 'next door' to our temporary engineering headquarters, and we could plainly hear Michael calling out the increasing loads being imposed on the specimens being tested. Then there would be a loud cracking sound, or a loud thump, to which would be added cheers from our group if the failure was particularly loud. These tests were being performed mainly for the Vought engineering department.

Increasingly now, members of the Vought managerial staff were dropping in from corporate East Hartford to visit the plant during lunch periods, so as not to interfere with work in progress, and usually when both Michael and Boris were absent. They had been testing for Vought, a full-scale hydraulically actuated retractable landing gear system, and, having been bothered earlier by an intruder fiddling with test rig controls and causing damage to one or two test specimens, they falsely labelled a dummy overhead control lever 'retraction lever'. It was located so that one had to stand directly under it in order to reach up and operate it. Just as Michael and Boris had planned, they met the culprit hurriedly leaving the lab, covered from head to foot with bright red hydraulic fluid.

As 1940 drew to a close, so did my first full year of helicopter experience. It had indeed been a memorable one, especially being admitted to Igor Sikorsky's 'inner circle'. Taking over engineering responsibility of VS-300, was the high point, and now I was Project Engineer on XR-4.

That brings to mind an amusing incident. During my second session with Igor, Michael and Serge, after Russ Clark had left and I had taken his place, the other three became so engrossed over the subject matter in hand that they inadvertently began to speak in Russian. After a few moments I turned to Igor and asked him in Spanish if I might join the discussion. All three turned and looked at me with puzzled expressions. Then, suddenly realising their *faux pas*, they laughingly asked to be excused. I do not recall such a recurrence.

During the time before I took over from Russ, when I was not yet associated with VS-300, I frequently had chats with Michael. During one of those chats I mentioned that I had constructed a small smoke tunnel at home. One of the models I tested was a form of trailing-edge, lift-increasing wing flap that was quite popular at the time because of its simplicity, just a section of the rear undersurface of the wing being hinged to move downwards. It was called a 'split flap'. However, it caused the wing to stall very abruptly at its maximum angle of lift, so I added a slot in front of it and rounded the front of the flap. The smoke tunnel showed the abrupt stall was eliminated, and instead the modification produced a smooth stall with additional lift. This interested Michael, so he arranged for a model to be made and tested, commenting that it was always a good idea to have one's name known to the top people at East Hartford. The tests did indeed duplicate the smoke tunnel tests. This was yet another kind gesture of Michael's.

By 31 December 1940 reconstruction of VS-300C-3 was well underway following the October accident, and it would soon be flying again. In the meantime VS-316/XR-4 proposal had been approved. United Aircraft's gamble in backing Igor's 'dream' helicopter, the first successfully controlled single-main-lifting-rotor type in the world, had actually borne fruit, with a contract on the way.

The next chapter covers 1941, one of the most productive and exciting periods for VS-300, as she finally faithfully proved her worth.

IGOR'S 'POSITIVE ALTERNATIVE TO CYCLIC BLADE CONTROL' HAD INDEED SAVED THE DAY, BUT NOT SOLVED THE PROBLEM.

Fig 56
*William Hunt in the new heelicopter department,
as photographed by Michael Buivid from his board
in the foreground.*

Chapter Four
1941

VS-300 Proves Her Worth

By January 1941 Mr Sikorsky's offices, the flying boat and helicopter engineering departments and machine shop, together with the construction areas, were at last all under the same roof, the S-44 hangar, with its front facing north.

A large east-west balcony at the south end of the hangar provided adequate room for Igor Sikorsky's offices, the staff engineers and the engineering department. Almost the entire area beneath this balcony was occupied by the machine shop, the remaining eastern two-thirds of the entire floor area being for production of the three S-44s for American Export Airlines. The remaining front half of the west side area was for VS-300 work.

We 'heelyites' were now tucked away in the south-west corner of the balcony. Our tiny area was partitioned off from the S-44 engineering department, and consisted of six draughting tables and my desk (Fig. 56). The first to join me was Michael Buivid, much to my delight. I considered it a privilege to have him, considering his long association with Igor and his extensive knowledge of mechanics. Shortly afterwards, Ray Coates, who had earlier asked to join me, became the second member. He was a large, rotund, blue-eyed, jovial Irishman. An excellent draughtsman, he was well versed in government draughting requirements and procedures, and never failed to maintain his good humour, no matter how involved the situation. I still recall one of his remarks, made at the time the Russians started their great counter-offensive. Ray commented that the reason the Russians were going to win was because only Irish Generals knew how to fight, and now they had Tim O'Shenko (Gen Timoshenko)!

Two major events, other than the move, occurred that January. The first was the receipt of the official contract from Materiel Command for the design and construction of the experimental VS-316 Observation-Training Helicopter, the Army's XR-4. Secondly the new VS-300C-4 was ready to be tested with her new 30 ft-diameter, three-bladed main rotor.

After warming-up VS-300C-4 on our flight-test meadow on an overcast and cold winter's morning, with Igor in his cold-weather flying suit (up-brimmed grey Fedora, woollen scarf, heavy overcoat and warm gloves) he gently lifted his pride and joy several feet above the ground and hovered for several minutes. Then he slowly tested the helicopter's pre-eminent superiority over its fixed-wing relative by flying forwards, backwards and then from side to side, ending up over the spot from which he had started with an obviously pleased expression.

After a recheck by Adolf Plenefisch and Red Lubben, Igor took off with increased assurance and was soon engaged in his favourite figure-eight series of manoeuvres, at ever-increasing speeds and altitudes, before landing some 15 min later.

He was generally pleased as he spoke about the more positive 'feel' that he had experienced throughout the various flight manoeuvres. This was especially evident during forward flight, as a direct result of the lighter disc loading of the main rotor owing to its increased diameter.

His final concern was to check sideways flight more thoroughly, as the wind had freshened considerably. Rising to about 20 ft, he started flying sideways, heading directly into the wind, apparently requiring no more skill than usual. But when he tried flying sideways directly against the wind he was obviously subjected to maintaining slower speeds than he had expected. This was mainly due to outrigger drag, but according to Igor there was still not enough lateral leverage from the horizontal tail rotors. Next Serge took his turn, concentrating on the sideways flying, and came back with the same opinion.

At the meeting later in the afternoon, Igor said he had come to the conclusion that the tail outriggers should again be extended. While it might cause a serious delay, he felt it was necessary to ensure that the best possible solution was found, as well as the limit to which the horizontal tail rotors could be separated. I had previously suggested that any further extension to the outriggers should call for an entirely new set, to which both Igor and Michael agreed. So back into shop went VS-300. The result was a slimmer, triangular and tapered pair of welded tubular outriggers, with another foot added to each side. It would be March before VS-300C-5 began test flying.

On 21 January 1941 Michael Gluhareff and Nik Nickolsky had an interesting meeting with top officials at the Langley Field Laboratories in Virginia. I include the following resumé of that meeting to show the actual paucity of background, experience and general knowledge concerning matters pertaining to rotating-wing type aircraft, and especially helicopters, even at the highest levels of our scientific aeronautical establishments.

'The Main Rotor Blade

1 The co-ordinates were available, for a specifically designed aerofoil section for rotating-wing type aircraft had been devised and windtunnel tested. The ratio of its thickness-to-width was 15 per cent, and it was capable of maintaining smooth airflow over its surfaces (then referred to as 'laminar airflow'), at positive angles to the airstream, generally associated with rotating-wing type requirements. It was capable of operating at rotor tip speeds in the 460–500 mph range, which would include the sum of both the rotational and aircraft forward speeds. Michael described the contour of the wing section as 'quite peculiar'. (Not to mention that it would be both difficult and costly to manufacture)

'**2** The use of trailing-edge wire may cause trouble if the structure is not very rigid in horizontal bending. The autogyro manufacturers have had considerable trouble with bent metal, or broken spruce trailing edges. (That is why VS-300's trailing edge was changed from thin aluminium to flexible steel cable on VS-300B.)
'**3** Neither tapering, nor progressively increasing the pitch angle of the blade from its tip towards its root, would prevent autorotation. For better autorotation,

maintain the aerofoil section close up to the root of the blade. (That has been done on both VS-300 and XR-4; no autorotation attempted)
'**4** It would be better not to use horizontal blade dampers. It is a very complicated arrangement. Autogyro manufacturers have still not solved that problem. (It was not a problem with the VS-300 noncyclic control system)
'**5** It was suggested that we use a really low-drag blade aerofoil section as a means of attaining smoothness in forward flight.
'Horizontal Tail Rotors
'**6** Horizontal movement of the blades about their vertical hinges is imperative unless they have extremely strong hubs, because of possible vibration in forward flight. (Which so far, had not occurred with VS-300.)
'**7** A two-bladed rotor was not recommended for the same reason as in item **6**. One, or three blades, in case of difficulty is recommended. (This also had not occurred on VS-300)
'General
No information is presently available regarding the best material or method of construction for the main or auxiliary rotor blades.'

Shortly after this meeting the following event took place.

Because of his usual mildness and dignity of manner, Igor Sikorsky would sometimes catch one by surprise. On 29 January 1941 he was to address the Institute of Aeronautical Sciences (IAS) in New York. It was to be a resumé of the progress achieved by his experimental VS-300 during 1940. Evidently he had previously started to write the paper, but more pressing matters had prevented him from finishing it. So that morning he rang up his office and left word for me to finish it and bring it down to him. This was an unexpected privilege, to say the least.

As arranged, I met Igor in the lobby of the Commodore Hotel, directly accessible from Grand Central railway station via an underground pedestrian walkway, with about an hour to spare. After he had finished reading my modest addition, made several notations, and warmly thanked me, we sat chatting for a while before departing for the IAS meeting. However, as I sat facing him, with my back towards the lobby, every now and again his eyes would become fixed upon some passing object behind me and his speech would trail off, or he would ignore my conversation. At the same time he would start making a curious little sound in his throat which signified something very pleasing to him was taking place. At the first opportunity I quickly turned my head and glanced in the same direction. I beheld a delicious example of femininity – of course! But I had sampled it too long, for when I turned back Igor was looking at me. I raised my eyebrows and we both smiled at each other.

This was the first helicopter meeting, before the founding of the American Helicopter Society (AHS), and the IAS had kindly arranged to have the meeting in their lecture theatre. It was well attended. Igor's presentation was remarkable for the many questions that were asked after it. One in particular has always been easy to recall. It came from Professor Picard, the internationally renowned free-balloonist, who had recently set an altitude record. He said that he did not see why, if rising vertically was so important, Mr Sikorsky did not turn his obvious talents to the use of lighter-than-air gas. Good-humouredly Igor responded: 'Because, Professor Picard, the heelicopter can, as directed, fly in any direction, including backwards, which even the damned mosquito cannot do'. This produced much laughter from the audience, including Picard himself.

This was also the occasion of young Arthur Young's first appearance before such a meeting, to demonstrate his theories pertaining to rotating-wing aircraft capable of vertical ascent by the use of rubber-band-powered models, fashioned mainly from aluminium cigar containers. He was roundly applauded. He also showed a movie of his very clever fly-by-wire models. Several years later, along with his pilot friend Mashman and sponsored by Larry Bell, they demonstrated the outstanding qualities of Bell helicopters.

The early months of 1941 were marked by a series of leaps and bounds from one project to the other. This curious situation was the result of having been awarded a government contract to design and construct an experimental aircraft which had yet to prove itself as being a worthwhile aerial vehicle in the first place. If that was not enough, the particular configuration chosen was a stop-gap design, in that, while it did perform reasonably well within the limitations of its particular configuration, it was not the configuration the military really wanted.

Fig 57 *The diminutive helicopter 'Design Office', 1941, showing Ralph Lightfoot up front, and Henry Wirkus busily engaged. It would not be long before Ralph Alex would be occupying the desk in front of, and to the left of Henry. Ray Coates sat just to the right of where the picture ends. Michael Buivid's board is to the left behind Henry.*

'Furthermore, gentlemen,' as Igor was wont to say, as VS-300 continued with its series of changes, so was it necessary to consider their incorporation into XR-4. But even this was not the whole story, because both Igor and Capt Frank Gregory realised that their credibility was also at stake, and depended on our being able to produce a practical solution in the form of a cyclically controlled single-main-rotor system that worked.

So, in January 1941 I was no longer Igor's 'Engineering Department'. I now had Michael Buivid and Ray Coates with me, soon to be joined by Ralph Lightfoot. As more detailed information became available on XR-4 requirements, weight estimates had to be revised upwards, and so did Ralph's estimates of the power required. It went from the 150 hp of the flat-six Franklin engine to the 165 hp of a radial Warner engine. This meant that my original design layout of the main rotor gearbox was now obsolete, as were the similar layouts for the tail rotor driving systems and the main rotor hub.

At about this time Ed Katsiper arrived upon the scene. A mechanical engineer, he had recently been working for Dr de Bothezat, well known for his earlier attempt (1924) at designing a multi-rotor helicopter for the US Army. It was unfortunately unsuccessful, but recently he had designed, built and test-flown a co-axial-type helicopter with the engine located between the lower and upper rotor.

Some time previously Ed had learned of Igor's helicopter programme. He had been interviewed by Serge Gluhareff and had been promised the top engineering position on the project (or so he thought), but apparently this had been forgotten. Anyway, Ed was willing to join the project under my supervision, so I put him in charge of the new gearbox design for XR-4, which was of considerable help, as was his designing of the cooling fan for the radial engine. Later on he cleverly incorporated the cyclic blade control system into the already completed non-cyclic main rotor hub. Much to his credit Ed was very co-operative, open to suggestions, and a fast yet accurate design-layout engineer. If he was disappointed, it never showed up in his work.

Another newcomer was a young draughtsman of Armenian descent who was both deaf and dumb, who Ray Coates immediately took under his wing, because of his eagerness to do his best and his draughting ability. In no time Ray was learning simple phrases in sign language.

I have already mentioned the importance of a mock-up of a new design as a means of determining the required space for humans and equipment. The particular areas of XR-4 involved were the control cabin and the centre section, which contained the powerplant, power transmission system, main rotor controls and the fuel and oil systems. It was necessary to get the drawings into the Experimental Shop as soon as possible, and by March the mock-up was well advanced and proving its worth.

Up to now I had been doing all the necessary preliminary stress calculations, but it became necessary to employ a full-time stress analyst. Dick Hansen therefore joined the XR-4 team, being in charge of, and responsible for, all stress calculations. His first major concern was the welded tubular steel fuselage structure. It so happened that I had to be away for several days on company business, and in the meantime Hansen thought he would pleasantly surprise me by reducing the weight of the fuselage structure, simply by means of increasing the 'end fixity' (rigidity) of all the truss tubes in the structure. This was to be accomplished by adding gussets on the ends of each tube, thereby allowing the wall thickness, or diameter, of each of the tubes to be reduced. Fortunately, the necessary drawing changes had only just been started by the time I got back, for the number of gussets required would have been impossible to weld in their clustered proximity to each other. This mistake was due to lack of experience, a problem that became increasingly evident throughout the engineering and manufacturing industry.

Another time-consuming factor now began to

Fig 58
XR-4 Tail rotor construction.

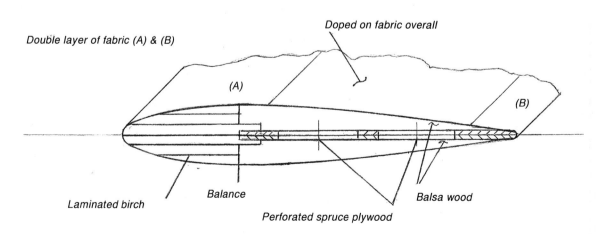

Double layer of fabric (A) & (B)

Doped on fabric overall

(A)

(B)

Laminated birch

Balance

Balsa wood

Perforated spruce plywood

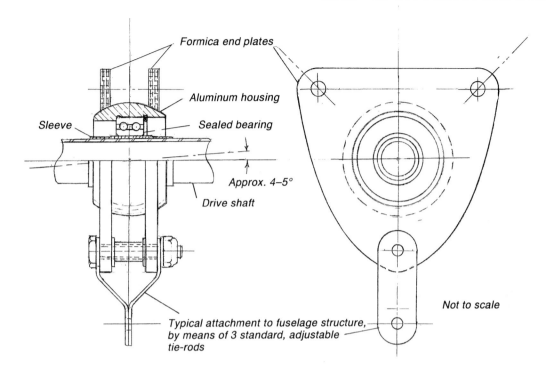

Formica end plates
Aluminum housing
Sleeve
Sealed bearing
Approx. 4–5°
Drive shaft
Typical attachment to fuselage structure, by means of 3 standard, adjustable tie-rods
Not to scale

Fig 59 *XR-4 – Suspended, adjustable alignment bearings on tail rotor drive shaft.*

emerge; governmental paperwork. When VS-300 was a corporate funded project I could bypass a good many required government procedures. However, the advent of the XR-4 military contract, although it allowed us better access to the necessary materials, meant that shop priority was still a problem and everything had to be done in triplicate. Moreover, everyone had to sign out a drawing before it could be released. And I had to start writing progress reports. I mention this because the 'invisible overhead' is not appreciated for its non-productive interference, not to mention the departmental 'kingdoms' that soon evolved.

I was now able to make three more design layouts for XR-4. The first was the new 8 ft 2¼ in-diameter three-bladed tail rotor, with its hub and controls, the second was the central tail-rotor gearbox and driveshafts to the two horizontal tail rotors; and the third was for the outboard gearboxes. It should be borne in mind that, at that point, the non-cyclic control system was still being considered the final system.

We all have our less-gifted areas, and so it was with Igor. Curiously enough it pertained to the matter of 'reading' and/or, mentally envisioning a mechanical drawing depicting either a particular part or an assembly-type design layout, insofar as being able to judge instinctively whether or not its proportions were acceptable relative to its proposed functions. Fortunately I discovered this problem early on, when he would question me regarding my reasons for the proportions I had depicted on my drawing. When I had explained this to his satisfaction, he would either accept it or say why he did not. I would also come across him carefully running his hand over a particular structural member or peering intently at a mechanism and visually sizing it up, so to speak.

I began by presenting Igor with a full-scale model of the proposed cross-section of a new tail rotor blade I had devised (Fig. 58). This would balance out at the desired point of its width, for aerodynamic reasons, without the need to use lead weights. Immediately his innate visual sense of proportion was motivated, and he readily accepted the idea. It obviously pleased him no end, but I can vividly recall an exception to the foregoing. This occurred when Igor 'suggested' increasing the diameter of a certain bolt by $^1/_{16}$ in. It meant re-proportioning an entire section of a design layout Michael had just finished, and he awaited Igor's departure with stoic, stoney silence and then said: 'Beel, this is real UMPH'.

The relocation of the tail driveshaft from on top of the fuselage to a lower level was due to the decision to use the more powerful Warner radial engine. This meant that the driveshaft would angle up from the main transmission, from about the mid-point of the fuselage centre section to the original location for the central tail gearbox, and required the sustaining tail shaft bearings to be located in space (Fig. 59). Owing to the increase in estimated weight, the rotor diameter was increased from 34 ft to 36 ft.

By the time I had finished the aforementioned design layouts it was well into the first week in April, and for the past few weeks Igor and Serge had been testing VS-300C-5's new lengthened outriggers. They both agreed that the change had been worthwhile, as the outriggers were lighter and the response was better, with less resistance, allowing a slight increase in forward speed.

Then, on 17 March, Lester Morris, formerly Commissioner of Aeronautics for the State of Connecticut (he had presented Igor with State helicopter pilot's licence No 1) arrived to join the VS-300 team and become its first official test pilot. For quite some time the management at Hartford had become increasingly anxious regarding the obvious risk involved in continuing to sanction Igor's role of chief test pilot, and he was finally persuaded to find a replacement. Happily, earlier on, Igor and Les had found sufficient mutual grounds of interest to warrant Les's appointment to the position.

Les attended his first VS-300 meeting in early April, at which time, due to VS-300C-5's improved performance, Igor informed us of two events he had been considering for quite some time, and which he felt could now be performed. These were the setting of an American helicopter endurance record and, then, a similar world record, at that time held by Germany. The immediate enthusiastic response amused and pleased Igor. It was decided to proceed with the necessary preparations immediately. They included careful fuel consumption tests, and the fitment of an additional fuel tank. At that time the helicopter had a single tank holding

approximately 6 gal, mounted up beside the main gearbox, on the left-hand side looking forward. It was sufficient for possibly a ¾ hr flight. Since there was no existing American helicopter endurance record, it was decided to stay up as long as VS-300 was running smoothly, or as weather conditions permitted. Hopefully that would be at least an hour.

By 7 April the extra fuel tank and its plumbing was installed, and the next day VS-300 went through several check flights to the satisfaction of all concerned, mainly going through the exercise of switching from one fuel tank to the other. The weather reports for the next 24 hrs were fair, with light steady winds, so Igor decided to have a preliminary fuel consumption test run, simulating the procedure to be used during the actual endurance record attempt.

On 9 April, a fair Spring day, Igor gently lifted off VS-300C-5a and proceeded to hover 4–5 ft up, in the 'ground effect'. This was done to warm up the engine thoroughly, check the flight controls and listen for any strange sounds at a safe hovering altitude, should there be a sudden engine failure. At that time there had never been a transitional recovery of a helicopter from power-off hovering to a normal safe autorotational glide, and this would not occur for some time. In fact, I used to feel very uneasy when Igor apparently thought nothing of hovering at 25/30 ft or so.

Igor slowly moved the helicopter forward, climbing up to about 25 ft, and started circling the meadow. Stopwatches were clicked to determine exactly a 15 min flight period, at which point, as arranged, he was signalled to return to the starting point. As he hovered just above the ground, the fuel gauge (a graduated glass tube) was checked for fuel consumption. VS-300 was found to be thirstier than expected, but Igor decided to continue for another 15 min, as there was enough fuel left.

The second 15 min again indicated the same rate of fuel consumption, so he landed. There was still sufficient fuel left for another 6/8 min before having to take fuel from the new tank, which meant there would be no fuel problem for at least a full hour. The helicopter was returned to the shop for a thorough check-up before the record attempt.

As mentioned earlier, Les Morris joined the VS-300 project on 17 March and had since then been acquainting himself with all the information available relating to helicopters. For the first time we had the opportunity of frequent discussions about the changes VS-300 had undergone and was going through. In fact, we rather enjoyed each others' company.

Igor had advised me that Les was going to join us, but on the day he arrived, somebody had apparently got the 'wires crossed', as no desk space had been arranged for him. I therefore suggested he share mine for the time being, as it so happened I was mostly busy on my drawing board at that time. Les evidently greatly appreciated this. He was now eagerly following every step of the preparation for the attempt at the US helicopter endurance record.

Finally, after a seasonal weather delay, 15 April dawned bright and clear, with a predicted steady wind that would increase to about 15 mph by early afternoon. It was quite perfect. The record attempt had been purposely kept confidential, just in case of failure. I was only able to witness the start, but Les enthusiastically recounted the event to me afterwards. As it was to be an official attempt, an official from the National Aeronautics Association, Mr William C. Zint, was present, as well as two local friends of Igor's to act as official witnesses, a Mr Goddard and Mr St John, both

from Stratford.

With Igor strapped into the pilot's bucket seat, Adolf engaged the driving pulley of a standard truck-type, battery-driven starting motor, with a drive belt that turned up all of the rotors to a speed greater than that of the engine starting speed. With everything whirling up to speed, Adolf called 'contact' and Igor responded 'contact' as he turned on the ignition. Adolf pushed the starter button and the pre-warmed engine started up. Igor was soon smoothly engaging the engine speed with that of the whirling rotors. With a wave of his hand he then grasped the collective pitch lever and steadily pulled it back until VS-300 gently lifted off, amid cheers and clicking stopwatches, to begin her first record breaking flight at exactly 3.08 pm. As a final precaution he kept the helicopter hovering only a few feet up as he checked out its control reactions while heading directly into the 15 mph wind, thus

---

Fig 60 *U.S.A. Helicopter endurance record, 1hr. 5min. 14½ sec.*
VS-300-C-5a – With extended new outriggers and 30ft. main rotor 15 April 1941.

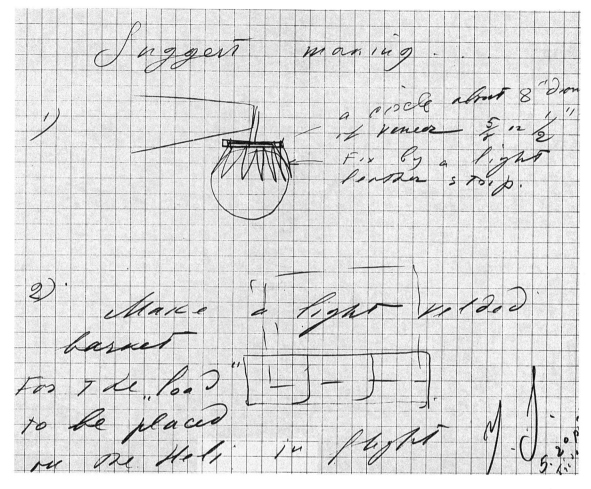

Fig 61

1) VS-300-C when first equipped with inflated rubber floats – and a canvas covered standard basket ball provided bow bouyancy!

2) The "light velded basket" was to demonstrate precise control when accepting or delivering a parcel. A bicycle package basket was used.

reducing power to a minimum. He then proceeded to make a series of slow circuits of the meadow at a height of about 10/15 ft.

As on the trials of the 9th, every 15 min Igor would return to the starting point and have the fuel consumption checked. The wind was obviously contributing to the noticeable amount of extra fuel remaining at each check-in, so at the third check-in Igor unhesitatingly said he was going for the one-hour mark. When finally signalled that he had reached his goal, he happily waved back and

proceeded to make a leisurely extra circuit of the meadow. VS-300, its engine still running smoothly, gently touched down, having established the first secure helicopter endurance record for her country by remaining airborne for 1 hr 5 min 14½ sec. The good news soon spread.

Several weeks before this happy event, Igor had said he was anxious to test the possibilities of an amphibious version of the VS-300, and asked me to look into the matter. Someone suggested that we approach the Air Cruisers Company which was successfully making inflatable pleasure boats, and there was also the MacKinley Company, which was marketing inflatable light-aircraft floats. Both were quick to respond to enquiries. The latter flew in with a two-seat Taylorcraft so equipped, and I was amazed at how smooth take-off, landing and water taxying was, when compared with with metal floats. They were not too sure of their time schedule.

However, when I contacted Air Cruisers and explained our intentions, the President, Mr Blood, came on the line and said he was sure he could attend to our needs immediately. I suggested that he contact Mr Sikorsky the next day, which he did, and he arrived the following day. While enthusiastically watching Igor demonstrate VS-300 he said to me: 'Just give me the necessary information, and I will have a set ready for you within a week'. Igor was delighted, and after we had discussed the various design requirements with Mr Blood, the necessary drawings were sent off to Air Cruisers the next morning.

True to his word, Mr Blood rang up to say he was personally delivering the floats the next day. It had taken only five days for his engineering department and shop to fabricate them. Furthermore, he was donating the floats to the VS-300 project for the privilege of supplying them.

In the meantime, Adolf had incorporated all the necessary changes to accommodate the two main flotation bags, plus a tail float. To be safe, Igor decided to add a basketball to the front end of the fuselage. (Fig. 61) To this was rather unceremoniously added a larger white plastic marine mooring buoy, after initial water trials started.

It was unfortunate that Maj Frank Gregory and Capt Haugen were both unable to be present at the endurance record flight. However, they arrived the following day, and, knowing that both officers were no doubt looking forward to flying VS-300C-5a with her latest changes, Igor made sure all was made ready for their arrival. First of all he wished to demonstrate his latest 'sales gimmick', to demonstrate the machine's precise control. It consisted of a 1-in diam. metal tube about 1 ft long, driven into the ground, into the top end of which was slipped a smaller diameter 6 ft tube vertically supporting a 6 in-diameter ring. A tubular horizontal probe, like a boat bowsprit, had been added to VS-300.

To begin the demonstration, Igor put the 300 through its familiar but now more precise routines. He then suddenly flew over to where the rod and ring was located, unnoticed until then, made a quick dead stop, took careful aim and put the probe through the middle of the ring. Lifting the ringed rod clear, he brought it over triumphantly for Frank Gregory to remove, which he did with an

appreciative flourish. This trick was very typical of Igor's innate sense of showmanship which, when combined with his obvious pleasure in performing, made it a delight to behold.

Incidentally, Gregory and Haugen were again returning from checking the much delayed Platt-Le Page XR-1 helicopter project in Philadelphia, which had yet to make its first free flight, and, as yet, both VS-300 and XR-4 had still not reached their definitive and final configurations.

While Gregory and Haugen were enthusiastically taking turns flying VS-300, Igor took me aside and asked me if it would be possible to install the new flotation gear by tomorrow morning. I said I would check with Adolf. When I put the question to him, I realised it might well be another one of those late, or all-night affairs (I always tried to be on 'stand-by' with Adolf and his loyal gang). Adolf smiled and said: 'Of course', and I reported back to Igor, who was obviously relieved and pleased.

Upon the conclusion of their round of flights, Gregory and Haugen returned with Igor to his office, where he asked them if they could spare the time to witness still another 'world first' before they left, because he had just been assured that the new flotation system was ready to be attached. The next morning they could witness the first-ever demonstration of an amphibious helicopter. The answer was a unanimous 'yes'.

Happily, the transition to the new flotation bags proved to be trouble-free, especially due to the splendid teamwork by Adolf, Lubben and company. So on 17 April 1941, VS-300C-5b was trundled over to the amphibious flying-boat ramp of yesteryear, as had so often been done with Igor's world famous creations, ready for its first waterborne launching upon the Housatonic River. It was a strange-looking craft at best, but now it had acquired a huge, fat sausage-like float, abaft the engine section on each side, plus a smaller version replacing the tailwheel (Figs 62 & 63). Igor wished to avoid the possibility, when hovering, of spray caused by main rotor downwash hitting the horizontal tail rotors, especially under windy choppy conditions, so he had had the outriggers angled upwards.

Igor had on his 'nautical flight suit' for the occasion, consisting of a large tan raincoat, a large, ill-fitting life jacket, plus his inevitable turned-up-brim grey Fedora 'helmet'. He was barely able to strap himself into the bucket seat owing to the extra

Fig 62 *17 April 1941 VS-300C-5b*
First ever amphibious helicopter is afloat,
Igor I. Sikorsky pilot.

Fig 63 *VS-300C-5b*
First ever amphibious helicopter is airborne.

bulk of his regalia. Adolf was also wearing rubber hip boots. But eventually -300 was powered-up and then slowly trundled afloat.

It took to the water like a duck, floating evenly on the main floats, with the tail float well clear of the water. With Igor satisfied that all was well -300, with all rotors whirling, was properly positioned and pushed clear of the ramp amid handclapping and cheers. Immediately Igor started taxying slowly forward to get well clear of the ramp area, and then proceeded cautiously to try out VS-300's water-borne behaviour.

There was only a steady light wind prevailing as

he readily and smoothly turned one way and then the other, slowly at first, made a full circle, then went backwards and forwards, several times at different speeds, without any adverse reaction from the floats. Finally, sideways movement was attempted several times, but without success. Only when crosswise to the wind would -300 slowly drift with it, like a boat. But she could be kept thus by using the vertical tail rotor. As expected, the horizontal tail rotors were not designed to tilt the dead weight of the helicopter sideways when it was not airborne.

However, no problems were encountered as Igor

Fig 64 *17 April 1941 – VS-300-C-5b makes first ever amphibious helicopter ground landing, after water landing.*

Fig 65 *Adolf Plenefisch's shop, maintenance, and field crew.*

ended the demonstration after making several water take-offs and landings, then unexpectedly heading for the high grass (Fig 64) meadow and making a perfect landing. Thus were completed the first amphibious manoeuvres by a helicopter. Further amphibious testing was postponed until more immediate matters had been attended to and problems had been solved.

While both Maj Gregory and Capt Haugen were very pleased to see that every effort was being made to improve VS-300, it was also obvious that they regretted the considerable penalty in air resistance caused by the ever-increasing span of the outriggers.

I now began to notice that, whenever that subject came up, it made Igor slightly uneasy. I mentioned this to Michael Gluhareff, and he agreed with me. We both felt that, while he would welcome a positive change for the better, he was still too conscious of the reasons for abandoning the initial full cyclic-type main rotor control system, mainly owing to Serge's accident as a result of insufficient control. The present non-cyclic control had enabled a very narrow escape from having his whole dream 'go up in smoke', so to speak.

Before the two officers left, Igor informed them that he was now sufficiently encouraged to try for the world helicopter endurance record, and this was well received. So it came as no surprise when a

Fig 66 *Investigating best location of longitudinal centre of gravity shortly before U.S. endurance attempt. Note out-riggers still have small amount of dihedral angle. Also long, weighted, front boom. (X) * Author*

day or so later he told us he had mentioned his intention to his friend, General Manager Charles McCarthy, who agreed that the attempt should be made. The date he had in mind was 6 May 1941, which left just two weeks to increase the fuel capacity and give VS-300 a thorough going over, plus test runs.

Rather than construct an entirely new fuel tank, an eliptical saddle-type extension was fitted on to the outer profile of the starboard tank. This provided an extra 3½ gal of fuel, which should take VS-300 comfortably over the 1½ hr required duration mark. Adolf had the engine carefully checked and serviced, fitting new driving belts for the cooling fan, etc, and after satisfactory tests and flight trials the helicopter was again ready for another new record attempt at her private airfield, the 'Meadow'.

As on 15 April, 6 May turned out to be a fine, clear day, not quite as windy as before, but a good steady 10 mph wind blowing. This time there was to be considerable media coverage, so Igor suggested that, as he was going to make a pre-endurance test flight, he would appreciate the press taking their close-up photographs then, before the actual attempt rather than during it, because it was essential to keep the area completely clear throughout the record flight. After both the press and Igor had satisfied their needs, he landed VS-300 and made a short speech. With his usual light humour he mainly addressed the press, assuring them that they would be witnessing nothing more exciting than what they had just seen, for the next 1½ hr. Most of the time would probably be spent just hovering, he said, but everyone was welcome to avail themselves of the refreshments provided.

In the meantime, Adolf and Red had carefully topped-up the fuel tanks. Igor strapped himself into the pilot's seat, firmly adjusted the Fedora 'helmet' on his head, then gave Adolf the signal to start up the rotors. The now familiar routine of 'contacts' were called, and VS-300 with all rotors 'GO', lifted off and was on her way with her creator for yet another 'first', with cameras and stop-watches clicking.

Despite the extra 30 lb of fuel and the lower wind velocity, VS-300 had no difficulty initially, with the aid of the air cushion, maintaining a stable hovering altitude of four or five feet. By maintaining this position Igor was able to reduce power gradually as fuel was consumed, without over-working or over-heating the engine. When the throttle setting became normal he then let the heli-copter automatically gain height as she became lighter, which she did until over 6 ft had been reached.

At that point the Master took over and started a series of slow circuits of the Meadow. By then VS-300 had been aloft for some 20 min. After a while the press began to get fidgety and first one, then another, started to try to get 'unusual shots'. No doubt beginning to sense boredom himself, Igor began every now and again to acquiesce with a smile to the press's signals to 'pose'. Thus the time passed more pleasantly for all concerned.

At the one hour mark Igor was signalled by Bob MacKeller with his display card, and a spontane-ous cheer went up. There were only another 20 min to go to equal Hanna Reitsch's German world record of 1 hr 20 min in the Fw-61 helicopter. As the 20 min slowly ticked by we began to form a rough arc in front of Igor (out of the rotor wash) as he hovered into the wind some 12 ft up, while Bob Labensky monitored the glass fuel gauge with his binoculars. There was plenty of fuel still available. After what seemed an extra long 20 min, Bob MacKeller happily displayed the anxiously awaited sign, just one minute later, 'World's Record – BROKEN – 1 hour 20 min', to a second round of cheers. Igor happily responded, raising his left hand momentarily from the collective pitch lever in a triumphant salute, while his tie wildly fluttered vertically against his right cheek (Fig 67).

From that point on, Igor brought VS-300 down again to the 4 ft level to take full advantage of the air-cushion effect, while Bob Labensky continued to monitor the fuel gauge with his binoculars. There was another cheer at the 1½ hr mark, when Bob Labensky gave Igor the sign that it was OK to carry on, which he acknowledged with a nod. He was actually hoping he could reach the two-hour mark, or at least come close to it. However, almost exactly at the 1¾ hr mark Bob noticed a change in VS-300's engine note, and after several minutes this became increasingly noticeable to him and Adolf from where they were standing, off to one side. Alarmed, Bob positioned himself in front of Igor and signalled him to land. As the helicopter's main wheels touched the ground, bringing a final cheer, it had been airborne for exactly 1 hr 48 min 56.1 sec, a new world record. As with the previous

endurance record, the National Aeronautics Association was represented by Mr Zint, plus a Mr Heinmuller. Again, Messrs Goddard and St John acted as official witnesses. For the first time, press coverage was not just local but national, including aeronautical journals. This was pleasantly surprising, especially for Igor, as it also included television.

Fortunately the engine noise that caused Bob such concern towards the end of the record flight was caused by a blown exhaust gasket, which was easily replaced.

Now another first was coming up, this time for Les Morris. He had been waiting impatiently since 17 March for his first lesson in helicopter piloting, when he would become Igor's third student. On 12 May he was advised that day had finally arrived. VS-300 had been thoroughly checked and was again humming her familiar tune. First Igor took her up for a short check flight, then Serge had a refresher, his first flight on VS-300C-5. Then at last it was Les's turn, as with a butterfly or two in his stomach (as he later told me) he strapped himself into the bucket seat and for the first time called back 'contact' and turned on the engine ignition switch, to become the fifth person in the world to pilot the world's first successful single-main-rotor helicopter.

Igor's final words were: 'Try it out gently, Les. Take plenty of time, and remember, above every-thing else, if you run into trouble, just throw the pitch lever forward and land.' After showing Les the normal throttle and collective lever positions necessary for take-off and flight, Igor left him to fend for himself. Les's initial trials and tribulations are best described in his own book, *Pioneering the Helicopter*. Suffice it to say that within several weeks of odd flight opportunities, with only some 2½ hr of total flight time, Les was already partici-pating in some of the test flying.

At this stage two problems were receiving major attention:

1 Improving the synchronisation of power input (throttle) with the collective pitch lever (main rotor) and longitudinal control (horizontal tail rotors), so that VS-300 would automatically rise or descend vertically on a level plane. While this had been improved upon, the linkage ratios were still not satisfactory, as each time the outriggers were changed it occasioned a change in longitudinal balance.

Fig 67A *Press interviewing Igor just before Record Endurance Attempt*

Fig 67
Note: Out-riggers are level again, left fuel
tank with added 'saddle', and Igor's
necktie! Bob MacKeller holding sign. New
and 2ft extended VS-300-C-5-3.

2 Igor was now determined to clear up the even more important mysterious 'wobble' problem, especially as it certainly would never be accepted by the military.

At our next meeting Igor showed us a list of manoeuvres that he planned to go through, wherein he would signal us as he started the next manoeuvre. Should the 'wobble' occur at any time he would quickly raise his left arm, and we were to try and estimate the relative directional position of the helicopter with respect to the prevailing wind.

Michael, however, suggested that because the tail rotors were horizontally disposed they did not provide any lateral stabilising force, but they would if the outriggers were angled upwards, as they were during the amphibious trials, thus providing a pendulum effect. This upward angle is called the 'dihedral angle' on fixed-wing aircraft. Michael also suggested that this change be made first, before the 'wobble' tests. Igor thought this over for a few moments, then slowly said the familiar: 'Perhaps you are right, Mikhailovich, perhaps you are right'. As this was a relatively simple adjustment, VS-300 was ready the next day.

The tests were run under gusty wind conditions, which was usually when the 'wobble' was most likely to occur, and it did, whenever the helicopter was turned away from heading directly into the wind, while hovering a few feet above the ground. After several wobblings Serge then went through similar manoeuvres and produced similar results, except that he found them more noticeable turning against rotor torque. It was decided that this was due to the fact that, when turning the fuselage sideways directly against both the wind and the main rotor torque simultaneously, the vertical directional tail rotor took so much power away from the main rotor that it caused VS-300 momentarily to stagger or wobble. Raising the tail rotors did not seem to have made any significant difference.

While Igor readily agreed with the reasoning used to arrive at the cause for that particular wobble, he felt there was more to the problem. He had just come to the conclusion that there was not one, but two types of wobble. 'Furthermore, gentlemen,' he said, 'the other one comes from the main rotor, and the only way to fix that is to raise the horizontal tail rotors to at least the same height as the main rotor.' The cause was main rotor down-wash on the tail rotors. This was one of those rare, on-the-spot and sudden judgments at which one can arrive after unconsciously having sought the right answer for some considerable time. His logic was immediately obvious to us, so the next immediate job was to get the outriggers raised to meet the requirements, as per my sketch Figure 68, dated 11 September 1941. This was to result in the VS-300C-5-3.

Progress with the XR-4

As I look back to the early part of 1941 and recall the intertwining of events that took place concerning the two experimental helicopters, the VS-300 and XR-4, it is almost like trying to remember a dream. So much of what I had originally done on the XR-4 design had to be revised, mainly owing to the revised weight estimate, which required a more powerful engine, plus the inability to proceed with a final outrigger design because of the ever-changing geometry of VS-300's outriggers.

When the main gearbox was approaching the end of its detail design, it became necessary to find an outside machine shop to produce the various components, and cost was a major consideration. We were working to a very limited budget (only $50,000 from the Government – everything above that would be out-of-pocket for United Aircraft), and we were on the low-priority list. But that was just the sort of challenge that happily took Bob Labensky back 23 years to the rented-hen-farm days on Long Island, when under somewhat similar circumstances, he had helped Sikorsky construct his first aeroplane in the USA.

Bob had an old friend who, in years past, when Sikorsky Engineering moved from College Point, Long Island, to Stratford, Connecticut, owned a small machine shop. This establishment was located some distance to the rear of his home, but on his own property. By now it had seen better days, and the workforce had dwindled to just the owner and his foreman. However, the machinery had been kept in good condition doing odd jobs turned down by larger concerns, so I accompanied Bob to see if his friend could still do the work for us. I fail to recall the owner's name, other than Ed, but Bob knew he had a fairly large vertical boring machine (something like a very large vertically mounted drill) with which he could machine the main transmission gearcase.

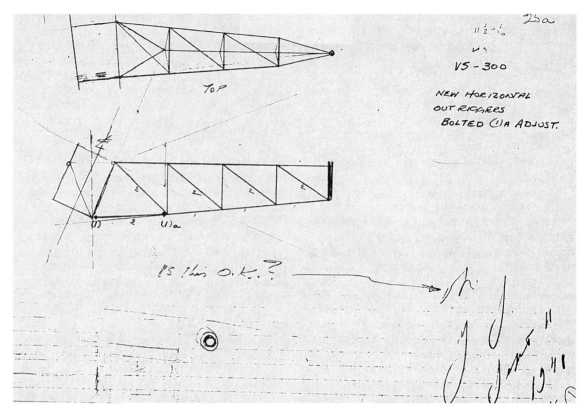

Fig 68 *VS-300 New raised out-riggers bolted (1)a adjust. To eliminate the "Vobble".*

After agreeing terms, and the manner in which the gearcase would be machined, we returned the next morning with two substantial aluminium castings, somewhat resembling squashed-down, sit-down lavatory bowls. To machine the upper rim of the gearcase horizontally, a 'fly-cutter'-type system was used, comprising a horizontal arm attached to the vertical boring spindle, with a vertical cutting tool mounted at its outer end. Thus, as the arm swept around, it would chip off a bit of the rim. Apparently, however, both castings were not clamped down firmly enough, and they began to move a very tiny amount each time the cutter arm swept around. This was not discovered until the transmission was actually being flight tested, when the gearcasing became excessively hot. Poor old Bob was terribly upset, especially as he had so proudly beaten the deadline set for the first official flight of XR-4. There is more to this story, which will be told later on, but I have included it here to illustrate more clearly the circumstances prevailing during that exciting period.

One of the new features of XR-4 main rotor hub would be the elimination of the cables supporting the rotor blades from a central pedestal, as on VS-300. Otherwise the hub was to be geometrically the same, with an inner horizontal flapping hinge and an outer vertical 'drag' hinge, except that the circular hub itself would be made of heat treated steel (to save weight), and would have a vertical outer flanged rim high enough to support a circular cover of the same diameter, keyed to it. In between the upper and lower surfaces, the flanged rim supported the three horizontal rotor blade-flapping hinges. On the periphery of the lower flanged unit, three 3 in-diameter horizontal resilient discs ('droop-stops') provided support for the three main rotor blades, in a slightly drooping attitude. The collective-pitch actuating control rod, with a three-pronged star at its upper end, would move up and down inside the main rotor shaft. The simplicity of the hub was due to the absence of the cyclic blade control system, which had been replaced by the two horizontal tail rotors, carried on outriggers. This was a joint Buivid-Hunt effort. Michael would become the main rotor hub specialist.

The welded structure containing the cabin, centre section, and rear fuselage attachment fittings was now ready to be bolted to the matching fittings on the rear section of the fuselage. The welded engine mount had just been released from the shop, and I was anxious to have it fitted to the engine, and then to have both installed in the central section to ensure that there were no misfits.

I received a summons from Serge, who was down in the shop. I found him standing next to the engine mount, which was lying with the engine mounting ring upwards, its four triangular fuselage attachment trusses held in place by nails driven into a wooden platform used to deliver it. 'Look Beel,' said Serge, 'the mounting ring is not complete. It will put stress into the engine case. Watch while I show you.' With that, he stood up on the ring, and the four unsupported rear fuselage trusses moved outwards. I told Serge I had a letter from Warner's chief engineer, saying that the engine ring cut-out was normal practice owing to the location of the carburettor, as the engine casing had been designed to take the stresses. Serge was not convinced. Several precious days were lost while the mount was returned to the shop (by pure luck the temporary welding jig had not been touched) and a yoke was designed; stresses were analysed; drawings made, checked and reissued; welding carried out, the work reinspected and the mounting redelivered, not to mention the cost of overtime. As the US Navy pilots were then wont to say: 'SNAFU' (situation normal, – all fouled up)! Never mind, even more fun was to follow.

With the engine mounted in place, its fuel and oil systems, controls, and cooling system with fan and cowling were next to be installed. Happily no major problems occurred, thanks mainly to Adolf and Ed Katsiper.

At about this stage Ralph Alex joined our team, and it was not long before he made his presence known with his enthusiastic if somewhat flamboyant manner of both dress and speech. Yet he was always very willing to put in the extra hours to get a job done, and properly supervised. So Ralph was put in charge of the electrical system; first on paper, then supervising its installation.

XR-4 was now screened off from the rest of the shop as it gradually began to take on her completed form. But time was beginning to become a worrying factor with regard to the date she would be finally rolled out. This was mainly due to uncertainty regarding the ultimate outrigger configuration which was dependent upon the forthcoming VS-300 tests and the solution of the wobble problem.

To be on the safe side, it was decided to finish the engineering based on the latest canted configuration, but to hold off any shop releases until the wobble problem was resolved. By the time the various shop and engineering items were well in hand it was the end of September 1941, and VS-300C-5-3 was ready to test the validity of Igor's

Fig 69
VS-300-C-5-3 Solving the 'Vobble' problem. Just before test flight. Late September 1941. Igor in Autumn flight testing apparel.

Fig 70
VS-300-C-5-3 this eliminated the 'Vobble Problem'.

hopefully final solution of the mysterious 'second wobble'. The cranked-up, reworked outriggers were now even more obvious than ever before. Nevertheless, we anxiously watched as the Master once again lifted off his brainchild. (Figs 69, 70 & 71)

The first test flight of VS-300C-5-3 was made on a typically windy north-eastern US autumn day, reminding one of cooler times ahead but just right for wobble testing. For twenty minutes or so the helicopter was put through every conceivable manoeuvre in every direction from zero speed upwards, including quick stops-and-goes, to try and induce a wobble. Upon landing Igor had a very satisfied smile as he said: 'I believe gentlemen, ve have solvéd the vobble problem'. But, as expected, the inwards tilting tail rotors produced a noticeable reduction in longitudinal control. Further test flights were carried out during the following days, as Serge corroborated Igor's reactions, performing similar manoeuvres.

It was then decided to have the engineering department incorporate the necessary changes on XR-4 outrigger drawings, with the two raised tail rotors set to turn horizontally but also having their plane of rotation some 2 ft above that of the main rotor, to make absolutely sure there would be no further interference with the main rotor downwash (Fig 72).

From the time of my first joining the VS-300 project when I knew nothing about helicopters, right up until the last two outrigger changes, I had been so busily involved with the various engineering changes, as well as supervising them, not to mention XR-4 activities, that I gave little more

than passing thoughts to the question of cyclic versus non-cyclic control systems. When I spoke with Michael it seemed that none of us was really happy with the present system. It seemed as though we had gone from the sublime to the ridiculous, rather than *vice versa*.

More frequently at that time, my thoughts kept returning to Serge's accident with the original version of VS-300, with which backwards and sideways flight was relatively easy to attain, without unreasonable vibration, while forward flight was attended by growing vibration as speed increased until it became unbearable. With the present non-cyclic system on VS-300, forward flight was apparently no longer a problem, especially now that the wobble had apparently been conquered. If such was indeed the case, it occurred to me that tilting the main rotor forward, like tilting an aeroplane wing, was the same in both cases, if done by tail controls. In other words, the whole aircraft was tilted, not just the rotor or the wing by itself. That must mean that the main rotor did not actually 'feel' it was being tilted; the revolving wing/blade was not being asked to change cyclically its present angle of pitch, or to depart from its existing plane of rotation relative to the rest of the aircraft. If there was some slight horizontal wing/blade disturbance, back-and-forth about the vertical hinge, it was minimal, and therefore, did not need any form of horizontal drag damping of the blade itself. The existing snubbers were sufficient. If my reasoning was correct, it became obvious that only a single horizontal tail rotor would be needed, rather than the present two, IF lateral cyclic could be reintroduced, thus eliminating the outriggers.

While it was true that the lack of sufficient lateral cyclic lateral control had contributed significantly to the cause of Serge's 1939 accident, I felt that the 'vertical blade-flapping restricters' also contributed to the accident by creating a rigid blade connection to the hub that induced a gyroscopic overturning moment as well.

On the other hand, it will be recalled that VS-300 could be flown sideways without inducing any additional vibrations. We also knew that, in order to fly sideways using cyclic blade control, far less tilting force was required, owing to the reduced aircraft inertia required to roll sideways about the CG. To me, the accident also indicated that the geometrics of the cyclic system should be such

Fig 71
VS-300-C-5-3
Look – no 'vobble'

Fig 72
*XR-4. The final outrigger engineering change
made on XR-4, just before the semi-cyclic
'Breakthrough' on VS-300-D-1. How lucky we
were to escape having to put up with this horror.*

as to allow for greater and more vertical movement of the control linkages between the azimuth tilting plate and the rotor blade control horn.

The next immediate thought was whether the military would readily accept such a change. I telephoned Michael one evening and asked him if I might pop over and see him ('chain of command' was very important to Igor's generation). 'Anything special, Beel?' 'Yes, Michael.' 'C-Come right over'. We carefully went over the whole proposition, including the impact it might have on the military, and Michael was both enthusiastic and supportive. First thing next morning, he arranged for a meeting with Igor. In the meantime I made some necessary drawings, and prepared an outline of the proposed changes to VS-300, including an estimate of the time required to make the changes.

The meeting was held after working hours, a favourite time for Igor, with less chance for interruption. In fact, it was customary for him to browse through the shop on his way out to go home.

Knowing this, I would take advantage of it from time to time; it always paid off.

At the meeting, which also included Serge, Michael led off by recounting his meeting with me and his immediate favourable reaction to my proposed changes to VS-300, which would eliminate the outriggers. He then turned the meeting over to me. This was the first time I was entirely responsible for calling a meeting, and also the first time that it was not Igor who was advocating a fundamental change to VS-300, not to mention the impact the proposed change might have on the XR-4 programme. Following the latest flight tests, which had resulted in the final repositioning of the tail outriggers after months of trial and error and had ultimately eliminated the wobble, VS-300 down-time and costs were becoming increasingly the most important items to be considered.

At the beginning of my presentation Igor, as usual, gave me his quiet but full attention, which was very reassuring. It was not long, however, before he was looking intently at my drawings, and started to question me. He readily recognised the great advantages to be had by removing the out-riggers, and also by placing the single horizontal tail rotor centrally, well out of the way of the main rotor downwash, and reintroducing cyclic lateral control. Nor did he question my

'HEELICOPTER' – PIONEERING WITH IGOR SIKORSKY

reasoning regarding the difference between non-cyclic longitudinal rotor reactions relative to forward flight and those necessary for proper lateral control. He asked if consideration had been given to the change in the relocation of the CG, with respect to the weight the single tail rotor would have to sustain without outriggers in addition to the thrust required for forward flight.

I assured him that this had been done. The use of an available XR-4 tail rotor would fulfil all requirements. It would be driven through a similar gearbox to that used to drive VS-300 vertical tail rotor. Fortunately a spare set of bearings and gears were to hand. Also, Carboni had assured me, our shop could quickly reproduce the simple gearcase from the original detail drawings. The reintroduction of lateral cyclic main rotor lateral control would be relatively easy, since it merely required freeing the existing azimuth plate and adding its controls down to the pilot's control stick. By now Igor was definitely indicating his increasing interest and pleasure by making that familiar little noise in his throat.

It was estimated that production, assembly and installation of the various items should not take more than two weeks. As this satisfied Igor's final concern, he did not hesitate in giving his approval. As the meeting ended, it was plain from Igor's relaxed enthusiasm that he, too, had been deeply concerned about the basic drawbacks and the uncertain future associated with the existing control system, and he warmly thanked us for having demonstrated our continuing confidence in his 'heeli' by bringing this very important suggestion to his attention. He finally remarked: 'Perhaps now, gentlemen, the problem of proper control has been solved'.

The present control system had indeed outlived its original, but nevertheless very important usefulness. Once again it would take Igor's calm courage successfully to sell corporate East Hartford on yet another change in mid-stream.

The following morning my meeting with Adolf and Carboni brought renewed enthusiasm at the prospect of making yet another significant change to VS-300. They also reassured me that the schedule for the changes would be met. This was of considerable relief to me, as certain events were taking place that were to affect the XR-4 project. By then, Vought had taken over complete charge

of the combined test facilities of the materials test laboratory, machine shop, and experimental department, of which George Reickert was in charge, and of great help to us 'heelyites'. The test laboratory, under Bob Labensky's management, had been the contented domain of Labensky-Buivid for some years, but first Michael Buivid had been transferred to the XR-4 project, and now Bob Labensky was being made redundant. To keep busy, he had recently been designing for VS-300 a welded tubular steel truss for relocating the vertical tail rotor higher up. Stoically, he was making the best of an unpleasant situation, but I sensed his feelings of uncertainty for the future, as he had been quite content with his lot until the Vought invasion. So, as we were going over his designs, I turned and remarked to my far older and experienced friend: 'Bob, by rights you should be the Project Engineer'. He looked at me, gently put a hand on my shoulder and said: 'Thank you'.

One ethnic characteristic of all those remaining who had been involved in Igor Sikorsky's early attempts to gain entry into the US aviation market was unfailing loyalty, not only to him and to each other, but also Sikorsky's to them. It therefore came as no great surprise when Serge advised me that Igor wished to make a certain change in regard to the XR-4 project, and would like to see me. Michael and Serge were also present. As of yore, Michael was the spokesman. The reason for this particular meeting was first to assure me that they were in no way being critical of my handling of the project. Rather, they were counting on me to help them out of a difficult situation, namely Bob Labensky's redundancy. Bob and Michael Buivid had been the backbone of Igor's support both before and after the VS-300 programme was established.

At that particular moment they felt it was most important that I remained in control of the VS-300 project, because the outcome of any changes being made on VS-300 directly affected the XR-4 project. However, in order to maintain Bob's status, the only comparable opening for him would be that of Project Engineer on XR-4. I was being asked to step aside (maintaining my status) with the understanding that, essentially, Bob was going to rely upon me to help him continue operating the project as I had. I accepted, as I already had a strong friendship with him. His appreciation, both immediate and subsequent, would become apparent, and later events would prove it to have been a wise decision for all concerned.

It was now almost the end of September 1941. Back in June, rumours had filtered up from Philadelphia that Platt-Le Page was running into problems with its XR-1. Apparently, Major Frank Gregory was getting rather uneasy about the number of times an expected 'first flight' had been cancelled. Anyway Igor, during a meeting at that time, suggested that Prof Sikorsky and I have a quick look at what might be the specification for a competitor to the XR-1, using a United Aircraft 450 hp Pratt & Whitney engine.

Several days later we came up with the following data: Engine, Pratt & Whitney Junior 450 hp at 2,300 rpm, cruise 300 hp at 2,000 rpm.

Weight 668 lb, Diameter 46.19 in, Length 42.38 in

Fuel consumption at cruise: 0.48 lb/hp/hr = 100 gal.

Four hours = 600 lb

Oil consumption at cruise: 0.25 lb/hp/hr = 10 gal.

Four hours = 75 lb

Gross weight to be aimed at: 4,000–4,200 lb; empty 2,735/2,800 lb

Useful load – 1,200 lb

Main rotor diameter: 44 ft; maximum rpm: 200 at take-off, 180 cruise.

Maximum rotor torque, 95,000 in/lb. = 290 lb tail rotor.

Pilot: 1, observer: 1 front, with rudder pedals only.

Clear moulded plastic nose section.

Landing gear: main gear travel inside fuselage.

Engine mounted vertically, with gravity feed for fuel.

Welded tubular steel centre section, sheet aluminium cabin section and tail cone, elliptical with tail shaft on top. Radio. Construction of main rotor similar to that of XR-4.

Depth charge and anti-submarine Sonar to be fitted.

It is interesting to compare a copy of the original sketch I presented at that meeting (Fig 76) with a later drawing of VS-327/XR-5.

I. A. Sikorsky, Igor's nephew, was usually referred to as 'Prof' before Alexander Nikolsky joined the old guard, as he was the only member with an engineering degree. From the very first time I met him I could only visualise him as the living embodiment of Mr Pickwick, the famous, kind-hearted and endearing character portrayed by Charles Dickens in his delightful novel *The Pickwick Papers*, in which he was the founder and president of the Pickwick Club. Not only did he physically resemble the illustrated chubby and balding character to an extraordinary degree, but in many ways he was Mr Pickwick. I shall never forget one hot, summer afternoon, when I dropped by to see him. He had just finished watering the lawn and flowerbeds, using a sprinkler nozzle on the end of the hose. There stood 'Prof' on the lawn, just in his swimming shorts, his left hand holding the sprinkler vertically so that it gently bathed him, fountain-fashion, while with his right hand he casually sipped a dry Martini.

'Prof's' computer was a 24 in slide rule (slip stick) rather than the more usual 12 in, because its 2:1 ratio permitted him to calculate to four decimal points instead of only two using the 12 in. I have always regretted that our paths did not cross more often during the period covered by this account, for it always was such a pleasure when they did. This quiet, unassuming man was never too busy to share some of his time with me.

The performance data that 'Prof' presented has unfortunately disappeared, but as I recall, he had estimated a cruising speed of about 105 mph in addition to the 4 hr duration noted above. We all agreed that this quick outline, although it was very limited and assumed that the all-cyclic main rotor had become a reality, had nevertheless strengthened our hopes that before long we would have the chance to prove its practicability. Any further work would have to come after we had found a successful solution to the control of VS-300.

At the end of September 1941 VS-300D made its maiden 'roll-out' on to the meadow, where it was first carefully inspected by us (including Les Morris) before being 'accepted' by Igor, who was obviously anxious to take it aloft.

Our major concern, of course, was the effectiveness of the redesigned lateral cyclic control. Incidentally, we had at last persuaded Igor to test this new control combination initially without the vertical flapping restricting dampers. Thus his first manoeuvre, after a slow, smooth take-off and slow climb to about 15 ft followed by a descent to about 5 ft, was a cautious attempt at sideways flight. Much to his and our relief he obviously had no difficulty in doing this smoothly, several times to either side, with increasing confidence and speed. Coming to a hover facing us, he gave us a satisfied wave, made a complete 360° turn and then a 180° about face, then gently tilted VS-300 forward,

Fig 73
VS-300-D

First flight with tail rotor in old location. No blade flapping restricting or lag dampers
(1) Lateral cyclic control
Note Les's awkward position of left hand on collective pitch lever.

Fig 74
VS-300-D-1

(1) Tail rotor moved to pylon after accident. Cockpit and centre section covered.

Fig 75
VS-300-D-1a

(1) Upper bar attached to lateral cyclic.
(2) Lower bar static.
(1) Indicates amount of movement for lateral control 0° hovering.

Igor is snapped snapping one.

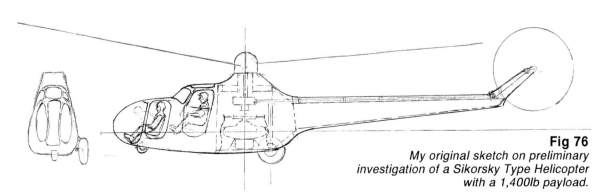

Fig 76
My original sketch on preliminary investigation of a Sikorsky Type Helicopter with a 1,400lb payload.

letting it gain speed and altitude. It was obvious that the Master was 'off and running'. Next came backwards flights, followed by stops and starts, then several circuits of the meadow at increasing speeds, finally going into his beloved figure eights before making a perfect landing. He switched off the engine and sat there a few moments before exclaiming, very precisely and emphatically: 'Gentlemen, this is a new heelicopter'.

Now, for the first time, I was experiencing the exhilaration of witnessing a successful demonstration of an entirely new VS-300 configuration that was entirely my idea, by none other than Igor himself. Admittedly VS-300-D was hardly a thing of beauty (Fig 73) with her single horizontal tail rotor perched inelegantly on top of a slender conglomerate of welded tubes that protruded upwards from the aft end of her unaltered rear fuselage section. It was obviously a quick 'make-do' structure to which, shortly afterwards, would also be relocated the vertical tail rotor, the main requirement being to locate the single horizontal tail rotor above any possible main rotor downwash. Apparently this had now been achieved.

The greatly improved lateral cyclic control was due, of course, to the leverage advantage of the main rotor itself initiating the tilt well above the craft's CG, rather than the two laterally disposed horizontal tail rotors, which had to twist-tilt the entire aircraft forcibly. Moreover there was no other disturbing control force with which the main rotor had to contend. Of equal importance, however, was the new cyclic blade control system, adapted to the original tilting plate, which provided the blades with increased angular control movement and control response. By eliminating the tail outriggers, two important reductions took place. The tail area was lighter, thereby reducing the force required to move the tail up or down, and there was a considerable reduction in air resistance. The net result was greater manoeuvrability and speed.

This latest flight control breakthrough, took place on a fine clear morning with a 10/15 mph wind blowing. After Igor's initial enthusiastic comments on VS-300's newly acquired behaviour, he made several suggestions regarding adjustments that had to be made. These mainly concerned the collective pitch synchronisation between the main and horizontal tail rotor, using the engine throttle, to produce a level vertical ascent or descent. After Adolf had made adjustments to the several linkages involved, Igor took off, and, after several vertical ups and downs and another rechecking of the lateral control, he was satisfied that VS-300 was ready for Les to lift-off the following morning. Les had been keenly observing the entire first successful flight and carefully listening to Igor's various comments regarding the new 'feel' of controlling VS-300D. On the morrow he would be initiating his first test flight of an entirely new control system.

Ever since his arrival that March, this had been the day for which he was waiting; his initiation into the art of aircraft flight testing and the evaluation of an entirely new configuration to the one which he had learned to control very successfully. So, when Igor asked him if he would like to be 'first up' that morning, one can readily imagine how eagerly he accepted the invitation. First Les was given a general run-down regarding what to expect from the new configuration, and told to monitor the longitudinal trim carefully when using the collective pitch lever, so as to go straight up or down in a level manner. As with Igor, it was suggested that Les begin by getting used to the feel of lateral control response.

Unlike so many of the earlier history-making test flights in the meadow, these took place on the outskirts of Bridgeport Airport. This was mainly because of the greater level area afforded, together with steadier wind conditions, it being well away from any adjacent large structures, as the wind was gustier than the day before.

Les's initial careful vertical take-off of -300D, lateral control testing and subsequent manoeuvres in all directions, a few feet off the ground, were all smooth and well co-ordinated. It was increasingly obvious that he was rapidly becoming, like Igor, comfortable with VS-300D, and that the decision to adopt the new configuration had been right. Les was indeed an exceptionally fine pilot. He ended his first test flight on VS-300D by demonstrating the precision possible with the new control system, slowly but carefully manoeuvring the helicopter until the main landing wheels were just ahead of the two sandbags, before setting down precisely a few inches ahead of them, as they had been before lift-off. The original idea for the sandbags was to prevent VS-300 from rolling backwards (it had no brakes), a precaution Les thought would help his initial handling of the controls before lift-off.

It was then Les's turn to express his enthusiastic response to questions, including those of Michael, Serge and myself. Igor's satisfaction with Les's answers was plainly visible. Both agreed that the outstanding improvements were in control response and smoother overall operation. This was especially true in sideways flight, where less control stick movement was required, as was the case when making banked turns in forward flight. Like Igor, Les had made no attempt at flying other than at speeds of 20/25 mph. He then said he would like to have a second go at increased speeds.

Les's lift-off on his second flight was more assured. This time he considerably increased the scope and speeds of the various manoeuvres he had previously made. Then he began making figure-eights that ended up at estimated speeds of 35/40 mph at some 20/25 ft, as he happily waved to us. However, as he came in to land, as he later admitted, he was somewhat overconfident as a result of the newly acquired feeling of freedom of heeli-flying, which he had never before experienced. He misjudged the precise location of both main undercarriage wheels by concentrating on only the left wheel. However, the right wheel was not in front of its sandbag but directly over it as he brought VS-300 down to earth. It quickly tilted over to the left. Les over-controlled to the right and the tail skid buckled as it hit the ground, as did the tips of the tail rotor, smashing its blades and causing excessive vibration. Instinctively Les switched off the engine. VS-300D immediately quietened down, rather tilted, as we all ran over to assist him.

Poor old Les was rather shaken but otherwise none the worse. On the other hand, he was obviously terribly humiliated because it had been his idea to use the sandbags in the first place. Quickly sensing Les's feelings, Igor reassured him by remarking that if that was the worst he ever did, he need not worry.

The net result from this accident was, at least, positive. For this was the second time the vertical tail rotor had hit the ground. This time it was decided to place the rotor out of harm's way on the horizontal tail rotor's support structure (Fig 74).

It is also worthy of note that lateral cyclic in no way caused any additional vibration, regardless of

the manner of flight. In fact, as flight testing started again, VS-300D-1, with the vertical tail rotor relocated higher up and closer to the height of the main rotor hub, was considered the smoothest version yet tested. For the first time Les was really thrilled by the manner in which he could demonstrate the machine. This also led to Serge again returning to piloting VS-300.

As higher speeds then became possible, directional instability (fish-tailing) was becoming a problem. First, a vertical fin area, using doped fabric, was added in the centre of the rearmost section of the triangular fuselage frame. Then this was progressively enlarged until it reached the centre section, where it proceeded to cover just the right hand side (Fig 73). Correspondingly, so both directional stability and speed improved, with the result that it was decided to enclose the other side of the centre section, and (at long last) the entire cockpit area. That was attractively done by Alex Krapish, now in charge of VS-300. The reduction in air resistance was immediately apparent, as Les was able to clock speeds in the 50/60 mph range, with good directional stability. (Fig 74)

It will be noticed that Les was already doing practically all the flight testing. This was, of course, exactly as intended. However, Igor never failed to keep abreast of any significant change by testing it personally, and his active mind was never without concern for any pertinent problem. His present optimism and enthusiasm in supporting a successful improvement was equally shared by all of us.

At Wright Field, Dayton, Ohio, Maj Frank Gregory at Air Materiel Command was also very pleased to hear the good news about how well VS-300D-1 was performing. It was not very long, however, before we were being gently reminded that, regardless of how remarkable VS-300's performance was, the basic military requirement remained that all flight control be attained by the main lifting rotor, other than that for anti-torque and/or directional control (or words to that effect). That is to say, as far as Frank Gregory was concerned, we had successfully returned halfway to a fully cyclically controlled main rotor. How about us finishing the job?

The dilemma facing both Gregory and Sikorsky was in a way unique. The Military, in good faith, had given us a contract to design and build a helicopter configuration that turned out to be not as

Fig 77 *XR-4 Main rotor hub. The 3 collective pitch levers (CPLs) (1), through the 3 CPL links (2) move the 3 blade control horns (5), when activated by top triangular unit (4) is moved vertically UP=plus, DOWN=minus pitch angle. At each end of the 3 levers (1) is a link (3), that is connected to the 3-armed, gimbal-mounted, cyclic blade pitch control unit (8), that is attached to the non-rotating, 2-armed lower swashplate unit (9), by means of a ballbearing, which in turn, is tilted by means of control rods (10) longitudinal rotor tilting and (10)a lateral rotor tilting, when activated by the pilot's flight control lever. Each outer end of the 3 flapping hinges (11) contains a vertical lead-lag hinge pin (13) to which is attached an inner blade arm (14), with a control horn (5), and rotor blade attachment fitting (14)a. Which is circular ring-type fitting, that mates with a similar fitting (7)a, at the root end of each rotor blade (7). (12) is the main rotor drive shaft. Ref. Fig 83 page 112 (same key numbers) . This bizarre arrangement actually worked! So it was never changed.*

fully developed, or as practicable, as either party, in good faith, had considered it to be. The ball was now in our court, and we had to make the winning play!

At this point it is necessary to examine how the foregoing was affecting the XR-4 project. Obviously, if cyclic control was indeed going to be used on the main rotor, we would have to make do with the existing non-cyclic hub. There was simply not enough time left to start from scratch, designing and making an entirely new hub and control system (Fig 77). Luckily, as mentioned

earlier, I had had Ed Katziper revise my original hub design to incorporate cyclic blade control. Basically, what he had to do was to devise a means whereby the originally simple blade pitch changing mechanism, comprising a three-pronged horizontal star on top of a push-pull rod (protruding from inside of the rotor shaft), which was provided with three vertical links that were individually connected to each of the blade pitch control horns, would be replaced by a cyclic blade control system. This Ed ingeniously accomplished, as per Figure 77. I jokingly asked him at the time whether a tarantula had inspired him. He said no, it was a

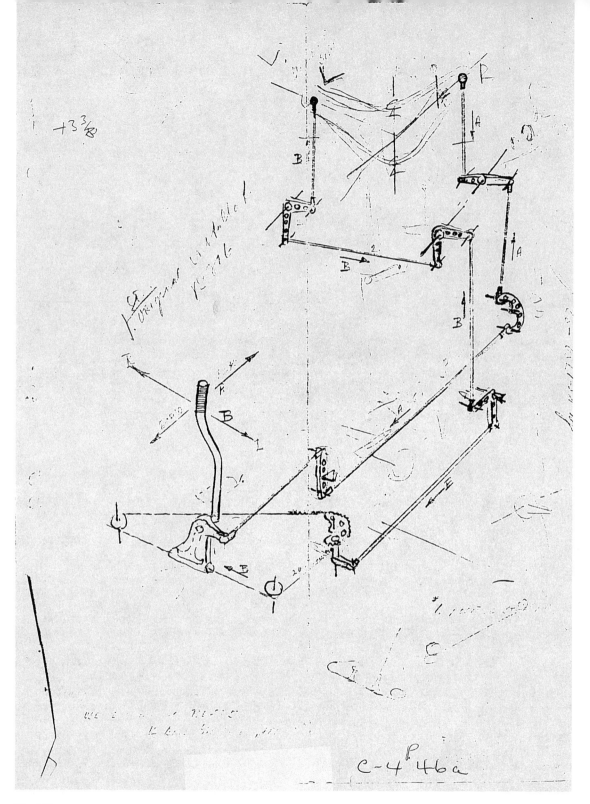

Fig 78
My original sketch for flight control system on XR-4.

fairground merry-go-round.

It now remained to work out the details of incorporating the complete control system from the pilot's control stick to the main rotor hub. I was helping Bob Labensky with this when I happened to mention that a chain-and-sprocket system would probably be the best solution for a particular section of the controls. The next morning Bob arrived with a bicycle chain and several different sizes of bicycle sprockets, and much to his amusement I actually incorporated a set (Fig 78). In numerous instances XR-4 was indeed a one-off specimen.

At this point, much of this type of engineering information was in the form of Engineering Orders (EOs). These were gridded, 8½ in x 11 in draughting pads with duplicating carbon sheets. The first sheet was transparent, and could be duplicated on a printing machine. They each had a printed order number. If properly signed by the project engineer they were accepted by the shop manager. This saved a considerable amount of time.

Before the decision had been made to evaluate VS-300 with a fully cyclic controlled main rotor, a new set of inflated rubber floats were delivered for us to try out. They were longer and smaller in diameter than the original ones, eliminating the need for fore and aft flotation bags. Both Les and Serge took turns flying VS-300 with her new floats for the first time, and the most pleasant surprise for them both was how easily the machine moved sideways on the water now that lateral cyclic of the main rotor had been installed, whereas it had been impossible so to do with the non-cyclic control system. Also, the new floats impaired VS-300's overall performance very little. (Fig. 79)

Serge was the last one to fly, and considering he had far less time on VS-300D-1 than Les, let alone had never flown it with floats, he was doing very well. He elected to make a final ground landing, rather than alight on water, to save the haul-out up the ramp. He began his final slow, vertical let-down from about 10 ft up, but apparently VS-300 was not quite level enough, for as the lowest float touched down she suddenly began to rock from side to side at an alarming rate, roughly shaking Serge. In a desperate effort to switch off the engine, using the switch located low on the pilot's left side (which also meant letting go of the collective pitch lever) Serge caught his coatsleeve on the knob of the engine throttle lever and the helicopter went up to

Fig 79
VS-300-D-2.
Les flies -300 with new longer, narrower floats.

about 25 ft under full power, at which point all rocking had ceased. This time, Serge had no difficulty reaching down and switching off the engine, and down he came, heeli and all! Slightly tail-down, the floats hit the pavement with a dull whump. The impact caused the two lower tubes, supporting the rear fuselage, to buckle upwards, and the vertical tail rotor blades rata-tat-tatted to pieces on the pavement.

As luck would have it these new floats were shock mounted to the fuselage, and the actual shock force of the landing was greatly reduced. Nevertheless, it was yet another nasty shock for poor Serge. Other than a bad shake-up he was not hurt, but it was still a close shave. In fact, I believe that this was his last flight on VS-300. The whole episode probably would not have occurred but for Serge's long coatsleeves. Curiously enough it was a centuries-old custom of dress, originating with the Mongol invasion of Russia. Long sleeves indicated that the wearer was upper class, and therefore above any form of manual labour. At the time it was still customary for Serge's generation in Russia to have their coatsleeves coming down to the upper knuckle of their thumbs.

For some reason or other a back-room boffin termed that side-to-side rocking 'ground resonance'. I have never been able to understand what was resonating what sound. Nevertheless, whatever it was it was abundantly there then, whereas it was not there with the non-cyclic outrigger system.

Apparently, what the pilots had not considered was the entirely different (more powerful) origin of the centre of side-to-side tilting (roll) now being initiated at the centre of the main rotor hub itself, by virtue of lateral cyclic blade control. With the non-cyclic control system, the horizontally outrigged tail rotors were far more limited in the amount of tilting force they could generate.

Thus the constant demand by the pilots for greater lateral control, by increasing the spread between the horizontal rotors. Also the origin of the initiating force was more nearly associated with the CG of the entire aircraft, thus greatly reducing the vertical leverage effect and the ability to tilt the whole aircraft, when water-borne, and move it sideways.

Actually, it was not quite as simple as that. For the foregoing ignores what happens to the aircraft when the pilot uses the vertical tail rotor as a directional rudder control. Not only does this rotor act as a rudder, but it also constantly counteracts the torque from the main rotor, monitored by the pilot. So when he adds a thrust force to the vertical tail rotor (or subtracts it from it), its centre of rotation (thrust) also creates a varying vertical tilting force, separately from the main rotor. This being the case, any one of those forces, or the simultaneous accumulation of them all, could also be directly influenced by downwash from the main rotor, whether the aircraft was water-borne or hovering, as it rebounded from a fixed surface upwards through the centre of the main rotor.

So if by chance one of the floats or main wheels should contact a surface first, there was a distinct possibility that, one way or another, any force or a combination of forces could immediately activate a reaction sufficiently great to rock the whole aircraft laterally in the opposite direction *ad infinitum*, from side-to-side and with ever-increasing intensity. The pilot therefore had to make certain when landing that the final vertical surface contact was made as level as possible, and fairly quickly, to forestall any oscillating. Many successful demonstration flights were made, both on floats and wheels, without further incidents. Never had starting or stopping forward flight been accomplished so smoothly. VS-300D-1 was a delight to watch and fly.

But Maj Gregory was anxious for us to give up the single horizontal tail rotor, in spite of its proven and desirable qualities (he never flew that version). There was no question but that Igor, Michael and I wished we could have pursued this avenue of endeavour much further. Indeed, I still feel that using tail control would eliminate the high hub stress forces induced by longitudinal cyclic blade control, especially in large helicopters. It would eliminate the need for carefully tuned, horizontal lead-lag dampers, resulting in smoother, more comfortable flight for passengers and crew. It was a typical case of 'the customer is always right'!

Thus the next order of business was to remove the horizontal tail rotor with its pylon, and reinstall (after two years of trials and tribulations) a longitudinal cyclic-blade control system for the main rotor. This also entailed designing and making an entirely new, lighter, triangular rear fuselage and a new aft landing skid, and installing a new longitudinal flight control system. In other words, back to square one. For Alex Krapish it meant being happily busy in the shop; for the rest of us, it meant we were two years the wiser. It was by then late November, and it would be several weeks before VS-300E was rolled out.

With regard to XR-4, its engine, cooling, fuel and lubricating systems, the main and tail transmissions systems, the main (full cyclic) and tail rotor hubs and controls, the main and tail rotors, and their flight controls were almost 'systems go', and apart from then attaching the main rotor blades, the helicopter would soon be ready for its initial ground runs.

It then became apparent what Igor had in mind when he had Bob Labensky take over as acting project engineer on XR-4. For between VS-300 and assisting Bob on XR-4, my time had been well taken up. However, a directive had been received from Air Materiel command at Wright Field, requesting us to submit a design based on similar requirements to those originally set forth for an Army Observation Helicopter, and referring to the VS-311 bid of April 1940, which the winning contender, the Platt-Le Page Company, was currently testing as XR-1.

Consequently, a meeting was held on 26 September 1941, where I was once again given the privilege of starting the preliminary design of an entirely new helicopter. The new company type number was VS-327, its military designation being XR-5. Anticipating the Army's desire for an

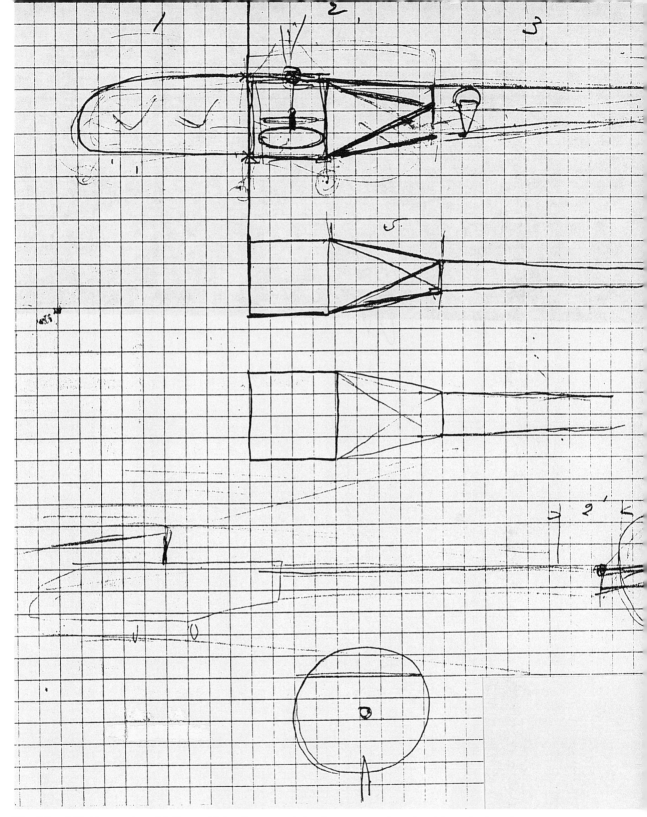

Fig 80 XR-5 meeting 26 Dec. 1941. Igor's original concept sketch of 3 main fuselage sections 1- 2- 3-. Ref. Fig. 76

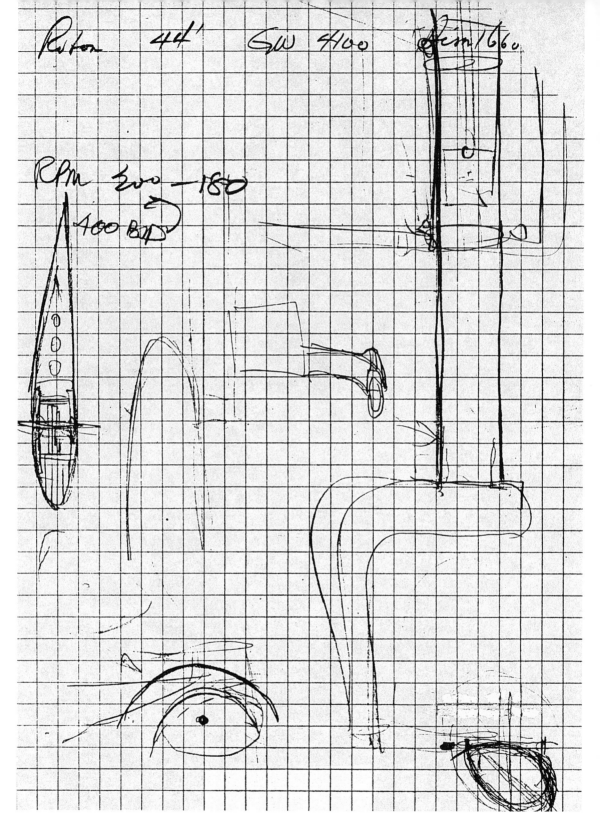

Fig 81 XR-5 meeting. 26 Dec. 1941. Main rotor – gross weight – engine and undercarriage.

all-cyclicly-controlled main rotor, as noted in the preliminary June meeting, VS-327 would be directly influenced by the test results from VS-300E, therefore incorporating full cyclic for both lateral and longitudinal control.

Since our June meeting, apparently, Igor had been led to believe by inputs from both Washington and Wright Field that money for additional helicopter research and development (R&D) was rather scarce. The very beginning of any new design or concept is usually preceded by rough sketches, as ideas are formulated by those involved in the initial stages. Igor had therefore spent considerable time and thought on the possibility of upgrading XR-4, including the structure, landing gear, etc.

The outset of that September meeting was consequently devoted to listening to Igor's proposal and suggestions. Our general surprise at this approach was evidenced by the rather subdued acceptance by Michael, Serge and myself. Michael, by virtue of his long and personal association with Igor, had the privilege of addressing him as, 'Igorianovitch' (son of Igor), and he went on to say that, while all of his

suggestions were quite feasible, he wondered if just another, larger XR-4 would be as appealing as an entirely new approach. Moreover, the military requirement for the observation helicopter called for tandem seating, with the observer in front. There was silence for a few moments as Igor looked intently at Michael. Then he smiled graciously as he repeated his oft-made comment 'Perhaps you are right' several times, as he reached over for his sketch pad and started to sketch his basic thoughts on the new approach (Figs 80 & 81). Our relief was evident.

One of the first considerations with the new design was the positioning and location of the engine. Igor still favoured having its driveshaft mounted vertically, directly under the main rotor hub and transmission, thus avoiding an initial right-angle gear drive. The vertical driveshaft then directly lent itself to driving a planetary geared transmission. In order words, this basically adhered to my original June sketch. It was taken for granted at the time that there would be no major problem in mounting the engine in this way. I therefore proceeded with the preliminary design while still taking care of VS-300 and, to a lesser degree, also helping Bob on XR-4.

In the preliminary stages of designing VS-327 – XR-5 I was in the process of changing the positioning of the CPL from the vertical, as on VS-300 and XR-4, to a more horizontal position, but still

Fig 82

XR-4. Automatic collective pitch and throttle increase/decrease with independent throttle monitoring.

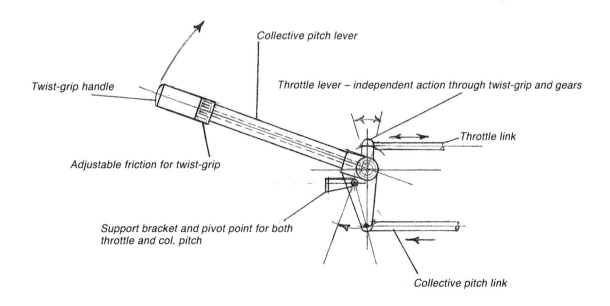

located on the left-hand side, next to the pilot's seat. The engine throttle was also in this location. My basic reason for the change was that the pilot would pull upwards, rather than backwards, as with a vertical lever, for vertical ascent, and downwards, not forwards, for vertical descent. In addition, for prompt adjustment of engine throttle to increase or decrease power independently, the handgrip on the lever could be twisted, similar to a motorcycle handlebar throttle.

I mentioned this to Bob, and he apparently promptly went out and salvaged a right-hand motorcycle handlebar, with its twist-grip engine throttle (shades of 1923). Shortly afterwards, with a very satisfied grin, he handed me the desired treasure, suggesting we attach it to the left rear leg of a nearby chair after having first determined its proper length and comfortable height for its operation. The *modus operandi* became instinctively apparent, as we would raise the lever and at the same time twist the wrist clockwise outwards, and the reverse when pushing down. We immediately brought in Les, who enthusiastically tried it out, and then Serge was similarly sold. Finally all four of us, with the chair, descended upon Igor's office, where, much to his amusement, Les demonstrated this latest breakthrough to him. Igor then 'test hopped' the new arrangement, readily agreeing to its advantages after going through the motions a number of times. He added: 'Furthermore, gentlemen, I suggest it is installed on XR-4 as soon as possible'.

It should be borne in mind that, at that time, XR-4 had been designed as a flight trainer. The trainee was therefore expected to occupy the right-hand seat, so as to have the flight control stick in his right hand, and the engine throttle and the CPL, separately, on his left. With the new system the CPL and throttle would be combined.

On the subject of flight controls, one seldom hears mentioned the fact that a helicopter can take off in the same manner as a fixed-wing aeroplane. That is with a running take-off, provided it has wheels. In such a case, it can take-off with a considerably greater load than it could lift vertically, with only a very short take-off run.

By the end of October 1941 I was getting well into the preliminary design of VS-327/XR-5, and as before with XR-4. Happily for me, as with XR-4 it was a one-man show. There were, of course, visits by Igor from time-to-time and Michael, and occa-

sionally by Serge. One visit by Serge still comes to mind. Igor had suggested 'perhaps' altering a particular line on the side view, which I did. A while later Serge suggested altering the same line almost back to where I had originally drawn it. With a chuckle I told him that Igor was responsible for that particular line, and Serge said 'Awh', raised his eyebrows, smiled and walked away.

On Sunday 7 December 1941 my wife and I were comfortably stretched out before the living-room fire, looking at the *New York Herald Tribune*, with classical background music being provided by WQXR New York. I was particularly interested in a large feature photograph in the rotogravure section, showing a spectacular flight formation of US Army Boeing B-17 heavy bombers flying over Diamond Head as they approached the Army Air Force Base on the island of Oahu, Hawaii. They had flown non-stop for the first time, direct from California, with fuel replacing the weight of their usual armament and only a flight crew aboard.

Suddenly the music stopped. A special announcement was to be made. An emotional voice told us that the Japanese had bombed Pearl Harbor. Such was the background to our feelings when, next morning, VS-300E was rolled out with its final basic flight control system, ready to be tested. One had to admit that she had never looked so smart, trim and balanced as she did with her new, lighter, tapered, triangular rear fuselage. A central, vertical expanse of doped fabric, down the length of the rear fuselage as before, also helped give her a continuous profile.

Les Morris's next series of tests were to be conducted, for the first time without the benefit of the Master at the controls. His first careful lift-off showed that VS-300 had a new bag of tricks to display, as she immediately started oscillating from side-to-side. Les quickly put the helicopter back down on the ground, and Igor suggested that the flight control system be carefully checked again before another flight was attempted.

After tracking tests were finished, in which the rotating main rotor blade tips are checked for consistent alignment, using the blade tracking flag, the flight control stick was unlocked. While the main rotor was still turning I then asked Adolf to move the control stick slightly from side-to-side as I stood directly in front, so that I could check the amount of tilt.

The first time he did so, not realising how sensitive the lateral control actually was, the resulting extreme cyclic reactions of the blades, as their blade tips whipped up and down, and the blades formed perfect arcs from each blade tip down to the flapping hinge, was beyond belief! I was so astonished that it took me a moment or two before I yelled 'Stop!' to Adolf. He reacted instantly, but was obviously puzzled by my agitation. After my explanation he gently repeated the motion. George Lubben, who was standing at right-angles to the rotor hub, signalled me to join him and said: 'Watch the tilt, it isn't at right angles to the fuselage'. He was quite right.

Igor and Michael came down, and agreed after a demonstration. The actual angle could only be visually approximated, but we made a mark on the pavement a measured distance from the centre of the rotor shaft, and compared it with a similar mark at right angles to the fuselage. This highly scientific arrangement produced an approximate angle of 9°, which was dubbed the precession angle. It was decided to reposition the lateral control input to accommodate the 9°. This angle becomes more apparent as diameters increase, because a combination of the blade's weight, with its outward pulling centrifugal force, air resistance (drag) and the radial distribution of its lift determine both its upward coning angle and precession angle. Moreover, if a vertical hinge is added just beyond the horizontal flapping hinge, as Sikorsky did, the drag component becomes even more important, as shall soon be seen.

For the next few days, despite adjustments here and there, VS-300 refused to co-operate, continuing to shake herself and Les as hard as she could. Finally, Les decided to 'go for broke', and right after lift-off he steadfastly kept nudging the helicopter forward for about 30 yards. He repeated this several times, but each time he tried to increase the forward speed VS-300 would shake even harder. Michael suggested frequency testing of the whole aircraft, and Igor agreed. Although the results were interesting, they shed no new light on the problem.

The human brain is without doubt still beyond full comprehension, for the basic cause of all this unwanted vibration was already known to us! While chatting with Adolf it suddenly occurred to me how free VS-300D was of any significant vibration with its single horizontal tail rotor. The main rotor and the whole aircraft were being tilted together, simultaneously, with no change in relationship. This was the basic original argument for changing to non-cyclic control, i.e. not cyclically changing the established tip-path plane of rotation of the main rotor blades from their normal right-angle (plus coning angle) relationship with the main rotor shaft to attain longitudinal control.

Cyclically disturbing a rotor blade's established rotational tip path plane automatically excites each rotor blade to move back and forth about its outboard vertical hinge, as it (Fig 83) tries to accommodate itself suddenly to the new, rapidly varying airflow pattern, especially in forward flight. Thus, we were asking VS-300 to respond to cyclically induced, horizontal blade movement, but without horizontal blade dampers. It was as simple as that. No wonder she objected so vigorously.

My next thought was what sort of hydraulic damper should be employed. I turned to Adolf and said: 'I think I might have the answer to all of this vibration problem. It is a horizontal hydraulic blade damper that initially allows but little movement to sustain the shock, then allows enough movement to establish the new blade position.' Our conversation was momentarily interrupted while Adolf attended to another matter. A few minutes later he responded with: 'What about an anti-shimmy damper, like they use on trucks?' I replied that I was not aware of that gadget. He went on to explain that they were used to stop the front steering wheels of large trucks from shimmying back and forth at certain speeds, and said he would bring one in the following morning. It was a hydraulic cylinder with an actuating piston rod, and was certainly 'husky' enough (as Igor would say) and from the enclosed data, it had a double-acting piston that was capable of damping shocks from both directions.

I had a meeting with Igor and Michael, who agreed with my assumptions and said that the anti-shimmy dampers should be tried right away. With three dampers in hand, some on-the-spot measurements and after some cutting and welding, Adolf and Red had fashioned three complete damper kits, including retaining frames and attachments, and had them installed on VS-300E-1 by the afternoon of 30 December 1941. A preliminary ground run-up and blade tracking check cleared her for Les to try out the next morning.

Thus, on the very last day of the year, it was with anxious anticipation that Igor, Michael, Serge, Les, Bob and I foregathered in the familiar

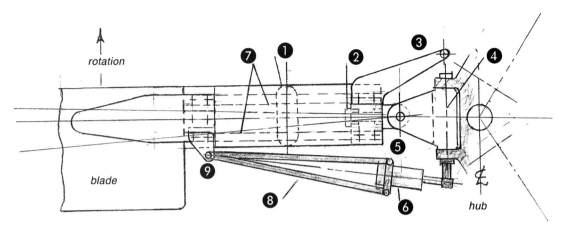

(1) Cross section
(2) Retention bearings
(3) Pitch control horn
(4) Horizontal flapping hinge
(5) Vertical lead-lag hinge

(6) Lead-lag damper
(7) Retention tubes
(8) Welded tube frame
(9) Ball socket joint

Fig 83 *VS-300-E-1 Hub with lead-lag hydraulic damper (not to scale).*

meadow next to the VS-44 hangar with Adolf and his ground crew, who already had the engine warmed up. It was a crisp, clear December morning as Les settled into the bucket seat, started the engine and engaged the rotors. After a preliminary checking of the controls he gave us a wave and gently lifted off and hovered smoothly, just clear of the ground then again several feet up. There was still no oscillation. Now slowly sideways, both ways, then backwards, and finally Les nudged VS-300 forward. She began to slowly gather speed, with hardly a quiver as she responded smoothly right through the old 'vibration barrier' and proceeded to make a complete circuit of the meadow. The flight ended as Les, with a broad smile, made a perfectly flared landing in front of Igor. As Les put it, it was like a miracle from the Dark Ages, how this simple expedient turned the trick. He entered in his log book: 'Flights were made forwards, backwards and sideways, and no wobble or resonance was discovered at any time'.

After the momentary euphoria had died down, Les was bombarded with questions. Yes, the transition into forward flight was still accompanied by a slight, short-lived tremor. The same occurred when slowing down before landing. Both instances

were not as smooth as with the single horizontal tail rotor. Otherwise, the control reactions were smooth when applied for sideways, backwards and hovering flight. The maximum speed attained, so far, was probably not more than 15 mph, which was well beyond the transition stage.

Eagerly, Igor took Les's place in the bucket seat and proceeded to repeat the same manoeuvres, with increased speed towards the end of the circuit, which also included several zig-zag bankings! He was both elated and greatly relieved, for once again, seemingly at the last moment, another rabbit had been successfully pulled out of the hat. He thanked us, including Adolf and his crew, for helping to make such a significant improvement, wishing us all a Happy New Year. His wishes were reciprocated. Then, turning to me, he quietly said: 'You were right again, Beel'. For me, there followed a very joyous New Year's Eve.

VS-300C

Belt drive ratio – $\dfrac{14}{8} = 1.75{:}1$

Gear ratio – $\dfrac{51}{8} = 6.375{:}1$

$\Big\}$ 11.15625:1

Rear horizontal rotor drive ratio – $\dfrac{4.5}{4} = 1.125{:}1$

Rear vertical rotor drive ratio – 1.28:1

RPM

Engine	Main Rotor	Rear Drive-Shaft	Horiz. Aux. Rotor	Vert.Aux. Rotor
2,600	*233	1,485	1,320	1,160
2,650	*237	1,514	1,345	1,182
2,750	*242	1,543	1,371	1,205
2,700	*246	1,571	1,396	1,227
2,800	*251	1,600	1,422	1,250
2,850	*255	1,628	1,447	1,271
2,900	*260	1,657	1,472	1,294
2,950	*264	1,685	1,498	1,316
3,000	*269	1,714	1,523	1,339
3,050	*273	1,743	1,549	1,361

* Tip speed 292 mph

As this momentous year of 1941 thus came to its promising end for Igor and his associates, it also meant that he was able to signal the long awaited news to Maj Frank Gregory at Wright Field that, in the last few hours of 1941 VS-300E-1 had broken through the last remaining barrier, thus fulfilling Wright Field's ultimate requirement; a fully cyclically controlled main lifting rotor about all axes. VS-300 had proved her worth! This, of course, meant completely eliminating the non-cyclic control system on XR-4. This proposal was happily received, readily agreed to, and accepted as done.

It took from 9 December 1939 to 31 December 1941 to rectify the basic faults inherent in the original VS-300 main rotor full cyclic blade control system. In other words, it took that length of time before the original basic problem was recognised and properly understood, which, inadvertently included the development of the best non-cyclic configuration. From now on it would be a matter of 'fine-tuning' the results of our efforts.

While 1941 had been a year of uncertainty for XR-4's final configuration, up until its last hours, 1942 was soon to change all that, when she was officially accepted by Air Materiel Command, with flying colours. Similarly XR-5 began to take form, soon to be followed by XR-6, and -300 had a whirl at being a two-seater, VS-300-F. 1942 would prove to be another gala year.

Before 'signing off' 1941, I must record a most memorable occasion earlier in the year, when Miss Helen Keller, that remarkable deaf, dumb and blind lady, together with her equally faithful mentor and companion, Miss Sullivan, visited us. Igor had invited them to 'see' him demonstrate the

first successful single-main-rotor helicopter. The demonstration took place during the earlier stages of VS-300's development, when it was non-cyclic. At Miss Keller's request, just a small group of us were privileged to witness the event.

Igor first described, in general terms, the configuration of VS-300 to Miss Keller. This was continuously relayed to her by what appeared to be a series of flickering finger tappings on her hand by Miss Sullivan, and Miss Keller enthusiastically, similarly responded with head noddings and smiles of understanding.

Next, Igor took the ladies on a walk-around tour of the machine describing in some detail some of the features, and Miss Keller, would from time-to-time reach out to pass her hand over them, also, through Miss Sullivan, asking a surprising number of questions. Igor asked her if she had any idea of the length of VS-300. She thought a moment and tapped out her answer, 'about 28 ft'. As I happened to be nearby, Igor turned to me and asked how correct that was. I replied it was remarkably close, only 2 ft more.

Finally came the flight demonstration. A wooden rod had been horizontally fastened to the top of the centre section, extending forward, ending next to the pilot's seat. A piece of rope dangled down for Miss Keller to grasp with one hand, while Miss Sullivan could communicate to her by the other hand, thus permitting Igor to explain each phase of the demonstration to her, while at the same time, she would be 'seeing' through the action of the rope. With the two ladies in their respective positions, Les started the engine. Immediately Helen reacted by marking time, as it were, with both feet. Then as Les slowly moved the helicopter through the four directions, both ladies were obviously thrilled as they followed its movements. However, when VS-300 rose gently vertically, Helen was so excited that she let go of Ann's hand, and marked time vigorously in utter delight. Obviously, Igor was both equally surprised and delighted with her uninhibited response, as was her audience.

Later Ann Sullivan remarked that she had never seen Helen so happily animated. Not to mention that she, too, was so very thrilled, for indeed she was partially blind herself. Her extraordinary patience and determination to save the soul of the despondent deaf, dumb and blind Helen Keller can only be appreciated by reading her book.

Fig 84
Les Morris pilots the XR-4 for its first flight, 14 January 1942.
Original tail section.

(1) Lead weight to bring centre-of-gravity forward, as even without
outriggers C-of-G was still too far aft.

Chapter Five
1942

First US Army Helicopter Accepted and Flight-delivered – XR-5 Design Approved by US Army and British Military and Production Initiated – XR-6 Design Approved by US Army and Navy – With Newly Acquired All-cyclic Main Rotor Control System, VS-300-Fa Gains a New Lease of Life, Ending Up as VS-300-G

The very first order of business for the New Year was getting XR-4 airborne now that VS-300Fa had definitely demonstrated the final practical solution for an all-cyclic, single-main-rotor flight control system. To meet the roll-out date for XR-4, it was necessary to come up with a similar version of the truck shimmy-damper used successfully on VS-300Fa as soon as possible. Working together with Michael Buivid, we came up with a simplified version, incorporating two major improvements proposed by Michael. The addition of a central oil reservoir on top of the hub let centrifugal force help to maintain a constant full capacity of oil in the cylinder, and two external adjustable metering valves, one on each end cap of the cylinder barrel, governed the exact amount of oil flow needed in either direction, caused by the horizontal movement of the rotor blade, to provide the correct amount of damping, rather than by the piston itself, as in the original shimmy-damper. The overall redesign thus simplified fine-tuning the dampers.

On 14 January XR-4 was ready for its first attempt to become airborne, with the new blade dampers and collective pitch/throttle lever, but without cabin doors and with an otherwise completely uncovered fuselage. Another feature which made XR-4's appearance somewhat grotesque, if not cumbersome, was that she still retained the rear portion of the original fuselage, which was designed to carry the two large out-riggers. This was because, almost up to the last moment, the final shape and requirements of the rear fuselage section depended upon the outcome of the concurrent testing of the all-cyclic main rotor control system on VS-300Fa (Fig 84).

Bob Labensky was now officially the XR-4 Project Engineer, and had chosen Ralph Alex as his assistant. Their engineering group, together with Adolf Plenefisch and his shop crew, had put in many extra hours getting XR-4 ready for its historical maiden flight. Furthermore, for Les Morris, it would be his very first experience at test flying a completely new, untested helicopter. As we were chatting while walking to the field next to the VS-44 hangar, where XR-4 was being warmed up, Igor mentioned the strange feeling he was experiencing, for XR-4 was the first aircraft in his entire career, bearing his name, which would not have him at its controls for its maiden flight. It was a unique milestone for both Igor and Les.

The day was overcast and cold, with several inches of snow on the ground and a light breeze, as Les prepared to board XR-4 for a careful pre-flight checkout. For the past two weeks, or so, he had been steadfastly practising the new technique required in using the combined pitch/throttle control lever with his left arm. This meant that he would be sitting in the right-hand seat in the cabin. Apparently this was because the demonstration rig that Bob and I had devised, and on which Les had practised, (à la XR-5) was left-handed. But for some reason Les forgot that XR-4 had only one pitch control lever, located between the two seats. Igor pointed this out to him as he started to enter the cabin on the left side. He hesitated a moment, then settled into the left-hand seat, realising too late, as he afterwards told me, that he should have heeded Igor's hint. However, with considerable extra concentration he gradually became adjusted to the new regime.

With engine started and warmed up, and the

Fig 85
XR-4a
This was the start of the second series of tests.
Note:
(1) That the cabin doors have been added.
(2) The side panels on the engine compartment have been left off, to help cool the gearbox.

(3) Only the left-hand side of the fuselage has been covered over, to test directional control, and/or stability.
(4) The weighted nose boom has been extended forward, to overcome tail heaviness.

Fig 86
Waiting for Les Morris.   *Alex*   *Buivid*   *Walsh*

rotors clutched in, Les truly began his new career as a test pilot. To start with, while four ground crew held on to the landing gear, Les cautiously checked out the engine controls and flight control behaviour. The main rotor blades were not properly balanced, causing sideways rocking, but nevertheless Les courageously kept pulling up on the collective pitch lever and twisting the throttle grip for more power. As XR-4 slowly lifted itself clear of *terra firma*, a cheer from us all went up with it, not the least of all from its creator.

Like a young mare experiencing a bit, saddle and rider for the first time, XR-4 started to buck and twist from side-to-side in a frantic effort to overcome Les's determination to regain control. We were all left speechless at the sight of such wild gyrations. Then as Les started to let it down it calmed down sufficiently to allow Les to make a safe landing, ending with handshakes and congratulations from us all. The total flight time was 3 min.

Obviously there were adjustments to be made, so XR-4 was taken back into the shop. All of the control loads were too high, especially the CPL, downwards, so a spring was added, providing considerable relief. It was mid-afternoon before Les, now determined to learn how to fly from the left side, made several more flights, each one with more confidence, as the controls loads were made easier to handle and the main rotor made smoother by careful blade angle readjustment. A remarkable total of over 25 min were logged on the very first day out, and steady forward flight had been attained.

Next time out XR-4 had a bowsprit in the form of a two-by-four wooden plank with a lead weight at its outer end, to bring its CG further forward, for without the tail rotors to lift up the tail section it was tail heavy. The cabin doors were installed, and doped fabric was added to the entire left-hand side of the tail section of the fuselage. This was done to check in-flight stability while flying forwards, sideways and backwards. The engine compartment was left open, as both engine and main transmission cooling were still not satisfactorily determined (Fig 85). At the time when the cooling fan for the XR-4 engine was being designed, the fact that the engine and fan were facing backwards, and that the air flowing from the fan would also be blown backwards, was not given too much thought. Moreover, as XR-4 first flew (Fig 84) there were no side, top

or bottom panels enclosing the centre section, or tail section, of the fuselage. It being winter time, whatever cooling air the fan was providing was apparently sufficient.

However, when XR-4 started to fly with her new, completely covered tail section and covered centre section, the engine started to overheat. This was caused by the lack of any rear enclosing panel in the centre section, which resulted in any air entering the centre-section area being sucked out through the open-ended rear end of the tail section, when the helicopter was flying forward. Once the rear of the centre section had been sealed off, all was well. This was so typical of the problems that make research and development engineering such an interesting area.

Over the next two weeks, no fewer than 32 test flights were made, logging a total of nearly 2½ hours. This was considered quite a remarkable achievement for such an entirely new type of aircraft, not to mention the abilities of the test pilot.

Happily, during this same period Frank Gregory, now a Lieutenant-Colonel, was able to make a visit, and enthusiastically watched a flight demonstration. He congratulated us for converting XR-4 to fulfil the requirement for an all-cyclically-controlled main rotor. During this same period Michael Gluhareff became the first passenger to ride in XR-4. It was now time for all the necessary changes to be made, and, except for a brief check flight on 7 March, she would not be on the flight line again until the end of March. All things considered, Igor was well pleased with the test results so far.

Just before the end of January another very important date occurred for me. On the 26th I was officially made Project Engineer for XR-5. Again I had been entrusted with the task of designing and engineering an entirely new aircraft. The little ceremony took place in Igor's office, along with Michael, and Serge. I was to go over to the personnel office the next morning to acquire a new badge, signifying my new appointment. I was joined by Ed Dudek, who had also been made Project Engineer, in charge of refurbishing the three VS-44 US Navy flying boats for VIP civilian transatlantic wartime service. It was a happy day for both of us. I was also still in charge of VS-300.

That day was also important for XR-4, for in the afternoon Igor called a meeting regarding the

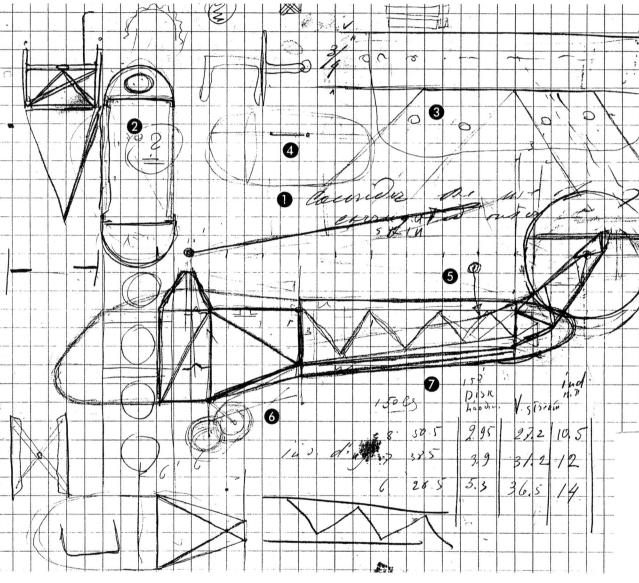

Fig 87 *XR-4-A*
*Some of Igor's and my thoughts sketched during
meeting on new tail section and handed to Bob
Labensky after the meeting.*

*(1) Note reads, 'Consider the use of corrugated
skin'.*
(2) Cross-section of proposed new tail section.
*(3) Side truss consisting of 'T' shaped aluminium
extrusions.*
(4) Outline of horizontal tail surface. (Ref Fig. 88)

*(5) Proposed use of a series of universal joints,
instead of gear.*
*(6) Lever type suspension for shock absorbers,
main undercarriage. (see Fig. 89) 36A Cantilever*
(7) Tail rotor performance calculations.
(8) Movable tailplane. (see Fig. 88)

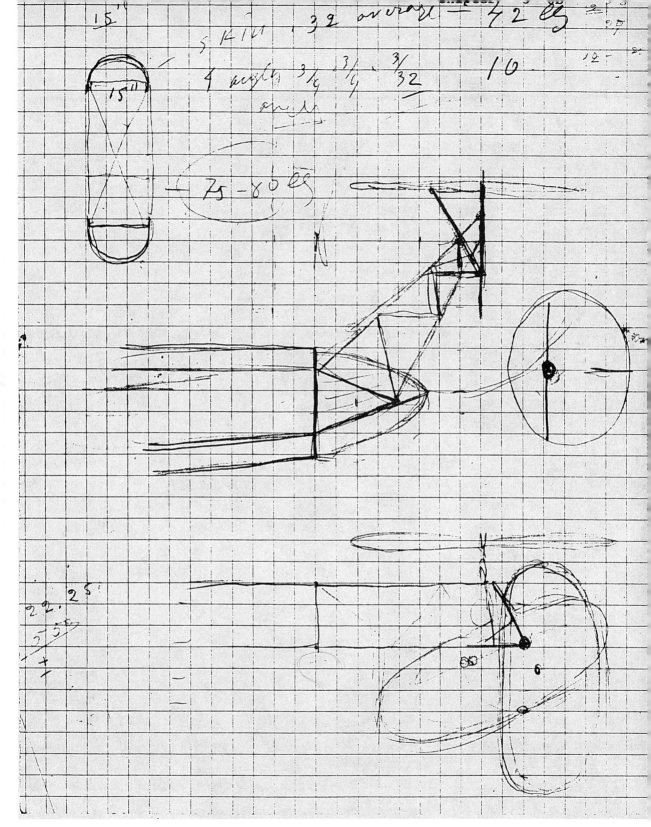

Fig 88 *Outline of movable horizontal tail*

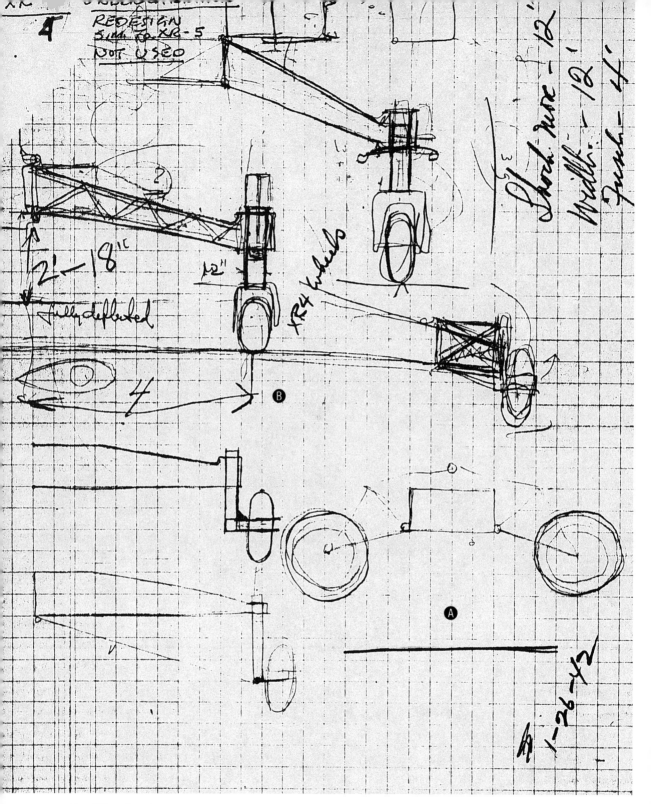

Fig 89 *A – Lever type suspension for shock absorbers, main undercarriage.*
B – Cantilever undercarriage.

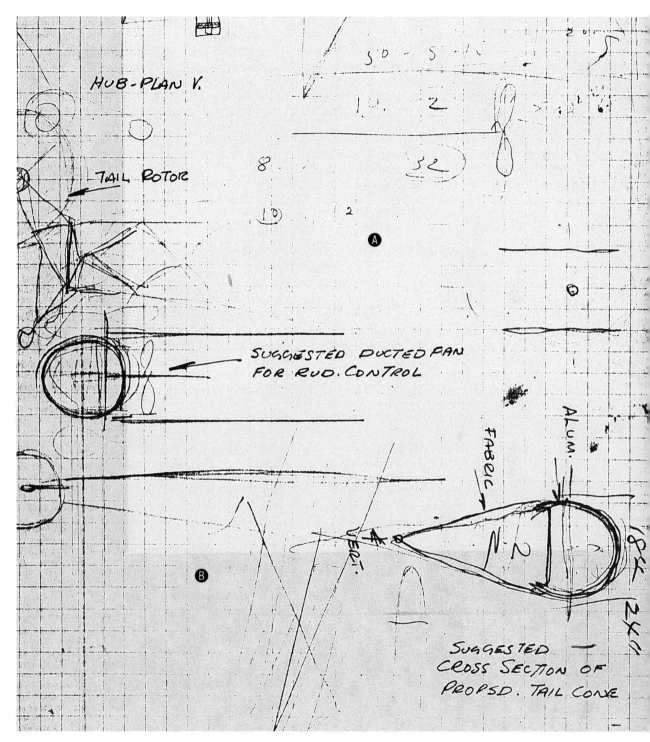

HUB-PLAN V.

TAIL ROTOR

SUGGESTED DUCTED FAN
FOR RUD. CONTROL

Ⓐ

Ⓑ

FABRIC

ALUM.

SUGGESTED
CROSS SECTION OF
PROPSD. TAIL CONE

Fig 90   *A – Ducted fan. B – Tail cone construction.*

changes being considered, including a new rear fuselage. Michael said that Igor wished me to attend, even though Bob Labensky was now Project Engineer, but it transpired that it was Bob who had suggested I attend, as there were still some areas of XR-4 with which I was more familiar than he was. Such, was Bob's humble loyalty and friendship.

As usual, Igor had been giving considerable thought to the various problem areas, and made some innovative suggestions for us to discuss. To lighten the redesigned fuselage he suggested a composite aluminium structure of extruded angles for the truss, covered with corrugated sheets (the well-known German Junkers method) riveted together. The final choice was mainly guided by what was most readily available; welded steel tubes and fairing battens, covered with doped fabric. Then, believe it or not, Igor wondered 'if perhaps we might consider trying the movable horizontal elevator on XR-4, before putting her back in the shop for refitting?' One just could not help but admire his perseverance. In fact, he actually ended up with a smile, as we did (Figs 88, 89 & 90).

Strangely enough, this time he won, as Bob felt that the amount of shop work required could be best handled now, and could then be incorporated in the new section if approved by Wright Field. Next the undercarriage was reviewed, and, as will be seen by Igor's sketches, he finally won again on XR-5! The present system was enhanced with a swivelling tailwheel, located further forward, rather than at the very tail end as at present.

Les had a harrowing brief experience with the horizontal tail surface. In a way, I am glad I was not present, from what Les later told me. He and XR-4 very narrowly escaped what could have been a fatal crash, as a sudden, strong gust of wind caught the tail surface and made the tail end thrash about violently. The helicopter almost hit the ground before Les could regain control (Igor was yet to give up).

Meanwhile VS-300 was making its latest test flights, with the all-cyclic main rotor control system. My old friend and neighbour, Alex Krapish (pronounced Kraypish) was now in charge of VS-300, Adolf and George Lubben having been transferred to XR-4 to take charge of its construction full-time. It may be recalled that Alex was one of the members of the original group who joined Sikorsky's engineering company on Long Island,

New York, in 1923. He had also designed and built several successful aeroplanes. He immediately made himself welcome with the remaining VS-300 crew with his quiet manner, good humour and endless accounts of his past aviation experiences, not to mention his ability to make practical suggestions regarding improving VS-300's performance.

Now that VS-300 was well on the way to becoming well mannered with the new control system, it was also necessary to reduce its weight and air resistance, and establishing the proper location of its CG, both vertically and longitudinally. Knowing Alex as I did, and not being required to go through official government channels, as the VS-300 was a company funded project, I needed only to supply him with the minimum of technical information in order to have any changes made. The next important change was to replace the rear fuselage, as it now only had to support the single vertical, directional tail rotor, this could be a lighter, more attractive structure.

Within a week VS-300G came into being. It also had a swivelling front wheel and a new rear skid, just to the rear of the centre section. The tail rotor was positioned so that its blade tips were well above the level of the lower tube of the triangular rear fuselage, providing additional ground clearance. However, the main reason for raising the centre of rotation of the tail rotor was to reduce the side-tilting force it produced when it was located well below the centre of rotation of the main rotor, as mentioned earlier when reciting the various forces simultaneously acting upon the helicopter as it approached the ground, at the moment of landing. This also had to be recognised and acted upon by the pilot at the same time, so directional control sensitivity, related to the amount of foot pedal movement required, needed adjustment because the lighter and slimmer tail required less force to move it.

The main rotor blades were removed and carefully weighed, and their spanwise balance points located. Then weight was added to the two lighter blades, so that they balanced at the same spanwise point as the heaviest blade. The blades were then whirl-tested, using the 'flag' and coloured blade tip system, and blade incidence readjusted. The final rotor run-up was decidedly smoother.

To find the CG of the entire helicopter, including the pilot and full fuel tanks, VS-300 had a weight scale placed under each main landing wheel and the

Fig 91   *Igor holds -300-G motionless as Alex Krapish replaces a 'damaged' wheel.*

Fig 92   *Les demonstrates precise control possible with -300-G.*

'HEELICOPTER' – PIONEERING WITH IGOR SIKORSKY

tailskid, with the helicopter level. Calculations placed the CG a few inches aft of rotor hub, so an 18 in-long tube was added at the front with provision for lead weights to be added to its front end. The amount added would be determined by the pilot's in-flight 'feel' of the control stick.

The top of the fuselage, aft of the main rotor shaft, was (2) faired in, and a vertical fin area was added to the new tail section, all the way back to the tail rotor. This was just a single vertical layer of doped fabric, stretched vertically upwards from the single bottom tube of the triangular tail section (4) (Fig 91).

When VS-300G was rolled-out she looked much neater than ever before. Igor was very pleased, and so was Les as he carefully took her up, slowly put her through the now familiar manoeuvres, then cheerfully waved to us as he came in for a landing. Les spent the next week or so testing VS-300G's control reactions at ever-increasing speeds, and so did Igor.

Owing to the pre-flight changes and careful rotor blade balancing, -300G was easy and comfortable to fly. Only a small section of the vertical fin, at the very tail end, was removed to provide good directional stability at high forward speeds, now in the order of over 60 mph. While -300G would never be

---

Fig 93

VS-300-Ga
Igor's only test flight with -300-Ga and its stabilizing horizontal tail surface. After which he decided, 'this system is not necessary'.
6 February 1942.

as smooth in translational flight as -300E with its single horizontal tail rotor, it was just as manoeuvrable. Les would demonstrate this by spearing the diaphragm of a 10 in ring, mounted on pole, dead centre! (Fig 92)

The final location of the CG was determined by adding more weight to the existing lead ballast up front. This was done in stages to test the effect of each new forward shift of the CG with respect to flight control reactions throughout the entire spectrum of flight manoeuvres. Les finally determined what he felt was the best location, but sought Igor's opinion. He was agreeably surprised at the overall improvement in controlling VS-300G. The final CG location was just about 2 in forward of the centre of the main rotor hub.

Having thus attained the optimum performance that could be expected of VS-300G, dear Igor, undaunted by Les's fandango with XR-4 and its horizontal tailplane convolutions, once again suggested testing a slightly different arrangement of the horizontal tailplane. (Fig 93 VS-300Ga) While VS-300Ga did not exhibit any violent reactions, the overall performance, which Igor himself tested, was disappointing, and he ruefully, finally remarked: 'I think perhaps, gentlemen, this system is not necessary'. Subsequently, however, other single-main-rotor helicopter manufacturers did, and still do, add small horizontal tailplanes for purposes of longitudinal trim.

From now on VS-300 was to experience a calmer, less hectic life, as such changes as she underwent were more at the pleasure of Igor. This, indeed, was no more than what he was entitled

to, or VS-300G, for that matter. VS-300G now assumed the role of a demonstrator of the world's first truly successful Sikorsky-type single-main-rotor helicopter, with either Igor, her master and creator, or Les, deftly showing off her unique repertoire and providing unparalleled fun for pilot and onlooker alike.

Les mainly devoted the months of February and March 1942, while XR-4 was being refurbished, to furthering his flight experience with VS-300G and the all-cyclic main rotor control. While important demonstrations took up part of this time, it also afforded him relaxed flying. On one such occasion he saw a small sailing boat becalmed on the river, not far from the Division's old flying-boat launching ramp. It had no motor, and was drifting with the current, plus tide, quite rapidly towards Long Island Sound. Sir Galahad Morris immediately turned his trusty steed in the direction of the stricken vessel, which, as he approached, he saw was manned by three young damsels in distress. Quickly positioning -300G, he aimed its main rotor downwash at the sails, and towards shore. With grateful handwaving the crew adjusted the sails as their little boat heeled well over to the welcome blast of manufactured wind, and the helicopter literally blew them safely to a neighbouring beach.

Apparently this episode, coupled with Igor's fertile mind, led almost immediately to his 'suggesting' that we make a movie of a similar 'rescue', for publicity purposes. This time an oarless, inflated rubber dinghy with hapless male (Red Lubben) was 'saved'. Les easily dropped a rope to the occupant as -300G hovered above him, and it was readily fastened to the bow painter. The helicopter was now supposed to tow the dinghy to safety while the movie cameras recorded the 'first helicopter air-water rescue, ever!', but Les suddenly found himself facing a dilemma. Firstly, he did not appreciate the actual surface speed at which the very light rubber dinghy was travelling owing to the combination of river and tide, plus considerable wind, all going in the same direction. Consequently, while -300G was towing the dinghy at a relatively fast surface, the over-the-bottom speed, being in the opposite direction, was much slower. Les finally recognised this and increased speed. Secondly, the dinghy was now out of his line of vision, and he could not see it wildly skittering from side-to-side, almost airborne, until it hit a

wave that catapulted its occupant unceremoniously into the river. The rescue launch, standing close by, really did rescue him. Gesticulations from the launch finally convinced Les to return to shore and land.

The next set of flight tests that -300G underwent, were made with inflated rubber floats. Control was found to be without any particular drawbacks, except for an appreciable reduction in top speed. Of particular interest to Igor was the ability to negotiate swamps, shallow water, slimy mud flats and tidal running waters, all of which Les actually accomplished. On the slimy mud flats the helicopter was able to move comfortably in any direction, much to Les's surprise. These tests were also made with rescue missions in mind. Flat roof-top landings and take-offs were also accomplished. One day we were running up -300G in what was obviously a rather high, gusty wind (not on floats) before trying some hovering flight. The helicopter behaved quite normally, and as a matter of interest I went inside and rang up the airport for wind velocity. It was 40–50 mph. The voice at the other end enquired: 'You aren't planning to fly, are you?', and I replied: 'We are flying the experimental helicopter'. Silence, then: 'I don't believe it – we've grounded the P-47s' (Army fighters – part of coastal defence).

There were two vertical tail rotor blade root failures that fortunately did not result in any bodily injury in either instance. One was with Sikorsky, and the other with Morris at the controls. The particular component involved, in both cases, was the axle attached to the root end of the blade, upon which were mounted bearings that allowed the blade to change its pitch and/or thrust. This part was 'Tee' shaped, with the top cross-bar having a rectangular cross-section, which was the retention section. The remaining vertical leg, or axle, was precisely machined to fit the bearing bores. In each case the failure occurred at the juncture of the cross-bar and the axle, where, apparently, upon close inspection, the machinist had not carefully cut the correct size junction radius called for on the drawing. Instead, very fine circular tool ridges interrupted the otherwise smooth surfaces. This was the perfect invitation for surface fatigue crack propagation. With proper inspection this part would not have been accepted. For the XR-4 tail rotor, and also for VS-300, I changed the basic design.

Fig 94 *31 March 1942, Les Morris lifts-off
XR-4a on her maiden flight with her new aft
section of the fuselage designed by Bob Labensky
in the 'Meadow' next to the S-44 hangar.*

In Les Morris's book *Pioneering the Helicopter*,
in reference to the foregoing tail rotor blade failures, he unwittingly made some ill-advised
comments regarding the type and quality, of the
engineering/design work that went into creating
VS-300, and/or the subsequent changes that were
made on her. As mentioned earlier, Russ Clark was
the first Project Engineer, and an experienced, top-
grade aeronautical design engineer. Similarly,
Carol Aumont was a top-grade mechanical engineer. The VS-300 always demanded top-grade
design, materials, construction and supervision,
not to mention that Igor would be the very first to
fly her. As regards my own contributions after I
took over from Russ, nothing went into the shop
without prior knowledge or acceptance from Igor
or Michael Gluhareff. And, I might add, there were
no more failures. Lucky?

On the morning of 31 March 1942, XR-4 was
rolled out for (Fig 94) preliminary run-ups. Facing
her was the date of 20 April; hardly three weeks in
which to prepare for a performance demonstration
before a US Army Acceptance Board before flying
her out to Wright Field. That demonstration was
to include the much-touted ability of a helicopter
to land safely power-off owing to its inherent
ability to translate automatically from power-on
flight to power-off flight. This is called 'autorotation'. We were all greatly concerned because
this manoeuvre had never been attempted on either
VS-300 or XR-4!

With this in mind, Les took XR-4 over to the
perimeter of Bridgeport Airport, across from
the plant, to have plenty of space to make the initial
attempts at autorotation. Air traffic at this airport
was very light, especially since it had become a military coastal defence area.

(Refer to page 39 Helicopter & Autogyro
diagram.)

Transition from power-on to power-off flight
means that the air has to change direction, from

being pumped downwards as it flows over the top of the rotor blade, power-on, to freely flowing upwards as it leaves the blades, power-off. It is therefore very essential, that the transition be as smooth as possible, while moving forward at a reduced speed. Prof Sikorsky estimated this speed to be in the region of 40-to-45 mph, and the necessary minimum height, 100 ft. Normally XR-4 would require somewhere between 10-to-11 degrees of blade angle for most flight conditions, but for autorotation it was estimated that only 4-to-3 degrees were needed.

What did all this mean to the pilot? It does not take much imagination to appreciate Les's feelings and thoughts, regarding his meeting the foregoing requirements, considering he only had a total of some 3 hr of flight time on XR-4, much of it very short hops of only 2-3 min. Now, with the new tail section, he had to contend with yet one more unknown reaction. In fact, Les considered this phase of his flight testing, the most difficult, in retrospect.

The XR-4 was still very much an unknown quantity, and considerably different from VS-300 to fly owing to its greater size, weight and resulting inertia (control input-to-time-lag-to reaction). Furthermore, Les had no one else with whom he could compare notes.

There were four important flight instruments, plus the flight controls, for the pilot with which to contend and monitor constantly:

Main rotor – rpm; engine – rpm; main rotor blade angle – degrees; air speed – mph.
PLUS
Rudder pedals – due to zero torque, power-off, on the tail rotor = zero thrust.
Collective pitch lever – down – for minimum blade angle.
Throttle twist-grip – reduce power.
Control stick – maintain steady, even glide angle, and final flared-out landing.

The two instruments, that together would indicate autorotation had been achieved, were the main rotor and the engine tachometers. Power-on, with the engine driving the main rotor at any safe forward speed, both tachometers will hold steady positions. Autorotation is indicated when the engine speed remains steady but the rotor tachometer indicates *increased* rotor speed.

Several cautious attempts were made on 3 April,

but because of the abnormal concentration required for each attempt to autorotate, Les suggested he have a short break between each, and that this time could be usefully employed making a series of forward speed runs, comparing XR-4's airspeed indicator readings with that of a pacing car. The average top speed recorded was close to 80 mph. These initial attempts to autorotate were actually more towards developing the technique required to induce smooth autorotation.

The next day, after several more 'dry runs', Les went up to about 200 ft and, at about 50 mph, maintaining that altitude, quickly but smoothly reduced main rotor blade pitch and power simultaneously by pushing down the collective pitch lever and twisting the throttle grip. XR-4 went into a smooth effortless glide, autorotating, without a shudder. Another very important hurdle had been cleared, but the safe landing still had to be accomplished. Before that occurred, Les made a number of autorotational glides to make sure he was not missing some important part that might improve his newly-found technique.

Apparently the gods of good fortune were still smiling upon us, for several days later Lt-Col Frank Gregory unexpectedly dropped in to go over the details of the forthcoming XR-4 demonstration. Les took him up for his first XR-4 ride, then handed the controls over to him. Frank was

Fig 95
Les Morris takes up Lt.-Col. Gregory for his first flight in XR-4A.
Walsh, Labensky, Gregory, Sikorsky, G. Gluhareff

immediately pleasantly surprised by the relative ease with which he was able to take over the control of XR-4. He continued to fly it for almost half an hour.

Encouraged by having, for the first time, the assurance and comfort of another seasoned helicopter pilot sitting next to him, Les, on the spur of the moment, announced that he would now demonstrate a power-off landing. Obviously pleased, Frank smiled and said 'OK', not realising it would be Les's first attempt! The result was a perfect landing. At last there would no longer be any hesitation on the part of a helicopter pilot to make an emergency, power-off landing. Thus encouraged, Frank was nothing loth in making a similar landing.

This is probably as good a place as any to define what is meant by a safe hovering height, even though it had yet to be demonstrated! In general terms it means that, to avoid a fatal crash landing, any helicopter hovering motionless (other than one rotor diameter above ground) that suddenly, and without warning, suffers a total loss of power, must have sufficient altitude, to immediately gain forward speed in order to keep the lifting rotor(s) turning (freely autorotating as described earlier) fast enough to maintain sufficient lift. This is accomplished by the pilot immediately and simultaneously pushing the flight control stick forward with one hand (to nose-down) and pushing down the collective pitch lever to reduce the pitch (lift) drag of the rotor blades.

However, as the helicopter pitches downwards and starts to increase its forward speed, it is also rapidly losing altitude before it has gained sufficient forward speed for the pilot gradually and safely, to increase the rotor lift (by pulling up the collective pitch lever) and arresting the loss of altitude. At that instant, the total vertical height lost, represents the minimum safe hovering altitude, under zero wind conditions. The amount of natural wind velocity prevailing reduces that height, thereby producing a plotted curve succinctly referred to as the 'dead man's curve'!

The minimum safe hovering altitude may also be reduced by the rotor disc loading (lb/sq ft of rotor blade swept area); that is, the total disc area divided by the total weight of the helicopter. The lighter the disc loading, the less the height required.

The final demonstration given to Gregory that day was weight lifting, when XR-4 lifted and hovered with the pilot plus three extra persons aboard, much to Gregory's satisfaction.

The next day brought cold, wintry weather, and a late seasonal snow storm. Since all air traffic was locally grounded, Les suggested to Frank that it would be a good opportunity to investigate what restrictions there were to helicopter flight under such conditions, and he agreed. After gaining special clearance from the airport they took off. Not having any provision for clearing the windscreen, they flew with the side windows open, but Les found that if he flew slightly turned sideways he could see quite well, especially downwards. This I was also able to experience, as Les took me up after Frank. A forward speed of 40–45 mph in light snow was about the maximum, and in the heavy snowfall that was reduced by almost half. What was most impressive was the pilot's ability to come to a stop and thoroughly inspect a possible landing area, before descending. Frank Gregory left encouraged and pleased, and looking forward to the demonstration.

The few days remaining before demonstrating XR-4's ability to meet the requirements set forth by the Wright Field Acceptance Board were a period of relief, and the releasing of pent-up emotions. For XR-4A had in effect finally demonstrated what VS-300 was supposed to have demonstrated on 14 September 1939, when Igor Sikorsky first lifted her off the ground. For those first brief seconds of free flight, the practicability of a cyclically-controlled, single-main-rotor helicopter was inconclusive.

Now, 2½ years after initial failure, Igor's patience, determination and his original concept had indeed been vindicated. Therefore, those of us who had the privilege of having shared his hopes with him welcomed this brief opportunity of sharing his enthusiastic participation in the events listed below. It was decided that they should be permanently documented on film, even though it might be decided not to include all of them in the final demonstration. The events were as follows:

1 While hovering several feet above the ground, have a passenger jump safely down. No parachute needed! Demonstrates precise control.
2 While hovering 30 ft above ground, deploy a rope ladder. Passenger can board or leave aircraft. Demonstrates rescue over land or water.

3 While hovering at 25 ft, deploy a single rope. Passenger can then slide down rope to safety. This so intrigued Igor that he insisted he be allowed to demonstrate it. Incidentally, he was one of those individuals who are quite fearless. Les started this act at 10 ft, but Igor, sitting on the floor at the cabin doorway with his legs dangling over the side, kept motioning Les to go higher. Les indicated at about 25 ft that he would go no higher, and Igor slowly and calmly descended, giving the rope a decisive waggle upon landing to indicate his safe arrival, as Les could not see him. Of course, somebody else took his place in the actual demonstration. This demonstrated passenger landing over any form of terrain, or water, in an emergency.

4 While hovering at 30 ft, have passenger lower a telephone to a person on the ground for two-way conversation. Demonstrates possibility of direct contact at greater height.

5 The first ever helicopter formation flying in the USA, (Fig 96) by -300Ga and XR-4. The -300G now sported a new stylish front section of the fuselage which was entirely Alex Krapish's design. This final finishing touch gave -300 the appearance of being something more than just an experimental test rig. With Igor flying his beloved VS-300 and Les in XR-4, they took off, performed several manoeuvres, then made several passes around the famous meadow before coming to a stop, hovering for a few seconds, and landing precisely together, like professional formation flyers.

With all the foregoing having been duly recorded on film, XR-4 still only had some 9½ hr total of flight time before the military demonstration.

The day of the demonstration, 20 April 1942, turned out to be a cold, overcast and windy day, with short periods of sprinkling rain. However, nothing worse was forecast, so it was decided to proceed as planned and in accordance with the requirements dictated by Wright Field. They specified that: 'The aircraft called for will be demonstrated by the contractor, at a flying field to

Fig 96 *The first ever helicopter formation flight in the U.S.A. VS-300-Ga and XR-4.*

be approved by the government, in the vicinity of the contractor's plant. Such demonstration shall be conducted by the contractor at his expense and risk, and shall prove to the government the airworthiness and structural integrity of said aircraft.'

The 'flying field' was VS-300's much-used flight test meadow near the VS-44 hangar. The official party consisted of Lt-Col Frank Gregory, Maj LB Cooper and Mandel Lenkowsky. Representing the Materiel Division from Wright Field Army Base were A.W. Morris of the Civil Aeronautics Authority, Cdr W.J. Kossler of the US Coastguard, L.M. Nesbitt, Wg Cdr R.A.C. Brie of the British Air Commission, Cdr J.H. Millar of the British Royal Navy, Col G.L. King, and Lt-Col P.E. Gabel of the Armored Force Section of the ground forces. A special 'time off' was granted to all who had participated in bringing XR-4 to its present stage of development, allowing them the privilege of witnessing the demonstration.

As Master of Ceremonies, Les addressed the gathering, saying they were about to witness a demonstration of the first successful military, Sikorsky-type single-main-rotor helicopter. With that he proceeded to take off from a 20-by-20 ft marked square like a jack-in-the-box, stopping abruptly 7–8 ft up and hovering motionless for several minutes. He then descended very slowly, settling gently down into the same tyre marks where he had taken off. Next XR-4 popped up to about 20 ft and hovered motionless again before Les demonstrated how easy it was, with a master pilot controlling, to fly sideways in either direction, stop, and fly backwards. Then he made a fast get-away forwards, a quick stop, hovered, and went down and up several times like a yo-yo, each time barely touching the ground. Finally, he made another slow, gentle descent and landing. The audience, respectfully attentive at the start, were now applauding loudly. I have never seen Igor happier than at that moment, as he congratulated Les. There was no doubt that Les and XR-4, had captivated every member of the official party. Frank Gregory was obviously very pleased and impressed. XR-4 looked most attractive in her silver paint and military markings. Bob Labensky and Ralph Alex had made a splendid job of it in 'engineering', and so had Adolf Plenefisch, George (Red) Lubben and their shop crew.

Having completed the first part of the demonstration with flying colours, Les then started the second part with one of Igor's favourites. He put a probe, in this case the air speed pitot tube, through the centre of a 10 in removable ring on the top of an 8 ft pole, and delicately lifted it off, then flew with it over to where Igor was standing with upstretched arm, so exactly that Igor merely had to lift it off the tube! Then, attached by a string to the same tube, a net bag containing a dozen raw eggs was held off the ground by one of the secretaries, standing directly in front of XR-4. Les deftly lifted the bag of eggs from her grasp, made a small circuit, and deposited the fragile load gently on to the ground. Evidently someone loudly remarked: 'I'll bet they are all hard boiled!' Hearing this, Bob Labensky walked over to the bag, removed an egg and broke it to applause and laughter. This left no question as to the ability of XR-4 to respond to all control requirements easily, quickly, and precisely.

A sample of helicopter utility, was the next event. Bob climbed aboard with Les and XR-4 took-off, made a small circuit to where Igor and Frank Gregory were standing, and hovered about 30 ft above them. Bob then lowered a telephone and carried on a two-way conversation first with Igor, and then with Frank. Bob also demonstrated how observation sketches could be delivered, attached to a weighted ring that slid down the telephone wire.

Rescue and/or retrieval in an otherwise inaccessible area was the theme of the next two events. Les flew XR-4 over to where Ralph Alex was standing in the meadow, and, hovering over him at about 30 ft, deployed a rope ladder which Ralph proceeded to climb with consummate ease, entering the cabin without assistance. After retrieving the ladder, Les flew round the field and back to the starting point, where Ralph deployed the ladder and returned to earth (Fig 97).

An alternative method of emergency delivery was demonstrated by having the passenger/rescuer/secret agent deploy a rope and slide down it into what could have been a small clearing in a forest.

Agility, and the safety of a power-off autorotational landing was the next important event. Catching the audience completely by surprise, Les made a rapid vertical climb right up to 500 ft, stopped abruptly, then peeled off to a shallow diving high-speed run, including steep turns, to about 200 ft. At that point XR-4 slowed down and went into a power-off glide, ending with a perfect autorotational landing.

Fig 97
XR-4a
Fearless Ralph Alex climbs up the dangling rope ladder, as Les Morris skilfully keeps XR-4 hovering motionless.

After this fast paced, dramatic demonstration, a bit of light comedy took place. Les took off with a passenger and flew to one side of the meadow, where a member of the ground crew stood holding a parcel, ready for emergency delivery. While the helicopter hovered at several feet, the parcel was handed to the passenger. Then XR-4 was flown to the opposite side of the meadow, where again it came down to a hover, low enough for the passenger, with parcel, to jump out and start running towards its delivery point. After this little skit, XR-4 demonstrated its extra lifting capacity by hovering with three-plus-pilot aboard.

Upon landing, as Les stepped out of the cabin and walked over to where a parachute was being held out for him to put on, it was announced that the XR-4 would now attempt to set a helicopter altitude record. The solid cloud layer was at about 10,000 ft, and scattered rain clouds were floating around as low as 3,000 ft. There was also an occasional sprinkling of rain that might possibly cause icing on the rotor blades.

Taking this all into account, Les felt that the immediate importance of meeting the 5,000 ft altitude that Frank Gregory had requested outweighed any of his present doubts. He therefore took off, heading straight into the wind with XR-4 climbing steadily and smoothly, towards a clearing between the lower rain clouds. Up past 2,000 ft –

3,000 ft – then 4,000 ft. Here it was much colder, but with everything functioning well, Les kept her steadily climbing at a slower rate until the altimeter passed the 5,000 ft mark and the clouds started to close in on him. It was an unofficial world record for helicopters.

However, unknown to those watching below, as Les eased down on the CPL preparatory to descending, his elation suddenly vanished. Without warning, XR-4 started to shake and turn at the same time. Instinctively using his old fixed-wing background training, he quickly pushed the control stick forward, and in a few seconds XR-4 went into a normal power glide. Upon reaching 2,000 ft he reduced power and blade pitch and went into autorotation, ending up with another power-off landing. As no one remarked about the behaviour of his flight, he said nothing. Later, Les reproduced the same flight conditions, and found out that lack of forward speed was the basic cause for the helicopter 'stalling'. Only his cool head prevented what could otherwise have been a fatal accident.

'HEELICOPTER' – PIONEERING WITH IGOR SIKORSKY

One other comment of Les's comes to mind. A few moments after he had experienced XR-4's sudden stalling behaviour, and was descending happily back to earth in a powered glide, he automatically looked down from some 4,000 ft. 'Down below,' he said, 'Bridgeport Airport was easily recognised, but XR-4 only needed that tiny little patch next to the plant to land on safely!'

After stepping out of XR-4, Les walked over to where Alex Krapish and his ground crew already had VS-300Ga ticking over, mounted on her twin airbag floats, to show the many additional possibilities for XR-4 if it was so equipped. Les quickly demonstrated the helicopter's unique ability to fly in any direction with airbag floats, making several landings and take-offs before flying over to the river to show her remarkable water-borne manoeuvrability. Finally he flew her back to make a perfectly executed vertical descent from some 30 ft in front of Igor Sikorsky and the government officials, all of whom promptly and enthusiastically congratulated Igor and Les, as well as Bob Labensky and Ralph Alex. The final round of applause from the members of the official party made it quite clear that XR-4 had been unanimously accepted.

Major Cooper agreed with Lt-Col Gregory's favourite comment: 'A helicopter will do anything a horse can do'. Wing Commander Brie said he had never seen such a remarkable demonstration, and that he would immediately signal his superiors in England the importance of what he had just witnessed. He was considered to be the United Kingdom's leading military authority on rotary-wing aircraft. This was my first meeting with Reginald Brie, and it developed into a close and lasting friendship. He made his final flight at the age of 93. In the mid-1920s he successfully demonstrated, for the first time ever, the practicability of rotary-wing aircraft (autogyros) for long-range naval observation, successfully operating from the deck of the Italian Navy destroyer *Fiume*, using a specially designed circular platform incorporating a special means of latching on to the autogyro's undercarriage; a Brie invention.

As far as Gregory was concerned, XR-4 was the most practical and advanced helicopter in existence. Such that right after the demonstration he sent the following message to Gen Carrol, Chief of the Engineering Division at Wright Field, Ohio.

Fig 98
Final float version of VS-300-Gb.

FLIGHT DEMONSTRATION OF XR-4 MOST SUCCESSFUL. THE CRAFT DEMONSTRATES ALL THAT COULD BE ASKED OF THE HELICOPTER TO SATISFACTION OF ALL WITNESSES. ALTITUDE REACHED DURING DEMONSTRATION, FIVE THOUSAND FEET, EXPECT XR-4 DELIVERY TO WRIGHT FIELD ON OR ABOUT MAY FIRST. GREGORY.

For the first time ever, the US military had a successful helicopter. Gregory also told us he would immediately recommend the adoption of air-bag type floats for XR-4, as a result of the VS-300's demonstration.

Later, during various discussions between the Sikorsky Division and Wright Field following the 20 April demonstration, Gregory was quick to recognise that this was a unique moment to capitalise on XR-4's demonstration success. He immediately started recommending that the military consider the helicopter for such duties as ocean convoy; coastal and harbour patrol; military observation and fire control; forest ranger work; liaison and communications; rescue, land and sea; and ambulance work. He earnestly advocated that the military possibilities of the helicopter should be explored to their fullest extent, and urged that the next step should be the procurement of service test helicopters similar to XR-4 without delay, to familiarise army personnel with the operation and maintenance of the helicopter.

Gregory further recommended not only that helicopter development should be expanded, but that experimental contracts be awarded to the Vought-Sikorsky Aircraft Division for helicopters having a larger load-carrying capacity than XR-4 (the YR-4 contract for pre-production machines specified a more powerful motor). All of the foregoing was contained in the report Gregory sent to Gen Carrol after the XR-4 demonstration. As he so correctly predicted at that time, the sceptics were confounded and the helicopter had been formally accepted as a military aircraft.

Following the demonstration on 20 April, all of the official party departed except for Frank Gregory. He was so elated by the events of the preceding few hours that he could hardly wait to fly XR-4 himself, so Les took him up for some dual instruction.

The next morning they went up again. This time,

however, it was obvious to Les that Frank was ready to spread, or rather rotate, his own wings. After landing, Les spoke a last few words to Frank, ending with 'take her up', then watched with pride as his very first pupil made his first solo flight in XR-4.

At first, there was a considerable amount of questioning between Wright Field and the Sikorsky group as to the wisdom of delivering XR-4 by overland transport, rather than by flying it to Wright Field. Frank Gregory was all for an airborne delivery, if made in easy stages with proper ground support. To this it was finally agreed, as well as the ground route to be taken by both the aircraft and ground crew (Fig 99). The date for the start would be Tuesday, 13 May 1942.

The chosen route was some 760 miles, rather than a shorter one of 560 miles which would have required negotiating some mountain ranges. There were to be eleven scheduled stops. The only really bothersome thought that filled everyone's mind about flight-delivering XR-4 was the overheating and/or possible failure of the main transmission. As already explained, that problem was caused by inadvertently machining the basic plane of the gearcase, where the top cover fitted on to it, somewhat off the true horizontal plane. Consequently the driving (small) pinion gear was not mating with the big gear at a true right angle, and was far enough out of line to cause friction heating of both the gear teeth and the supporting bearings. As a precaution, therefore, a complete extra gearcase was taken along.

In order not to stress the main transmission unduly, it was decided to fly XR-4 at an altitude of approximately 1,000 ft at 60 mph. This was to be the first true cross-country flight of a helicopter in the USA, and possibly the first helicopter delivery flight in the world.

The ground support crew, with a large, round yellow identification dot painted on the roof of their car, included Project Engineer, Bob Labensky, his assistant, Ralph Alex, Shop Foreman and Crew Chief Adolf Plenefisch, and company transportation chief, Ed Beaty, as self-elected chauffeur.

In the few days remaining before XR-4 departed for Wright Field a general air of enthusiasm prevailed amongst us, though we were not without some apprehensive feelings as well, especially Les,

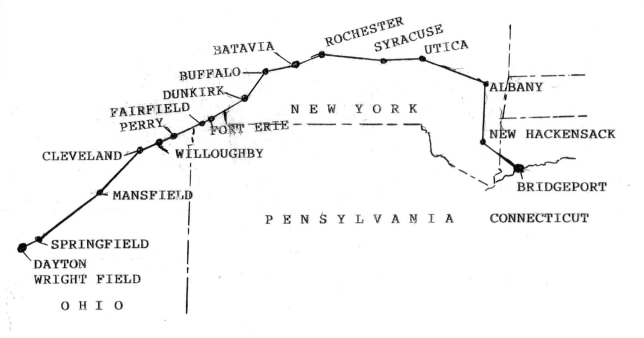

Fig 99 *Route of XR-4 helicopter delivery flight, 13–18 May 1942.*

who knew XR-4 better than anyone else. He had not yet had one continuous hour of flight time in her, so the prospect of flying for five consecutive days, possibly requiring some 20 hours of total flight time, which was about the total time the XR-4 had flown to date, was daunting. Furthermore, Les had not practised any cross-country flying at all. To remedy the latter problem, on 8 May Les flew from the home base of Stratford to West Haven, some 12 miles, back and forth four times, thus establishing another first true cross-country flight for a helicopter in the USA. In all, some 5 hr of extra flight time were put in during the 11 days before leaving for Wright Field. Most of this was devoted to checking out various adjustments on XR-4.

The full story of XR-4's epic delivery flight is recounted in Les's book *Pioneering the Helicopter*, but a brief account is given here for completeness.

With final approval from Adolf Plenefisch that all systems were 'go', XR-4 was rolled out on the beautiful spring morning of Tuesday 13 May 1942, with the temperature at about 80 degrees Farenheit and a gentle breeze. All hands were there to wish Les 'bon voyage' as he settled himself into the now familiar left side pilot's seat, though this time he wore a parachute pack that would also serve as a not-too-comfortable seat cushion. Adolf and crew

already had XR-4 warmed up and the main rotor was ticking over. Several of us walked over and gave Les a well-wishing handshake which he obviously appreciated. Meanwhile, Igor was giving the helicopter a careful final scrutiny, still not entirely convinced that flight delivery was the most expedient method. Nevertheless, he was gratefully proud of this moment as he warmly shook Les's hand, reminding him of the historical significance of the occasion.

Amid cheers and farewell waves XR-4 lifted off from its birthplace for the last time. But it did not leave before saying goodbye with a low, high-speed run above us and a pull-up over the factory as it headed westwards to a new home in Ohio. Simultaneously, the ground crew made a rapid exit to the highways to maintain visual contact between pilot and ground crew as much as possible. If Les followed the precise route marked on his map, he would be able to land in any small area should any trouble occur. The first day's destination was Syracuse, New York State, via Danbury, Connecticut, with a scheduled stop at New Hackensack. There, the welcome sight of Red Lubben greeted Les, who had spent a worrisome flight watching the oil temperature gauge of the transmission go slightly past the danger mark. He had also bucked a 16 mph headwind that reduced his over-the-ground speed to 45 mph. After a thorough inspection by Red Lubben, XR-4 headed north towards Albany, the State Capital of New York, flying at 1,000 ft and arrived uneventfully at Albany Airport. Les flew directly to a parking spot beside other aeroplanes, up against a fence, completely confusing both the operations tower and airport ground crew.

The next leg from Albany to Utica, up the beautiful Mohawk Valley, at 1,000 ft at a steady 60 mph, was flown over fertile farms. Hens made a wild dash to the nearest shelter, and humans popped out of homes and barns to gaze in wonder at the strange sight of their first helicopter, wending its 'secret' and leisurely way overhead.

Les was now obviously having fun at each airport. Upon arriving at Utica Airport he flew slowly sideways up to the front of the main hangar, stopped, then hovered motionless for over a minute before gently landing. Again the onlookers were incredulous as they walked over to greet him.

The final leg to Syracuse was started in the late afternoon, and was a beautiful flight but for the transmission oil temperature running at some 15 degrees centigrade above the 80 degrees danger mark. However, thanks to a light tailwind they arrived safely at Syracuse Airport 15 min ahead of schedule. This time they were shown to their allotted parking space by a guard trotting several feet ahead of XR-4. Thus ended the first day of the delivery flight; 260 miles covered in 5 hr 10 min, averaging 50.33 mph, establishing new helicopter records for distances flown and continuous flight time.

Several hours later Bob and his crew arrived, relieved that all was well so far.

The second day, 14 May, started as another fair day, and hopes were set on getting as far as Cleveland. The next immediate stop would be Rochester, New York State. Les took off and started to follow the ground crew for a while, but found that he was having to fly too slowly, so he speeded up to 60 mph at 1,000 ft. It was not long before Rochester Airport was sighted, and Les started his descent towards the front of the hangars. As he was landing in front of an open hangar he saw several workers suddenly make a dash to the rear, evidently expecting a crash landing.

A guard appeared and suggested that Les taxi XR-4 up beyond the hangars to the control tower. Naturally, Les lifted her a few feet and proceeded sideways up to the tower in front of the dumbfounded guard. Arriving at the tower, he brought her up to the level of the controller's window and looked in at him while hovering motionless. The

man was so astonished that it was several moments before he grinned and flashed the green landing light. Then Les slowly disappeared vertically, to land in front of the tower.

At Bob's suggestion, owing to the persistent overheating of the main transmission, the large access panels to the transmission and engine, on each side of the centre section, were left off. Hopefully, this would help to cool the transmission.

I believe it was at this stop that a bearing oil seal was found to be leaking. Bob solved the problem by fashioning a temporary seal from the brim of his felt hat.

The weather forecast promised headwinds and electrical storms, so XR-4 and its 'yellow dot' escort started off together for Buffalo, the next stop. Approaching Batavia, the mid-checkpoint, the threatening weather in the direction of Buffalo prompted Les to look for a safe place to land and wait the storm out. However, he lost 'yellow dot' somewhere in the Batavia traffic. Not knowing on which of the two main highways leaving Batavia the other might be, he switched back and forth between them fruitlessly. Finally, he found a grass plot between two farm homes, and one of the owners kindly let Les use their telephone (in case of separation, a predetermined Batavia telephone number was to be used by both parties). The storm having passed, Les prepared to leave, but his hosts, not having seen him land, were very concerned as to how he could safely leave such a small lot, as were several neighbours. When XR-4 just went straight up for 50 ft, all he could see were open mouths. Buffalo was safely reached by flying around another storm. When the ground party arrived it was decided to stay overnight, as there were so many storms around.

The third day, 15 May, was overcast with low clouds and headwinds up to 20 mph, with scattered showers forecast. Finally, a late morning start was made with Cleveland, Ohio, as the target destination, via Dunkirk, New York; Erie, Pennsylvania; and Perry, Ohio.

Visibility was less than a mile, but this was safe for a helicopter, as when a tall radio tower suddenly appeared through the fog it could be easily avoided. Visual contact with the ground was difficult, but upon reaching the shore of Lake Erie it was easy to follow the parallel highway that 'Yellow Dot' would also be using. Dunkirk Airport eventually came into view, and the usual landing in front of the main hangar was followed by a Plenefisch inspection. Since the transmission appeared to be holding its own, Les decided it would be safe enough to take a passenger to the next stop, at Erie. The toss of a coin won Ralph the honour of being the first helicopter passenger to cross a State boundary. Upon landing safely at Erie the weather forecasts were so discouraging that it was decided to play safe and stay over night. Weather permitting, Cleveland Airport could easily be reached the next day.

On day four, 16 May, a noon take-off was soon aborted owing to unusual sounds from the transmission. Bob got on board to help listen for any further transmission noises, but as none occurred they flew on to Perry, the next scheduled stop. This was the roughest section of the whole journey, with headwinds gusting from 12–30 mph. However, much to Les's surprise XR-4 'chopped' her way through it with little discomfort.

At Perry 'Airport' there was no fuel, so Les pressed on to Willoughby, where the refuelling for the flight to Cleveland was accomplished. During the short hop to Cleveland the weather improved. The Cleveland Airport tower gave Les the green light to land, presuming he would make a conventional aeroplane landing, but Les meandered down the hangar line until he spotted familiar figures, including Igor, happily waving to him. Meanwhile, the chap in the tower was frantically motioning 'DOWN'! XR-4 settled neatly in between some parked aeroplanes. Igor's emotional greeting with Les included great relief, as so much depended upon XR-4's safe delivery.

Sunday 17 May 1942, the long-awaited day that would herald the longest cross-country flight-delivery of an experimental military helicopter, dawned bright and sunny, partly cloudy, with a light breeze. The destination was Wright Field, Dayton, Ohio.

As arranged, Igor would accompany Les for the short hop from Cleveland to Mansfield. As soon as they were on course, Les handed over control to Igor, and with but a few instructions during the next few minutes, Igor was in complete control. Les's only inputs from then on were navigational, all the way to Mansfield. The inputs were occasioned by the problem when flying at such a low height (1,000 ft) over considerable areas of unbroken forest, of not having sufficient height for

an emergency landing. While this did not seem to bother Igor, Les was only too aware of the dangers. So as not to embarrass Igor, Les would keep making excuses that, somehow or other, they had got off course, and he would deftly steer him around the forests. Approaching Mansfield, Igor turned the controls over again to Les, as he had never landed XR-4.

The fuel pumps were surrounded with parked aeroplanes, so Les landed off to one side. There was, however, a rectangular area to the side of the pumps, approximately 75 ft square. Since nobody seemed to be interested in solving his problem, and XR-4 was still ticking over, he just took off and landed next to the pumps, much to the consternation of some of the bystanders but to the utter delight of Igor.

The next section to Springfield would be the longest (92 miles) of the entire trip, and while the transmission was still functioning, albeit on the hot side (outside temperature was also rising), it was decided to keep the helicopter as light as possible, so Les flew solo. Fortunately the trip passed without incident, with airspeed at 60 mph and altitude 1,000 ft.

As XR-4 came over the airport Les spotted a small aeroplane that had just landed and was taxying to the hangar at the other end of the runway. Dropping down to within a few feet behind the unsuspecting pilot, he followed him. As the pilot turned to park in front of the hangar, he finally saw XR-4 and came to an abrupt, bewildered stop. This caused a number of people to appear suddenly as XR-4, still hovering a few feet up, awaited the signal to alight. Then somebody signalled to move to the right, then to the left, and finally straight up. At which point the signaller threw up his arms in mock despair.

Having properly parked XR-4, it was not long before an Army AT-6 Training aircraft arrived from Wright Field. Its pilot was Lt-Col Frank Gregory, who had flown himself over to be on hand to welcome Igor and Les. Earlier, Frank had left Wright Field in a Boeing B-17 Flying Fortress to try and intercept XR-4 on its way from Mansfield, but he was unable to spot the low-flying helicopter, mainly owing to the difficulty of locating only a small fuselage, as the rotating wings were practically invisible at a distance.

After happily greeting each other, Frank and Les impatiently awaited the arrival of Igor, who had joined the ground crew. As soon as they arrived, the two side panels were installed for the formal arrival at Wright Field. Amid happy handshakes all around, and with Igor her creator and Les her chief test pilot at the controls, XR-4 made her last take-off of the delivery flight to Wright Field. It was indeed an historic departure. Then Gregory took off in the AT-6, followed by Bob Labensky in a chartered aeroplane. They soon passed XR-4, arriving at Wright Field in time for Gregory to take charge of her historic delivery.

Barely half an hour after take-off Igor and Les were scanning the skyline for the first glimpse of Wright Field. Suddenly an excited and joyful Igor called out 'There it is!' His keen eyes had spotted it first. As XR-4 started to circle the buildings, Les felt that the helicopter should end its epic flight with a proper signature. So, like the take-off five days earlier, he 'peeled off' and made a low high-speed diving run in front of her new home, with a smart pull-up, circling back and landing before the official welcomers and cameras, with Igor waving happily. Thus yet another historic milestone was reached in Igor Sikorsky's remarkable career. Along with Gregory to officially greet XR-4 were Colonels Carroll, Bogart and Craigie.

A resumé of this historic flight includes a total elapsed flight time of 16 hr 10 min; total air-line miles covered, 761; 15 consecutive sectional flights (not counting the abort at the Erie–Perry leg); an overall average over-the-ground speed of 47 mph; and an average distance between stops of 50.73 miles. Unofficial helicopter records were established for: American helicopter air-line distance – 92 miles; flying over four different States en route; and the first inter-State passenger flight. In addition, the world helicopter endurance record of 1 hr 50 min was exceeded.

On the next day XR-4 was scheduled to demonstrate its routine performance for the benefit of the Commanding General at Wright Field, Brig-Gen A.W. Vanaman. Orville Wright had been invited to attend as a special guest. According to Les, it appeared that the whole Operations Headquarters personnel had turned out as well.

While this was all very flattering for Igor Sikorsky, Les Morris, Bob Labensky, Ralph Alex, Adolph Plenefisch and Ed Walsh, XR-4, tired from its epic flight, really needed a complete going-over before any further demonstrations took place. So it was with considerable misgivings as to how much

longer the transmission would last that XR-4 was rolled-out, following an all-too-quick inspection.

That particular day was hot and moist, with almost no air stirring. Furthermore, XR-4 would have to operate from very hot concrete 800 ft above sea level, which meant that less power would be available. However, with minimum fuel and flying solo, Les somehow managed to coax the helicopter through a good demonstration. As a concluding highlight, Igor held up his famous Fedora hat and Les deftly speared it with the protruding pitot tube, much to Orville Wright's delight.

Next came a short ride for some of the officers, finally ending with Brig-Gen Vanaman. As he was above average height and weight this was asking a great deal of XR-4, but the helicopter astonished all of those most concerned by 'rising to the occasion' with a mighty effort. When Les gave her full throttle she 'struggled free of the ground and staggered away', to use Les's own words. Thus formally ended XR-4's flight delivery saga, much to the amazement and approval of all concerned.

Perhaps of greatest significance was the presence of Orville Wright, after whom, and his brother Wilbur, this very important airfield was named. Within less than 40 years Orville had seen an aircraft carrying over 100 passengers (the Dornier Do X), and racing aeroplanes surpassing 400 mph. Now Igor Sikorsky, standing next to him, was starting a whole new cycle of helicopter development with the successful single-main-rotor (Fig. 101).

For the next three days following the demonstration XR-4 was finally able to undergo a thorough overhaul, including the installation of a new transmission. The original transmission was returned to the Sikorsky plant for inspection and possible rebuilding.

The ensuing months were very busy ones for XR-4 and Les, as various utility tests were undergone before she was finally officially accepted by Materiel Command at Wright Field on 30 May 1942. Then followed an intense period for Les, training the first military helicopter pilots in the USA, plus Wg Cdr Brie of the RAF. At the same time he was involved in helping to write the first instructional manual for student training in helicopters.

Those 'students' included D.M. Kilpatrick, M.V. Lee, L.A. Cooper, P.E. Gable, D.D. Viner (Igor's nephew), C.A. Lindbergh, C.A. Moeller,

Fig 100

The Sikorsky Team L – R   O. Wright – *   L. Morris   B. Labensky
E. Walsh – Mech.   A. Plenefisch   I. Sikorsky   R. Alex   Chf. Test Pilot   Proj. Engr.
              Crew Chief   Creator   Asst. Proj. Engr.
            XR-4a   * Co-inventor of first successful airplane.

Fig 101

17 May 1942, Igor Sikorsky hands over XR-4a to Col. Frank Gregory, U.S. Army, witnessed by Orville Wright.
This unique historical moment was captured just after Les Morris, accompanied by Igor Sikorsky, had safely flight-delivered, for the first time ever, a helicopter to the U.S. Army, at Wright Field, Dayton, Ohio.

F.A. Ericson, F.W. Peterson, C.T. Booth, H.H. Hermes, F.J. Gable, J.G. Ray and E.A.H. Peat.

The acceptance of the helicopter by the US Military was largely the result of a visit to Wright Field by Gen Arnold, Chief of the US Air Forces, on 7 July 1942, when, because of his keen interest resulting from XR-4's demonstrations, he attended a special demonstration which Gregory arranged for him. While he was non-commital at the time, he later enthusiastically embraced the need for rapid expansion of helicopter testing and procurement, including larger types such as the XR-5.

An unexpected display of dedicated teamwork had made the demonstration possible. Only four days before Gen Arnold arrived it was discovered that a clogged lubricating line in the main transmission had caused severe overheating and damaged the main and pinion gears. As there were no spare gears available, this meant having the repair done at the Sikorsky plant and getting the reassembled transmission back into XR-4 within four days. This was accomplished by Bob Labensky and Ralph Alex in spite of the Sikorsky plant being closed due to the Fourth of July Holiday. Qualified machinists had to be found who were willing to work around the clock. Finally, two extra airline seats were purchased to transport the reassembled transmission back to Wright Field in time for Adolf Plenefisch and Ed Walsh to install it overnight, and have XR-4 ready for the demonstration next day.

On 23 July 1942 the following telegram was received from Wright Field:

DOCTOR I.I. SIKORSKY, VOUGHT-SIKO-RSKY AIRCRAFT DIVISION OF UNITED AIRCRAFT; TODAY THE XR-4 PASSED THE ONE HUNDRED HOUR MARK AND COMPLETED THE PRIMARY TRAINING OF FIVE AIRFORCE OFFICERS TWO OF WHOM SOLOED THIS MORNING. FEW EXPERIMENTAL AIRCRAFT HAVE ACCOMPLISHED SUCH A RECORD IN THE SHORT SPACE OF TWO MONTHS. I EXTEND MY SINCERE CONGRATULA-TIONS TO YOU AND THE MEMBERS OF YOUR ORGANISATION WHO TOOK PART IN MAKING THIS POSSIBLE.
BRIG.-GENERAL A.W. VANAMAN, WRIGHT FIELD, OHIO.

XR-4 still had some five months of testing to undergo to an evaluation of all the newly formulated military roles that might be applicable to direct-vertical-lift aircraft. This was accomplished on 5 January 1943. While I would dearly liked to have participated in the latter part of this programme, I had the satisfaction of seeing what I had started brought to a most successful conclusion by Bob Labensky, with Ralph Alex's assistance.

It is now necessary to turn back to 26 January 1942, the day I was officially made Project Engineer on XR-5. Actually, the Corporate Body at East Hartford had decided to back Sikorsky, insofar as corporate funding of the preliminary design was concerned, as far back as 26 September 1941, gambling on the Army's enthusiastic response after accepting XR-4 and their recognising the need for a more powerful and more useful next-generation model. The company's designation was VS-327, and by early February 1942 the Army began planning for a new and larger Sikorsky helicopter designated XR-5, which they nicknamed the 'workhorse'. On 8 May 1942 Brig-Gen Echols recommended to Materiel Command at Wright Field that immediate authority be granted for the procurement of two experimental XR-5 helicopters from the Vought-Sikorsky Division of the United Aircraft Corporation.

By 26 January 1942 the basic configuration and dimensions of the VS-327 had been arrived at, and I had started to make full-scale design layouts of the major mechanical components. As the heart of the helicopter is its main rotor hub, with its controlling system, this was my first design area. Early one morning, as I was descending the stairs from the engineering department to the machine shop, whom should I meet but Igor. Cradled in his arms was a large, three-bladed propeller hub weighing over 50 lb. I offered to carry it for him, but he declined, thanking me, adding that he wished to see me as soon as I was free. When I entered his office I found him going over some sketches he had already made, with the hub next to him on top of his desk. As usual he had latched on to an idea and was anxious to discuss it, in this instance with me, since it concerned the VS-327's main rotor hub.

What he had in mind was providing a method of rotor blade retention that would permit placing the horizontal flapping hinge with the desired amount of offset from the centre of the hub (see Fig. 102), yet provide ample room for large-diameter hinge

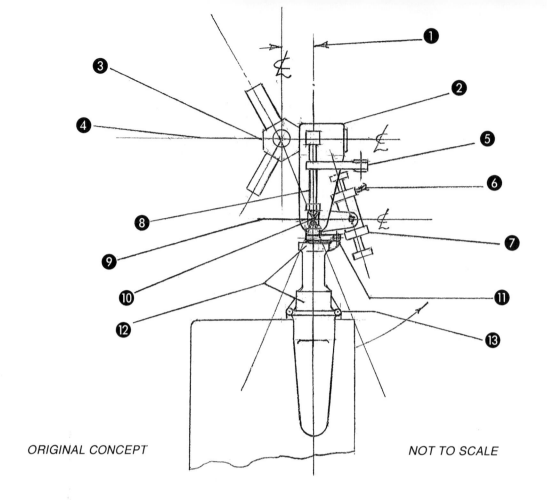

Fig 102 *XR-5*
(1) Hinge offset   (2) Flapping hinge link   (3) Hub – three axles   (4) Horizontal flapping hinge
(5) Blade pitch control lever   (6) Oil line from tank to damper   (7) Hydraulic lag damper
(8) Pitch control torque tube   (9) Vertical lag hinge   (10) Universal joint   (11) Blade pitch control
(12) Pitch/thrust bearings   (13) Blade attachment

ORIGINAL CONCEPT

NOT TO SCALE

bearings. Thus was the basic design feature of the hub handed to me, to be included in the final design (it also eliminated the need for a separate hinge pin). I was allowed complete freedom on the rest of the design. This episode demonstrated Igor's innate sensitivity towards other's feelings when suggesting a change that required complete rethinking and/or redesigning. A rare gift.

These personal moments with Igor Sikorsky, when there was no one else to interrupt us, I treasure the most. The fact that he too enjoyed them made them even more memorable. As engineering firms were growing beyond a certain size, it would not be too long before the days of allowing an individual with initiative and ability to create and carry out a complete aircraft design and then be put in charge of its construction would be

phasing out. I suspect that Igor was sensing that, too.

In connection with the hub itself, the preliminary stress calculations had to be made, and also, owing to the unconventional geometrics involved in this particular design, the relative movements of the parts from both flight and control imputs had to be calculated. In the latter respect, Nik Nikolsky greatly helped me by working out the necessary formulae to calculate those movements.

When designing a helicopter, unlike a fixed-wing aeroplane, it is indeed more like a mechanical bird, in as much as the only static structure is the fuselage, and that would also be revolving but for the anti-torque rotor.

I was therefore determined, as much as practically possible, to reduce the entire aircraft to a series of easily handled subassemblies. This would avoid the need to work inside restricted structural areas, and also avoid the need for any section of the aircraft to wait for subassemblies to be added to it. In other words, it would reduce the overall time between the experimental and production aircraft, wherever possible, by including as much production design as was feasible. The big exception was the main rotor blade, since the ultimate goal was an all-metal type and this would require much initial testing.

Also involved was an entirely new concept for cyclically controlling the rotor blades, in which I proposed using a double-acting chain-driven screw-jack requiring the very minimum of moving parts. I was rather proud of this effort, but while Igor was well pleased with the concept, he still

expressed a preference for three jacks, rather than the two that I suggested, even though, as he admitted, it would increase the weight of the system. His request was quite in line with his usual (Fig. 103) conservative judgement. With the change incorporated, I was able to release the very first XR-5 design layout to the stress department before detail drawings were made of the various parts.

Although we had not yet received any formal document from Wright Field, we had been, and continued to be, in close touch with them through Lt-Col Frank Gregory. I proceeded with the preliminary design in such a manner as to have as many of the important mechanical systems in full-scale design layout form completed, and stress-checked, before receiving a formal contract. In the event this proved to be a great time saver.

Fig 103 *Cyclic blade control Schematic – original concept*

(1) Double-acting Jack screws   (1a) Screw Jack links   (2) Collective pitch control (L)(T)   (3) Fore-aft rotor (T) tilt control   (4) Lateral rotor tilt control (T)   (5) Non-rotating scissors (L)   (6) Non-rotating (L) (7) Azimuth tilting socket (L)   (8) Rotating UPR tilt star (L)   (9) Ball-bearing (L)   (9a) Inner race static (L)   (9b) Outer race rotates   (10) Hub driven scissors (L)   (11) Rotor drive shaft   (12) Top of gearcase   (13) Idler sprocket (T)   (14) Link to blade pitch control

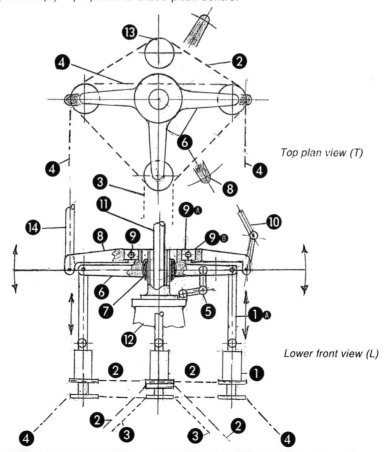

Top plan view (T)

Lower front view (L)

'HEELICOPTER' – PIONEERING WITH IGOR SIKORSKY

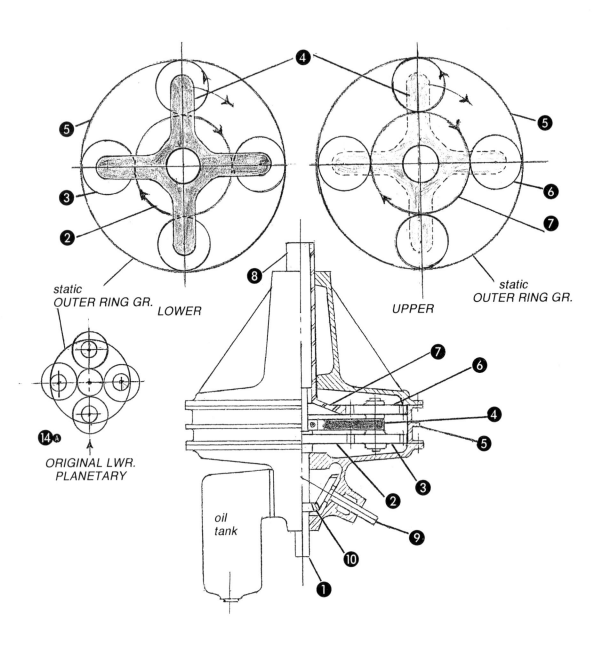

static
OUTER RING GR. LOWER

static
OUTER RING GR.

UPPER

ORIGINAL LWR.
PLANETARY

oil
tank

Fig 104
Main transmission (schematic)
The LOWER input shaft (1) drives the sun gear (2) which turns the planet gears (3) that are mounted under the follower (4) and run inside of outer ring gear (5), thereby moving follower (4). The UPPER planet gears (6) mounted on top of follower (4) now become the drivers of the output

sun gear (7) that turns the output shaft (8) approximately 10 times slower than (1). The tail rotor output drive shaft (9) is driven off of the input shaft (1) through gears (10). Thus when power failure occurs, the autorotating main rotor, then drives the tail rotor.
N.B.: The number of planet gears is optional.

142

An earlier incident regarding Nik explains the coolness with which he had received the news of my becoming a member of the special few involved with VS-300. One day, while he was standing by my drawing board regarding some particular matter, I suddenly felt his hand on the back of my head, moving upwards from my collar to the top of my head. I pretended to ignore this. From then on he became more friendly. After Nik left, Michael Buivid told me that, in old Russia, fine soft hair denoted good breeding.

As I was still the only engineer formally associated with XR-5 project, any other engineering time allotted to the XR-5 was strictly out-of-pocket for United Aircraft, and therefore had to be kept to a minimum. Furthermore, the Army was having some difficulty in finding funds for what was considered, at that time, such a low-priority item as an experimental helicopter.

Since the main rotor hub was attached to the upper end of the output shaft of the main transmission, and its cyclic controls were attached to the transmission gearcase, the main transmission thus became an integral part of the hub; its controls, rotor shaft and main transmission assembly, a feature I had deliberately designed as a complete subassembly to be fed into an assembly line. In fact, the complete helicopter comprised a series of subassemblies with jig controlled, matching attachment fittings that readily allowed them to be bolted together. This was already routine in the automotive trade, where precise jigging was a once only cost that was soon amortised. Thus the main transmission was the next full-scale design layout to be tackled.

The basic system of gear reduction finally decided upon is called epicyclic (or planetary). It consists of an outer static gear (with its teeth cut on the inside vertical rim), upon which rotate smaller (planet) gears, motivated by the central, smallest, high-speed input (sun) gear (Fig 104). This is generally considered to be the most efficient and compact means of speed reduction. In this case, by placing two such gear reductions one above the other, the desired total speed reduction was achieved within the smallest possible space.

Concerning mechanical systems, I would like to digress here for a few moments. In Igor Sikorsky's mind, mechanics apparently immediately generated but one thought – simplicity. On many times I heard that gentle voice say: 'I believe, gentlemen,

vot vee need here is a seemple leetle mechanism'. This was usually accompanied by a faint smile, and a twinkle of the eye. Gear manufacturers' representatives were also known to have chuckled when hearing Igor make that statement, and one sent him a memento for his office desk. It consisted of two mating gears, mounted on a small mahogany pedestal so that they could be rotated. Each gear had but one tooth! This was made possible by generating a shallow vee tooth on one gear that overlapped a similar tooth on the other gear. I wonder if Igor's family still has this gem? I know it greatly amused him.

When considering any speed gear reduction, if at all possible it should consist of but 'von beeg gear, and von leetle gear' according to Igor. This is clearly illustrated in his patent 1,994,488 of 27 June 1927. It was also the original configuration I used in designing XR-4 when the vertically mounted, flat, six-cylinder 165 hp Franklin engine was initially chosen and was later used on XR-6.

On another occasion Igor enthusiastically and dramatically explained to me what he considered to be the ideal method of constructing an experimental gear reduction. 'Take two husky, substantial cakes of Dural (aluminium), place the gears in between them with their bearings to support the input and output shafts, and bolt the top and bottom Dural cakes firmly together, [then with his right hand demonstrating and his voice softly trailing off] and around the outside just a dre-e-e-e-e-e-eam of a thin Dural skin cover.'

At that time I was in the midst of designing the XR-5 main transmission, and Igor was once again making more frequent, but always welcome, visits to my draughting table when he made the following totally unexpected comment: 'I would like when my son comes to work here, that he would work for you'. It took me several moments to gather my thoughts before I managed to say what a great privilege that would be for me. Unfortunately it was a dream that never came true, but it was so typical of his inspiring way of expressing his approval.

For some time I had been hinting at the need for additional assistance, so it was my good fortune to be able to welcome aboard Ed Katzenberger, who was soon to become Assistant Project Engineer.

More detailed information on XR-5 was now being requested by Wright Field, so that they could more properly describe their requirements. For instance, they were looking for a top speed of some

120 mph and an operational altitude of 6,500 ft. The helicopter was to lift-off vertically over a 50 ft obstacle in zero wind, and had to remain airborne for over 3 hr with a useful load of 1,100 lb at an all-up weight not exceeding 4,000 lb. Basing our calculations on original estimates, we optimistically signalled 'OK'!

By the time 8 May 1942 came around I had finished all the preliminary full-scale design layouts of the mechanical drive system. The basic reason for doing this at that particular time was the lead-time necessary to get the close-tolerance, heat-treated machined parts ready for assembly within a scheduled timeframe. In addition, deflection tests of the completely assembled gearbox, usually performed by the gear manufacturer, were needed as a final check to detect any possibility of undue gear tooth misalignment before the complete assembly was subjected to test running under Service loads.

My experience with the XR-4 transmission system taught me to accept nothing but the best workmanship. The usual 'lowest bidder' approach by the purchasing department was just too risky, and backyard machine shops were out of the question. From then on all of our helicopter transmission orders went to such firms as the Gleason Gear Co. in Rochester, New York, with excellent results.

This calls to mind an incident which occurred after the XR-5 main transmission design had been approved by the Gleason Co. and was being detailed. In retrospect, it was the beginning of something that ultimately greatly influenced ensuing XR-5 project decision making, but first let us recall the circumstances prevailing in June 1942. It was the beginning of the end of the Sikorsky flying-boat era, marked by the refurbishing of the three redundant VS-44 US Navy experimental aircraft for VIP transatlantic service by American Export Airlines. This had helped to keep Michael Gluhareff busy, and for Michael, unlike Igor Sikorsky, it meant facing a not-too-promising future. This was because Michael's outstanding design contributions to the world famous Sikorsky flying-boats were aerodynamic. They included creating the particular wing profiles that permitted greater loads to be carried faster and further than ever before. Unhappily, none of this was applicable to the main rotor blade profile of a helicopter.

While Igor's loyalty towards Michael never wavered over the years that followed, it was difficult for him to find a comfortable niche for Michael. Nevertheless, during the time I had the privilege of working directly with him, I never had a more trusting, understanding, appreciative or loyal friend than Michael.

In a way, it was understandable that Michael, being at a loose end, upon the arrival of a bright young mechanical engineer named Miller Wacks in the XR-4 engineering department, should show him the XR-5 main transmission design. By then this had been approved not only by Igor, but also be Gleason's chief engineer and the bearing manufacturers. Detailed engineering drawings were well on the way. Out of the blue, Michael came to me one day and asked me to review a considerable change to the lower portion of the transmission, namely the reduction of its diameter. So doing, he claimed, would reduce aerodynamic resistance. I soon found out that Igor had approved the idea. Apparently neither of them fully appreciated the extra time and expense required to incorporate the change (shades of Serge and the XR-4 engine mount) or the truly insignificant drag reduction.

I suppose I should have won, but at what cost? It had pleased Michael immensely that he had made a contribution. It was hardly the way for a Project Engineer to run a project of which he was presumably (according to the engineering manual) 'in complete charge', but such was the nature of the existing 'pecking order'.

Miller Wacks went on to make his mark in many ways. He joined Bob Labensky on the XR-4 project, then became Bob's assistant on XR-4, was Project Engineer on YR-4 and later became Chief Development Engineer.

As already mentioned, XR-5 was basically composed of three major sections, the front cabin section; the centre section including the main rotor hub, main transmission, powerplant, fuel system, undercarriage and controls; and the tail-cone section with the tail rotor drive and control system. Obviously the centre section, being the most complex, was the starting point, so our next major component was the powerplant, comprising the engine, the universally-jointed driveshaft, the cooling fan, the cowling, the engine mount and the clutch, as a complete subassembly mounted with its output driveshaft vertically.

Upon contacting our companion, the Pratt & Whitney Engine Division and informing them that

I would like to discuss the vertical installation of the 450 hp R-985 engine in the XR-5 helicopter, I sensed a lack of enthusiasm. At the subsequent meeting I was told that the lubricating oil would seep into the cylinder heads, and that the fuel distribution would be impaired due to the need to add a second 90° bend to the carburettor air intake. As I drove back to the office a thought occurred to me. But before I spoke to anyone I rang the Curtiss-Wright Engine Co, got through to their Sales Manager, and asked him if he could find out from engineering if there would be any particular problems involved in mounting their 500 hp engine vertically in a proposed helicopter. He said he would let me know on the morrow.

By mid-morning next day I was advised that there should be no problems, and that they would very much like to work with us on it. I thanked the caller very much, and said that I would respond shortly. I then apprised Michael and Serge of what I had done, which they found quite amusing, and asked them to stand by while I recontacted Pratt & Whitney in East Hartford. I spoke to the same people as before, and advised them of what I had been told by Curtiss-Wright. There was an ominous momentary silence from the other end (Michael and Serge were both smiling), and then they said: 'We will call you right back'. In no time Mr Willgoose, head of P & W engineering, was on the line. Early next morning I was back in East Hartford, and Curtiss-Wright was quite disappointed.

Pratt & Whitney was, of course, under considerable pressure at that time, owing to war orders. Moreover, the company was not particularly anxious to divert its limited manpower on to the then little-known helicopter goings-on in Stratford. After initial apologies, however, its engineers were soon studying the basic installation requirements, and three weeks later I was watching the final test run. Much to the pleasant surprise of all concerned, the extra 90° intake bend in the carburettor, along with the other dubious items, resulted in a far smoother-running engine that even produced more horsepower at its rated rpm!

In fact, the additional 90° air intake bend turned out to be a very simple sheet metal steel weld. Apparently, the concern had been caused by the time it had taken to successfully design the original single 90° turn before a smooth intake airflow was attained.

While I was attending the meetings with Pratt & Whitney, Willgoose asked me if I would like to see the next-generation radial engine, as it might interest me when considering the next-generation helicopter design. As a preview he kindly took me through the machine shops and assembly area, where assembly line methods were already well established. It was a fascinating and rewarding experience. We then entered the secret engine test area to the accompaniment of a surrounding, low muffled sound of untold numbers of engines being simultaneously tested. Each individual engine test could be viewed within its test cell through large soundproof windows. Those engines not illuminated from within at that moment were silhouetted by the ghostly, pulsating mixture of bluish-off-white light produced by their exhausts. We finally stopped in front of a cell with its curtains drawn. The deeper murmur coming from behind it was quite noticeable.

As the curtains were drawn aside I found myself completely overwhelmed by sight of the largest, radial air-cooled engine then in existence. Generating almost 4,000 hp it consisted of four banks of nine-cylinder radial engines, each bank skewed clockwise, a single cylinder over, from the one in front of it, for cooling purposes. Dubbed the 'corncob', it was mounted on a welded tubular steel 'dynafocal' engine mount. That meant that the whole engine floated on flexible shock absorbers so oriented that they all focused upon the actual CG of the complete engine, including its propeller. A Pratt & Whitney patent, this system greatly reduced fatigue stresses on both engine and mount. It was an unforgettable sight, 36 cylinders seemingly effortlessly humming away. The four-barreled carburettor was about the same size as an airline 'carry-on' valise!

When asked my thoughts regarding this engine being mounted in the next-generation helicopter, I replied, offhand, that I would be hard put deciding just where to locate it, let alone determining the size of anti-torque tail rotor required.

Regarding the 'corncob', the Vought Division designed, and built in its experimental shop, a secret pressurised, aeroplane for very high altitude performance testing of that engine. If I recall correctly it also had to do with superchargers. Whatever its final intent, the whole programme never got into active service.

The next XR-5 component connected with the

engine driving system was its clutch. I was looking for something light and automatic, to eliminate a pilot function, and by sheer luck I found one. What was more, it could be combined with the engine cooling fan, which also helped to act as a form of flywheel (I used a NACA engine-compressor-type fan). The cooling fan was of a type in which the diameter of the circular central area, to the outer rim of which the many fan blades were attached, was 69% of the overall diameter of the fan, so the inner area was free to be used for the centrifugal clutch. Originally there were two concentric vertical rims. Facing the inner sides of these rims were small, spring-loaded weights. As engine speed was increased, centrifugal force would automatically press the weights against the inner rims and thus start turning the main rotor. Conversely, below a certain engine speed the springs would automatically disengage the weights from the inner rims and the main rotor would be brought to a full stop by means of a disc brake attached to the output shaft from the main transmission which drove the tail rotor. Operated by the pilot, it was the first use of such a system on a helicopter.

The engine on XR-5, was the same as used on the US Navy Vought OS2U Kingfisher single-float observation aeroplane. Happily, the diameter of the front air intake of the OS2U engine cowling was large enough to accommodate the complete XR-5 fan-clutch assembly, so the only rework necessary on the cowling was to shorten its length; a considerable saving in cost and time. While we were waiting for the formal contract we had also been advised that helicopter experimental money was not easy to find in Washington. In the meantime, however, sufficient engineering information was coming to hand to permit Adolf Plenefisch and Red Lubben to start putting together a full-scale mock-up (see mock-up photo Figure 105).

In splitting the fuel required into two separate tanks and placing them well apart, fore and aft in the centre section, my intention was to provide a means of trimming the helicopter longitudinally by selecting from which tank to draw fuel. Furthermore, slender upright tanks with internal baffling would reduce lateral sloshing and allow maximum usage of fuel available. Both tanks were protected by stainless steel firewalls.

An additional longitudinal trimming feature was a remotely controlled, pilot-actuated screw-jack that could tilt the main transmission-rotor

hub assembly fore and aft. (3)

To facilitate powerplant maintenance, the centre section had arched side truss members. These provided maximum clearance for cowl removal, engine maintenance, etc., (4) and also, by laterally hinging the engine mount, the entire engine could be swung out and worked on or removed. To (5) service the main transmission and rotor hub area, a large fold-down work platform, hinged to the top horizontal centre-section truss, was provided. To top it all, the entire covering of the centre section consisted of quickly removable panels.

The two streamlined cantilever undercarriage legs, together with their vertical hydraulic shock absorbers and the main wheels, (6) were bolted to the basic bottom welded tubular truss unit. Also to this were bolted all the other various sub-assemblies, including the swivelling tailwheel and the tailcone (7) (8) supporting structure, as well as the control/observation cabin. (9)

Around July 1942 an amusing incident occurred. Lt-Col Frank Gregory, on his periodic visits to check on progress on XR-4 and/or XR-5, would sometimes stay with the Nikolskys. On one such occasion he asked Nik what sort of exclamation he could use, in Russian, that would be appropriate, for example at the end of a conversation or a meeting. After a moment's thought, Nik suggested a Russian phrase. Frank repeated this several times, prompted by Nik, who tried to make Frank's broad southern accent sound something like Russian. 'Yes', said Frank, 'I kinda like that', repeating it again.

Next day, Igor, Frank, Michael and Serge Gluhareff had gathered around my draughting table so that I could explain to Frank what had been added since his last visit. Finally, having satisfied his curiosity, he majestically waved his right arm and proclaimed: 'That looks just fine' and repeated the Russian phrase. There was a momentary silence as Igor fashioned a faint smile while making that curious little sound in his throat. Michael tittered, and Serge blushed. Apparently I registered a complete blank. Then Igor quietly suggested that we go to lunch. On the way, Frank took Michael aside and asked him if he had said anything wrong. 'Oh! No!' said Michael, 'All you said was "streamlined tit!".'

In mid-June Igor Sikorsky, for the second time, received an historic signal from Materiel Command at Wright Field. The War Department

Fig 105

Model XR-5 Full scale mock-up.
(1) Engine – fan – clutch – unit.   (2) Fuel tanks.   (3) Fore/Aft rotor trim-tilt screw jack.   (4) Side arched truss allows engine to pivot sidways on bottom hinged mount attachment points, for repair, or removing.   (5) *Fold-down service platform, had not been installed.   (6) Cantilever main landing unit.
(7) Rear, swivelling, landing gear.   (8) Tail cone attachment ring and mount.   (9) Pilot's and forward Observer's cabin (dual controls).   (10) Basic lower structural unit (see Fig. 109).   (11) Main rotor drive transmission, and tail rotor drive. Right side   (12) Engine oil tank.   (13) Pilot's flight control stick. Collective pitch lever to left.

was going to place a formal contract with the Sikorsky Division of United Aircraft for the largest-ever single-main-rotor Sikorsky helicopter, the XR-5. This long-awaited news was accompanied with a desirable mock-up inspection date of mid-August 1942. It was just the kind of inspiration we all needed, not to mention Igor's pride of accomplishment.

While in no way wishing to downgrade Lt-Col Gregory's consistent enthusiasm, salesmanship and perseverance in promoting the unique military usages of rotary-wing aircraft to our Military High Command, the picture would not be complete without giving equal honours to our staunch Allies from 'across the Pond', who similarly responded to

the equally urgent 'signals' being sent to them by Wg Cdr Reginald Brie of the British Air Mission in Washington D.C. This dual appeal to our Congress resulted in a contract calling for the delivery of four experimental XR-5 helicopters, two American and two British, for a total sum of just under $1,000,000, the greatest sum yet invested in rotary-wing aircraft development.

At a previous meeting with Igor and Michael, with both the foregoing and the mock-up in mind, I suggested we make the mock-up as complete and realistic as possible, excluding the tailcone. Without hesitation they gave me the 'green light'. I was also promised any extra help that was needed.

It meant that I was given the privilege of

preparing the XR-5 mock-up presentation, both as to descriptive material, as well as actually conducting the presentation before the Mock-up Board. Furthermore, Igor informed me that this was to be entirely my responsibility, and that neither he, nor Michael, nor Serge would be present. That automatically relieved all three from having to deal with unfamiliar details, and relieved me no end.

Adolf Plenefisch and his crew made a splendid job of it, and on 14 August they were openly praised by the members of the military inspection delegation, who remarked that they had never inspected a mock-up that included, so completely, all the necessary equipment. They also commended the extra attention paid to both maintenance and pilot/observer needs. The fold-down maintenance platforms for servicing the hub transmission area were especially popular items. Likewise, the extra vision provided for both the pilot and observer (especially the latter, with optional dual flight control) was greatly appreciated. The only item we failed to include for the observer was a lap-held map clip-board, which was furnished to the exact dimensions requested within the hour.

Provision was made for carrying two capsule-type litters on each side of the centre section for air evacuation of wounded or emergency rescue. On the underside of the centre section were attachment points for bomb racks for anti-submarine warfare (a British suggestion). As Frank Gregory put it: 'She was originally to have been a look-out in the sky, but now she is apparently to be an all-purpose helicopter – a real workhorse'.

Apart from the mock-up inspection, there were detailed discussions over other preliminary design layouts presented for review before detailing.

Several days later we received word that Wright Field was well satisfied with the reports received from the Mock-up Inspection Board, and we were instructed to proceed with detail engineering and production, which, as noted, we had already started. However, that was soon to be proved easier said than done.

The USA had by then been officially at war for nearly a year. What bothered me then, as it still does today, was the astounding lack of industrial preparation before 7 December 1941, in spite of all the warning signals coming from German-occupied Europe from 1936 onwards. As a minor history buff I have concluded that, while the world

stage does indeed change its scenery and/or locale, the show backers, stage managers and actors refuse to change the play's plot. Meanwhile, the brain-washed public audience dutifully pays the price of admission.

By the end of August 1942 I had acquired some additional help in the form of eight draughtsmen, but only one of them had any aircraft experience. In other words, because of the low priority of our helicopter programme, it was going to be difficult to hire experienced engineers. In fact, as time went on, Ed Katzenberger and I found ourselves running an aircraft draughting class. In spite of this, drawings for shop fabrication started to come from the draughting department in July. Since there were no drawing checkers available, that task also fell to Ed and self, with Ray Coates lending a much needed experienced hand. Ed was also a great help in screening possible applicants. One of these was a comely lass who had come down all the way from Boston, Massachusetts, in response to our advertisement for a 'tracer'. Her experience, unfortunately, had to do with 'tracing' deeds in a law office.

The problem of acquiring the proper materials for structural and machined parts also became a series of hurdles to be negotiated. This meant that a constant revision of schedules had to be maintained. It was a very busy time for all of us, but it was not long before a keen team spirit started to evolve.

It was indeed fortunate that we had chosen the simple, well established fabric-covered welded tubular steel structure for the R-4 programme, as these materials, and fabrication methods, were in adequate supply. It was also one of the least costly systems to maintain or repair in the field. Therefore the same reasoning was applied to XR-5 as much as possible.

There was an ever-increasing demand in the aircraft industry for lighter and stronger materials. This, in turn, inevitably increased overall costs, as well as causing delays in availability. We were therefore forced by circumstances to turn to alternative structural methods and/or material.

Since the Vought engineering department faced the same situation, but was far more knowledge-able regarding possible alternative market sources than we were, it proved of considerable help. Particularly with regard to XR-5's tail structure. Since I had chosen a simple, circular cross-section

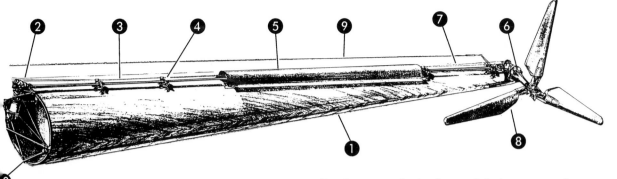

Fig 106 *The complete tail cone unit.*
(1) The entire tail cone structure is made of thin, laminated-wood veneers, resin bonded on a mold, using external vacuum pressure, while being cured.
(2) Electric generator driven off tail rotor drive shaft.
(3) Tail rotor drive shaft.
(4) Self-aligning sealed bearings.
(5) Removable inspection cover.
(6) Tail rotor gear box.
(7) Tail rotor pitch control cable operates screw-jack inside gearbox.
(8) 3-bladed tail rotor with hinged blades (Fig. 107).
(9) Radio antenna.
(10) Tail cone mounting ring (see Fig 109).

tapering down to where the tail rotor and its gear drive were attached at its very end, so it was dubbed the 'tailcone'. It was originally designed to be fabricated as a thin sheet-aluminium skin riveted to four internal longitudinal channel sections supported by, and riveted to, a number of flanged rings. The front end was bolted to the centre-section welded truss by its mounting ring.

While this design used a well established concept, it did require priority materials and fabrication tools. Vought's structures department therefore suggested that I consider an approved cold moulding, laminated-wood-veneer system. The firm was located in Brunswick, New Jersey. Our tailcone was just what the firm needed; a military contract. They had duplicated a Piper Aircraft light, twin-engined Apache model using their system of moulding, even including the engine cowlings, and I was able to inspect it. The evident precision and simplicity of the entire structure resulted from the vacuumed air system used, creating a completely even (Fig. 106) pressure on the adhesive-soaked laminations that were being bonded.

Furthermore, the basic metal design concept for XR-5 could be easily adapted, including the attachment points, as the production model would eventually revert to a metal structure. After another meeting with the Brunswick engineers, an exchange of all necessary data was accomplished, and to which delivery dates were agreed. Igor and Michael were well satisfied with the choice of the alternative wooden tailcone. Not only did it perform well, but in addition, the removable panels covering the entire centre section were also moulded, being provided by the Dolan company.

These laminated-wood panels covering the centre section, which the Dolan Co. provided for the first four experimental R-5s, were non-flammable. Also, like the temporary wooden tailcones, they were considered, and ordered, purely because of the existing shortages of metals and shop facilities. By the time the third and fourth XR-5s came along, the Dolan forms were used to make the panels from aluminium, as it was found that, when servicing the powerplant section, with frequent removal and replacement of the wooden panels, the corners containing the fasteners were vulnerable to rough usage and liable to crack or break off.

As mentioned earlier, the tail blades for XR-4 had been made by the Dolan Co in nearby Deep River, Connecticut, and the firm was also to supply the blades for XR-5's tail rotor. Paul Dolan, an accredited engineer, had been of considerable help to me with the design of the tail rotor blades, regarding the application of special techniques relative to wood laminating and the choice of wood best suited to a particular application (Fig. 106).

The next major component to be considered was the main rotor. My original design layout for XR-5 main rotor blade was similar to that for XR-4, but, as with the original metal tailcone, it would involve using priority materials. This was mainly due to the larger-diameter rotor, together with the greater loads involved. Both Igor and Michael agreed to

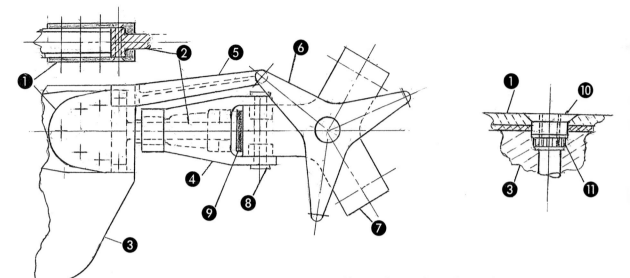

Fig 107

General Arrangement XR-5 Tail rotor hub (not to scale)
(1) Blade retention – root fitting
(2) Blade pitch axle
(3) Blade root
(4) Pitch bearing housing
(5) Blade pitch control horn
(6) Upper pitch control star linked to (5)
(7) hub
(8) Flapping hinge mounted on bearings
(9) Blade flapping limit stop
(10) Special flush-headed nut – serrated (11) to grip wood – made in our own shop.

my considering an all-wooden basic structure except for the stainless-steel-cable trailing edge with metal retaining clips, the overall fabric covering, and the metal leading-edge abrasion strip, which used a special nickel alloy with an adhesive backing (Fig 108).

As with the main transmission sub-assembly, as well as the tailcone, I assumed that, as the Project Engineer, I would be permitted to influence the selection of a particular supplier. Especially if a unique service was being offered, along with precision, attention to detail, and the supplier's involvement in the design of the item; in this case the design of the ribs. Using Paul's method of precisely press-forming thin wooden laminations I was able to design a unique method (patented) of attaching the fabric to the ribs. This also provided the necessary flanged areas needed for glueing the

ribs to the laminated wooden leading-edge spar, and at the same time assured more than adequate strength to sustain the rotor-blade operating loads.

Apparently the eagle-eyed government agent in our purchasing department took notice of our having selected a 'sole source' once again by choosing a specific supplier, and he promptly objected. This time the department would have to send out bids. After a week had passed I enquired as to the status of the bidding. No supplier could provide the ribs, let alone the complete assembly. Finally a furniture manufacturer, I think in Virginia, was awarded the contract for the leading-edge laminated spar. The results were crude (far too much glue) and considerably overweight. Paul supplied the ribs.

Incidentally, upon receiving the contract the furniture manufacturer's representative left a company brochure on my desk, with less than half-price mark-downs. Perhaps the foregoing events will give the reader some idea of the silly extra-curricular activities that sometimes helped to 'make my day'.

These blade sets were difficult to match-balance, but because they were on the heavy side they were actually smoother than the final Y-contract production blades. This was due to the greater centrifugal, outward-pulling, stabilising forces of the whirling blades. By the time the Y-contract came along, material and shop availability was becoming more stabilised, and the production blades were more like the R-4 blades, with tapered, tubular steel spars.

The molded, laminated wood, removable panels covering the centre section, that the Dolan Co. provided for the first four experimental R-5s, were

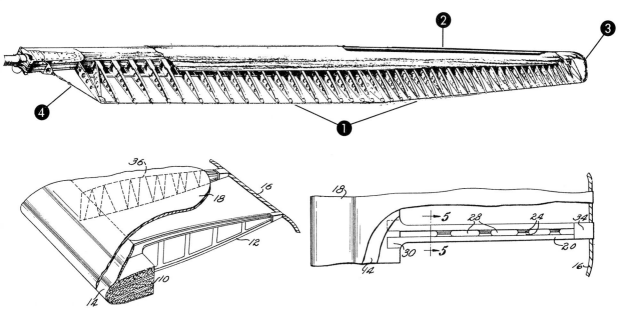

Fig 108

XR-5 main rotor blade unit (patent issued WEH)
(1) Main blade assembly.
(2) Metal abrasion strip bonded to leading edge
(3) Solid balsa wood fairing at blade tip.
(4) Turnbuckle to tension trailing edge cable.
(10) Laminated leading edge blade spar.
(12) The molded veneer ribs were made in two
separate halves and attached to the leading edge
spar (10) top and bottom by flanges (30) and to
each other by virtue of the mating vertical stiff-
ening depressions (24). Thereby forming a series
of slotted openings (28) through which the lacings
(30) can be passed directly from top-to-bottom of
each rib. Thus securing the covering fabric (18)
over the rib flanges (20). Since the stitches are
parallel with the airflow, and when the cloth is
drawn down between the rib opening (28), the
covering tapes over the depressed stitching,
result in exceptionally smooth surfaces.
(14) Leading edge veneer overlaps rib flanges
(30) top and bottom providing added bonding
strength.
(16) Trailing edge stainless steel cable is held in
place by metal clips (34) and tensioned by turn-
buckle (4).

non-flammable. Also, like the temporary wooden
tail cones, they were considered, and ordered,
purely because of the existing shortages of both
metals and shop facilities.

What actually happened, was that by the time
the third, and fourth XR-5s came along, the Dolan
forms were used to make the panels out of
aluminium. It was found that when servicing the
power-plant section, and after frequent removing,
and/or, replacing the wooden panels, the corners
containing the fasteners were vulnerable to rough
usage. They would crack, or break off.

In the engineering department, the burgeoning
XR-5 project now required extra space, and as
Project Engineer I was supposed to have my own
office. However, none being available, I suggested
that I occupy the area where the office was to be
located. Frankly I preferred to be in full view, as
well as having a full view of those working on the
project, and thus be readily available. I now rated
a secretary, and was most fortunate in acquiring
the greatly appreciated services of Miss Framson,
who so admirably took care of the rapidly ex-
panding project, which was soon to include two
attractive young females to augment draughting
requirements. With Ed Katzenberger also occupying the same 'office area', we three were able to
maintain a smooth running, mini command centre.

Shortly before making the foregoing move, I was
at my desk when I heard the sound of an aeroplane
unusually close. As I turned and looked out of my
window I saw a US Army P-47 fighter crash into
the outdoor storage area for jigs and fixtures. As it
so did it came apart at precisely the mating points
of the major subassemblies. The two complete
outer wing panels flew apart to left and right, then
the propeller, engine and its mount broke off as the
aircraft hit a large jig, causing the fuselage to flip
upwards. At that point the whole rear section separated from the complete centre section just aft of
the cockpit, vaulted over the centre section and,
upon contact with the ground, the extreme tail end
assembly (fin, rudder and tailplane) broke off.

The complete centre section ended upside-down.

Miraculously, the cockpit area was untouched. The sliding canopy had been opened ready for landing, and the pilot's unconscious head protruded downwards, two feet or so above the ground. It just so happened that two chaps from the shop were there, inspecting a particular jig. One of them had a sharp pocket knife, and was able to cut the pilot's safety harness. There was barely enough room as they worked feverishly to rescue the pilot, expecting the fuel from the ruptured fuel lines to burst into flames at any moment. As the pilot was being safely removed, the airport ambulance and crash team arrived from across the street. The various portions of the P-47 were soon covered with fire-retardant foam and the pilot, still unconscious, was carefully placed on a stretcher and rushed to the hospital. He suffered only minor head injuries and a broken collarbone.

A post-crash inspection revealed that only the port wing flap was in the correct lowered position for landing, as the control cables to the starboard flap had been severed (sabotage?). This had caused the port wing to stall as the pilot made a steep left turn at low altitude to line up with the airport runway on his final approach.

As mentioned earlier, Bridgeport became a coastal defence area soon after war was declared, and, according to availability, various types of fighter aircraft were stationed at the airport, just across from the plant, at one time or another. The P-47, compared to the other types stationed there, was the most difficult to land owing to the location of the cockpit. As the pilot increased the nose-up attitude of the 'plane it would correspondingly reduce his forward view of the runway, until, at the vital moments just before touchdown, it could disappear completely.

At the outset, pilots had but the minimum of flight instruction before they were put on active duty, especially with regard to learning the technique of short runway landing that was required at Bridgeport. As a result, wash-out (crash) or aborted landings by first arrivals were so frequent that the P-47s were finally withdrawn. The twin-engine Lockheed P-38s were faultless.

It was during this same period that the colonel in charge of the coastal defence unit, while making a practice flight in a P-47, went into a high-speed dive above the airport. The aircraft inadvertently went through the 'sound barrier' (beyond the speed of sound – 650 kts (760 mph) at sea level), producing a muffled boom which many of us heard, followed by a high-pitched screaming noise from the over-speeding engine (at this point the aeroplane was out of control). Then came a dull thud, and silence. Later I inspected the impact area, just a few yards from a private home just beyond the airport boundary. There was a round, shallow depression in the ground, and all that remained of the fighter above ground level were the outer panels of the wings and a short portion of the tail section. The rest was buried.

By the end of December 18 more personnel had joined the XR-5 project, only three of whom had previous aircraft experience. The Hunt-Katzenberger-Coates Draughting School, as you can well imagine, was thriving. An additional six engineers belonging to the electrical/radio section were available to any project needing their skills, bringing the total up to 31.

Drawings for shop fabrication started to come from the Engineering Department during July (so an old memo tells me). At about this time I began making somewhat louder noises with regard to the urgent need for experienced personnel to check the ever-increasing number of drawings. Somebody suggested that the Personnel Office run an advertisement in the local paper for two retired machine-shop foremen, needed as drawing checkers. In no time, anxious to help the war effort, two excellent applicants were chosen, and immediately shop questions/complaints were noticeably reduced.

Actually, what really sparked the foregoing was Bob Labensky kindly offering to help clear the 'log jam' and inadvertently marking up the original drawings with indelible pencils, instead of using checking prints. The personnel involved came to me in utter horror at seeing their earnest efforts defaced; especially for one of them, as it was his very first proud effort. Bob was mortified, but was readily forgiven.

The basic master jig on XR-5 was that which would determine the exact attachment points on the bottom, welded, tubular truss, of the centre section. When all the other subassemblies were bolted to this truss, it would form the entire centre section, as well as support the cabin, pilot's seat, landing gear, tailcone, engine mount and transmission-hub assembly mount (Fig 109 assembly centre section).

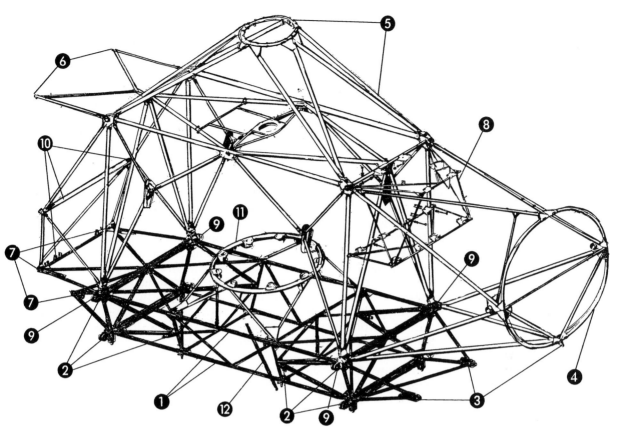

Fig 109

Completely assembled centre section XR-5.
(1) Basic lower weldment (dark) onto which all the other following subassembly weldments are bolted, or to each other.
(2) 3-point main landing gear attachment, fore or aft.
(3) 3-point rear landing gear attachment.
(4) Tail cone attachment mount and ring.
(5) Main transmission mount and ring.
(6) 2-point upper control cabin attachment.
(7) 3-point lower control cabin attachment.
(8) Radio communication racks.
(9) 4-point basic lower weldment attachment points.
(10) 4-point pilot's seat attachment.
(11) Engine mount and ring.
(12) Removable structural tube for engine installation.

After carefully going over the foregoing, together with Adolf Plenefisch and George Lubben, they assured me they could produce the basic master jig. I knew that George had experience in draughting, so I provided him with a table and all the necessary equipment near my desk in the Engineering Department, so that he had ready access to any information he might need. After several days George had a centreline drawing dimensionally indicating all the required attachment points, which were carefully checked, with their appropriate tolerance limits. That, George said, was all that was needed. The picture of the jig itself was firmly in his mind. I believed him. With that, he was 'off and running' with his own hand-picked crew. The saving in engineering time and paperwork was impressive, as was the rapidity with which the jig was made ready for fabricating the basic centre section unit, and finished in time to receive its other subassemblies. It was a strictly non-union type operation.

With 1942 drawing to a close, the XR-5 project was well on its way, mainly because of the good team spirit that had quickly developed, not only within engineering, but also within the shop and between the shop and engineering. Also in December, the first stork's arrival would soon take place at 'chez Hunt'.

This eventful year for Igor Sikorsky's 'heeli-copters' was highlighted by the XR-4 delivery flight. It also indicated, with its proof of acceptance, the age of the practical helicopter had finally arrived.

Of equal significance during that same month of

May, were the decisions arrived at by Air Materiel Command regarding the future role of the helicopter. The first was to buy enough follow-on YR-4 (Service evaluation) helicopters; the second, after YR-4 evaluation, was to incorporate refinements and/or improvements in the R-4 production model that would result in greater versatility and utility; the third was to build a larger Sikorsky helicopter, the XR-5.

In the final event, however, it was decided at a later meeting, on 16 September, not only to continue the R-4 series, but to buy four new, advanced experimental models designated XR-6 based dimensionally on the YR-4. This called for an additional budget of $500,000.

In the meantime the US Navy through Cdr M.N. Fleming of the Navy Bureau of Aeronautics in Washington, D.C., had submitted a request for four YR-4s. Learning of this, Lt-Col Gregory had a meeting with Cdr Fleming, apprised him of the Army's decision, and convinced him that the Navy would be better off, in the long run, buying the XR-6, because of its superior performance and increased utility. This resulted in the Army buying five XR-6s for $800,000, with the US Navy supplying 53% of that amount for three XR-6s. The Navy also agreed to having all five helicopters built entirely to Army specifications, thus reducing the overall costs. Later, owing to changes requested by the Army, the deal ended up with the Army contributing 57% of the total costs. Also, because of the more ready availability of the YR-4, with increased horsepower, the British ordered both YR-4 and R-4 models.

Having been Bob Labensky's able assistant on the XR-4, Ralph Alex was promoted to the position of Project Engineer for the super version of XR-4, designated XR-6, using the same main and tail rotor system as the production R-4. A full-scale mock-up was to be built immediately. This was a splendid new opportunity, and a challenge for Ralph.

As his assistant, Ralph chose an accredited architectural designer, Donald Plumb, who had recently joined the engineering department. He brought with him a more experienced form of judgement which was of considerable help to Ralph, but he had no prior aircraft experience, of which I was aware. Nevertheless, between them they produced an eyecatching design, rather than a functional one like XR-4. I do not wish to infer, by that remark, a negative viewpoint on my part. However, although I only had time for quick glimpses of the mock-up as its construction progressed, I did begin to get the impression that ease of maintenance had, perhaps, taken second place in certain areas.

This reminds me of the distinctly different design approaches between two famous British RAF fighters of the Second World War, the more functionally designed Hawker Hurricane designed by Sydney Camm of Hawker-Siddeley (Sir Thomas Sopwith's) Company, and the more eyecatching and elegant 'Spitfire', designed by Reginald Mitchell of the Supermarine Company. The former was considerably less costly to build and maintain, than the latter.

While in no way do I wish to appear to belabour the point, but in the recent obituary, at the time of Sir Thomas Sopwith's death, at the age of 101, it contained the following historical facts. London (AP) – 'When the Air Ministry couldn't make up its mind in 1936 about a new breed of fighters, Sopwith ordered his factories to build 1000 of the rugged eight-gun Hurricanes designed by Sidney Camm.'

'The Air Ministry bought them and the Hurricane formed the air backbone in the 1940 Battle of Britain. In that battle it destroyed more enemy planes than all the rest of the air and ground defences combined, including the faster Spitfire.*' * at high altitude (my comment). To be quite fair, it must be added, that there were only some two-to-three squadrons of Spitfires available at the very beginning of the Battle of Britain. However, they were never the major element in defeating the German threat, as the news media would have you believe. Necessary design changes in the all-stressed skin construction were costly, especially in total time required, to be included in the production line. The wings were so thin that installing more powerful armament necessitated introducing drag-producing bulges outside of the normal wing profile. The cockpits were cramped, except for medium or smaller size pilots. Baling out usually meant rolling over, to ease exit. Elegance can be costly. Amen.

Nonetheless the XR-6 passed the Army/Navy Mock-up Inspection Board with flying colours. Frank Gregory enthusiastically described her as looking like a streamlined, crooked-neck squash gourd with a rotor and wheels added.

Early on, Ralph had been given the green light to use a stressed-skin type of light sheet metal (magnesium) construction. It was considered a reasonable assumption at that time that thinly gauged aluminium sheeting would also be readily available by the time construction was due to start.

However, Ralph did look into the possibilities of using a then new material consisting of very thin glass filaments that could be formed into a thread of any desired diameter to produce woven cloth. Called 'fibre-glass' cloth and/or matting, it could be layered-up on a form to a desired final shape and thickness. It would then be saturated with a special self-curing liquid resin. The result was a very strong and light material for use in aircraft, as long as it was not used in primary structures (though even that day would eventually arrive). The fibre-glass manufacturer was located in California. Undaunted, Ralph was granted permission to investigate the possibility of having the two cabin doors made out of the new material. During a business visit he was on the telephone to Serge Gluhareff at the home plant when, at the end of their conversation, they were suddenly cut off. In those wartime days a transcontinental telephone conversation was strictly 'priority'. After considerable difficulty Serge was able to recontact Ralph and simply said: 'Hello – is that you Ralphy? OK Ralphy, bye-bye Ralphy.'

Fig 110 *XR-6. An early test flight.*

Basically there were but two major structural units to the XR-6. The main one was a single, structural, sheet-metal flat-topped bottom deck unit that supported both the control cabin and the centrally located main rotor, powerplant, fuel, etc,

plus the lower attachment point of the tailcone and the external undercarriage units. The main shock absorbers were located within the structure, and serviced through hand holes with removable deck covers. As in XR-4 and -5, a welded tubular steel structure mounted on the bottom deck unit supported the engine/transmission/main rotor system and the upper tailcone attachment point. A moulded paper base cowling covered this area.

The tailcone was of sheet metal construction. Its front end cross section was a vertical ellipse that tapered down to a circular section at its extreme end, where the tail rotor and its gearbox was attached. The tail rotor driveshaft ran inside the upper contour of the tailcone, which was a separately hinged section for maintenance purposes. Its internal structure consisted of formed sheet aluminium bulkheads and longitudinal stringers riveted to the outer sheet-magnesium skin.

The cabin frame was glassfibre, as were its two doors. The one-piece moulded nose section was made of clear vision Plexiglas that afforded excellent vision for both the pilot and his observer/passenger, who were seated side-by-side. The pilot's controls were identical to those of XR-4. The high frequency radio transceiver communication system was located on a shelf directly behind the seats, at about shoulder level. There were also pocket-like containers for the stowage of charts and personal items. Dual headphones were also provided.

A stainless steel firewall separated the cabin area from the powerplant. The engine was a 245 hp air-cooled, flat six-cylinder opposed Franklin, pressure-fan cooled. It was mounted vertically, driving the main and tail rotors through a planetary-gear-type transmission by means of a universally-jointed shaft. The main rotor hub was redesigned because the original XR-4 hub was non-cyclic, longitudinal and roll control being achieved by the two horizontal tail rotors.

Cooling air for the transmission and the engine was taken in and emitted through side-panel openings, as was the engine exhaust. The undercarriage consisted of two main wheels mounted on cantilevered, tapered tubular struts, attached by hinges to the bottom structure, and one swivelling rear wheel. A fourth small auxiliary anti-noseover wheel was also swivel mounted. There were provisions for carrying two capsulated external litters, one per side, and/or bomb racks.

XR-6's estimated gross weight was under 2,600 lb, the top speed over 100 mph, and it had a 714 ft/min rate of climb.

Following the demonstration of the float-equipped VS-300Ga on 20 April 1942, Igor would mention, every now and again, what had been apparently on his mind for a long time; namely the possibility of perhaps making a two-seater out of VS-300. He well realised, of course, that everybody was very much engaged with the XR/YR-4, XR-5 and XR-6 projects, but when, shortly before Thanksgiving, he mentioned the idea again, I had a quiet talk about it with Alex Krapish. How about surprising Igor with a complete shop and engineering package, and leaving it to Igor to get the necessary approval? Alex was delighted with the idea, as were Michael and Serge Gluhareff.

Needless to say, Igor must have had numerous thoughts and ideas pass through his mind on how to provide the necessary extra lift, which we estimated as being at least some 160 lb. After some time spent trying to second-guess what might be the most acceptable to Igor, it was decided to go to a two-bladed main rotor, and only move the pilot sufficiently forward to allow for a flat piece of plywood as a seat for the passenger, with another on which to place his feet. The basic requirement was not to exceed the then all-up weight, with pilot, of 1,285 lb plus passenger, making it a total of 1,445 lb, if possible, since the engine was not capable of more than an all-out maximum of 92 hp.

When designing a helicopter main lifting rotor, the ratio of the total circular area (disc area) of the revolving rotor is divided into the total area of the rotor blades, and this is called the solidity ratio. For VS-300F with three blades this was .052. However, by maintaining the same ratio with only two blades, the width of each blade was increased by half the width (chord) of the discarded third blade. This increased the individual blade area in the outermost one third of the radius, which is the fastest moving and therefore the largest lift producing portion of the blade (it was of constant chord). The net gain in lift was achieved by virtue of being able to use a smaller angle of blade incidence to produce the same amount of lift, with less resistance. Thus less power was required than with the three-bladed rotor while turning at the same speed. So the power saved could be used to increase lift, by increasing the blade incidence until it used up all the power available. The calculated net lift

increase amounted to almost 200 lb, which we felt ensured a safe enough margin for error.

The increased chord of the blade also meant that the blade profile could be more accurately fabricated. To reduce air resistance further, the blades were to be waxed and polished.

The new hub would slightly increase the offset of the horizontal flapping hinge, to allow for the more forward location of the CG. Two of the existing horizontal blade dampers were used. With the CG shifting further forward, the tendency for VS-300 to pitch forward (nose down) would be greater. By increasing the offset hinge leverage (also referred to as the flapping hinge), it would require less cyclic control force to overcome this nose-down force. The whole two-bladed system can now be seen at the Bradley Air Museum in Hartford, Connecticut.

Moving the pilot's location forward did not require any structural change, but it did mean that the pilot's controls and instruments also had to be relocated. This was a relatively simple task for Alex.

On the morning of the day before Thanksgiving Day I had prints made of the engineering changes and held a private meeting with Michael and Serge, as a preview before my presentation. Michael had already arranged to see Igor right after closing time that same afternoon. The staging of that meeting was entirely Michael's, since he knew well the best way to present Igor with a surprise.

First Michael discussed, along with Serge, a matter of common concern with Igor. After that was attended to, he announced that he would like Igor to listen to an interesting suggestion that I wished to present to him. As I entered his office with a roll of prints and a folder, his usual friendly smile greeted me. But when I announced the purpose of my presentation he enthusiastically asked me to proceed. It was not long before, greatly to my relief, he was not only supportive of the suggested programme, but obviously delighted with the engineering details presented, by reason of the many questions he asked and the answers he received. I was supported by both Michael, and Serge, and accompanied, from time-to-time, with that curious little tell-tale sound in his throat, denoting pleasure.

His final remarks concerned his great appreciation of our continued support of his interests, and he said he would certainly immediately direct his thoughts to the possibility of carrying out the suggested programme. I believe there was a comforting feeling between all of us when, after a friendly handshake, we left for the holiday. It was also heartening to see Igor once again enthusiastically looking forward to the possibility of test flying his beloved VS-300, as well as prolonging her life.

Soon after Thanksgiving, Igor announced that the programme had been approved, since most of the shop work would be accomplished by Alex Krapish and his small crew. Needless to say, Les Morris also welcomed the prospect of additional flight testing, and Alex looked forward to additional work on what to him had now become his proud personal charge.

In retrospect, 1942 was the most exciting and most productive of the war years. VS-300G had become the first truly successful, fully cyclically-controlled single-main-rotor helicopter. The first military contract for a Sikorsky helicopter, for XR-4 had been placed, and Les Morris had given a remarkable demonstration of XR-4 and VS-300G to the joint military observers on 20 April. This had been followed by the first flight delivery of a military helicopter, XR-4, and its official acceptance at Wright Field. Then came the first official military helicopter training course, originated and instructed by Les Morris. The follow-on YR-4 contract was followed in May by the go-ahead on XR-5, followed by the contract for four XR-5s. Finally, there was the contract for five XR-6s.

Reviewing 1942 from a more personal point of view, engineering gradually evolved into the forming of three separate 'inner circles' actively engaged simultaneously on the three military projects (I was also still Project Engineer for the -300). Unfortunately these teams were not really collaborating with each other, and this was symptomatic of what was eventually to become the source of unnecessary engineering problems. As Assistant to Igor, Serge Gluhareff held what one might call the position of co-ordinator of the engineering department. He reviewed project reports, and was tied in with personnel requirements.

The Vought-Sikorsky Engineering Manual proclaimed: 'The Project Engineer is in complete charge of the Project'. Apparently, this became a source of increasing irritation to Serge, for there was emerging a tendency for him to resent this control. One day he remarked to Ralph Alex: 'You Project Engineers think you are leetle Tsars'. Both

Ralph and I tried to get things done more rapidly by bypassing the system, but by the end of the year there was a noticeable increase of instances in which Serge would make a decision over our heads.

Curiously, the steady hand of Igor was missing here. What was obviously lacking was a timely meeting of the minds to collaborate in reviewing common problems, both short and long term. If nothing else, it was a lesson in management that I realised I was not applying to my own project. From then on, every Friday I had a joint meeting with my project group leaders, right after work. It gave them a greater sense of responsibility by their collaborating among themselves, enhancing the team spirit all round. I checked daily in both the shop and engineering.

Socially, Michael Gluhareff's friendship, both during and after business hours, never wavered. During the warmer months, when my family returned home to Brooklyn, Connecticut, (I would usually join them at weekends) he would sometimes ask me to join him for a swim, or to dinner at his home with his charming wife and family. He and his wife spent a weekend with us in Brooklyn, where we introduced them to our friends, to the delight of everyone. Several times we went flying together locally, as he liked to keep his hand in.

Brother Serge, a bachelor, although friendly, did not have the natural out-going warmth of his older brother. However, during the winter months, when my wife was with me, he did come to dinner several times, and during the course of the evening he would relax with us. We both felt that Serge missed a normal home life. I later found out that we were the first acquaintances, other than those in the Russian community, from whom he had socially accepted an invitation to dine at their home.

Some time ago I had a slight altercation with Serge, and apparently he had mentioned it to Michael, since I reported directly to Michael and he asked me not to be too concerned. He then went on to tell me that Serge would have times of depression. Apparently Serge had gone through a rather wild youthful period, while sowing his oats, with little parental restraint. Michael's interest in aviation, and his taking Serge under his wing, so to speak, had finally led Serge to finding enough interest in helping Michael to design and build a glider, and then learn, after Michael, to fly it. They next reworked the glider to accommodate an engine, and learnt to pilot it, and this made Serge

'HEELICOPTER' – PIONEERING WITH IGOR SIKORSKY

mend his ways. This was the beginning of Michael's continuing role as his brother's Keeper.

As the years went on, Serge became increasingly more religiously inclined and introspective. While Michael became a very important part of Igor's burgeoning aircraft construction, Serge maintained his position in it mainly because of Igor's personal sense of loyalty, and his appreciation of Michael's outstanding contributions. This relationship continued right up to the very end for all three.

Michael and Serge had a pet personal project for a postwar four-seat amphibian. It seemed to me that it was really a thoughtful way for Michael to provide Serge with a spare-time occupation. They had built a mock-up of the central hull, cabin and wing area in Michael's cellar, and they showed this to me, together with some of their drawings. They wondered if I might like to help them with its design. I said I would greatly appreciate the privilege of so doing, and would look forward to that time when VS-300 was retired. To that they willingly agreed.

I have just been reviewing my 1942 notes, and suddenly realized that I have failed to include several interesting flights that Les Morris made. The first one occurred during his time at Wright Field as the first military helicopter instructor. One of his early pupils was a Maj L.B. Cooper, a seasoned Army pilot. Les had been demonstrating how to make properly banked turns, and he signalled the major to take over the controls and make a series of similar turns, which he proceeded to do. Meanwhile Les relaxed, diverting his attention to the passing scene below him. Suddenly the major loudly exclaimed 'Hey!', startling Les out of his reverie. He pointed in utter amazement at his rudder pedals and asked Les: 'Who is operating these?' Neither of them were! The tail rotor, uncontrolled, had found its own self-determined neutral operating blade angle, and was thus automatically providing the necessary directional stability (equivalent to required vertical tail-fin area for a fixed-wing aircraft). That meant that the pilot merely needed to move the control stick sideways in the direction of the desired turn, and it would cause XR-4 to bank and turn automatically in the desired direction; a totally unexpected advantage. Furthermore, whenever the control stick was brought back to its normal neutral position, XR-4 would automatically smoothly straighten up and

assume its new directional course, without any fishtailing from side-to-side. In fact, banking turns of up to 70° could be safely made in this manner, and immediately became a part of the training curriculum.

Next, on a particularly foggy morning in March, at one of our VS-300 meetings which then included Les, Igor brought up the subject of fog flying in a helicopter. The upshot was the decision to try it out in the next available fog, and record the event with a movie camera. Within several days a dense, heavy fog, lazily rolled in off Long Island Sound, reducing visibility to about 100 ft. All local aircraft were grounded. Les took off from the usual area next to our building, the VS-44 hangar. This meant that at the start of the flight he would be unable to see the familiar trees and old farm buildings bordering the shoreline. He was then to proceed southwards over unpopulated marshlands as a safety precaution. He had no compass or radio. Initially, flying slowly within sight of the ground, Les had no problem negotiating the familiar trees and buildings. However, after a short while he realised he was quite disoriented. Determined not to panic, he proceeded more cautiously, and finally identified a large dark object that loomed up ahead as a familiar tree. He then decided to turn round, as he now knew well enough the direction towards home base.

Several other fog flights were successfully made. The final judgement was that while it was possible, helicopter fog flying (blind flying) required careful training with appropriate instrumentation, and voice contact with known ground stations.

Finally, some night flying was also done by Les in XR-4 which had the necessary position lights. The most rewarding were made by the light of a full moon on a clear night, as ground objects were clearly identified. Despite low overcast and wartime 'dim-out', moving traffic was still readily spotted. Normally, when flying over the countryside during peacetime, a large white arrow with an N at its tip, could be easily spotted on the top of barn roofs. Les suggested fitting a remotely controlled, powerful spotlight, which could be pointed either forwards for terrain guidance or directly downwards for emergency landings.

Igor thought it might be interesting to see what difference there might be in the noise level if a car muffler was installed in VS-300. It was really amazing to hear just the swishing of the main rotor, with only a brief fluttering beat from the tail rotor as additional manoeuvring thrust was applied. This was because the tail rotor was relatively lightly loaded and slow turning. There was loss of power, however.

So that brings us to the end of 1942, which I will terminate in a light vein. I shall call this, 'A sign of the times'. A newly acquired hand on the assembly line of the Vought F-4U Navy fighter 'plane, had been given the order by his Foreman, to remove a certain upper surface wing rivet, it being not properly installed. Quite some time later, he appears before his Foreman, and proudly presents him with the offending rivet. Exclaiming, 'Well, there is the rivet!' The Foreman meanwhile, having been otherwise occupied, replied somewhat testily, 'What rivet?' – 'Why the one you asked me to remove, and I had a really tough time trying not to damage it' came the reply. With that, the Foreman blanched, trying not to believe what was forming in his mind, while he dashed over to look at the spot where the offending rivet, now tightly clasped in his sweaty palm, reposed. There, to his horrified gaze, he saw a neat half-inch diameter hole through the surface of the wing!

After reviewing this chapter, the after-thought occurred to me, of some of the pleasant summer after-hours spent sailing on Long Island Sound with Art Hunt (distant relation), on his 'all bright' (unpainted, but varnished) all mahogany, 25ft sloop, including picnic suppers prepared before hand by his devoted Mother.

Or the equally delighted moonlight sailing with Bob Labensky, on his 26ft Cat Boat (it had but one, very large, gaff-rigged mainsail at its stem), that had no auxiliary engine. Bob was a true sailor, so auxiliary power was produced by manning two very large oars called 'sweeps', operated from the aft cockpit.

One evening the wind failed, just before the tide changed. Oh yes! We heave-hoed mightily against the ever-increasing tide rate, but to no avail, and we were also too far from the marina. So we 'dropped the hook', and retired to the cabin bunks to fitfully sleep, until the wee hours of the morning, when the tide changed.

Fortunately, the Dockmaster at the marina, surmising our predicament, upon our unscheduled non-arrival (we had no radio) had called the Buivids with whom Bob lived, so no alarm was raised.

Figure 111 shows Henry Wirkus, also from my home village of Brooklyn, Connecticut, attaching a bundle in a particularly tough terrain, while Les Morris hovers -300 precisely overhead. Henry graduated from the Putnam, Connecticut Trade School's Aeromechanical Course, and through Igor's generosity, he had the privilege of joining Alex Krapish's -300 team, in charge of engine maintenance, etc. He proved to be a splendid choice.

Fig 111
One way to render aid where even the helicopter may be unable to land.

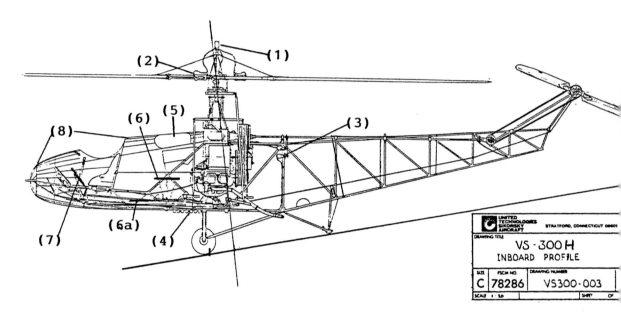

Fig 112
(HUNT) FINAL ARRANGEMENT OF VS-300-H – AS FLOWN WITH 2-BLADED ROTOR

(1) Central oil feeder tank (Buivid)–to hydraulic blade dampers (2)
(3) Oil circulating pump to (4)– Finned tube radiator.
(5) Rear cockpit – (6) – Seat. (6a) Floor board.
(7) Collective pitch lever (Krapish) also shape of front section (8)

Chapter Six
1943

VS-300-HVS-300-H with Two-bladed Main Rotor – Interlude –
XR-4 Lands on SS *Bunker Hill* – XR-4 and YR-4 land on
SS *James Parker* – First Lift-off of No 1 XR-5 – VS-300 Retired –
XR-5 No 1 Accident – First Flight XR-5 No 2

While the last day of 1941 witnessed the triumphant first trouble-free flight of 300, incorporating the much sought-after, fully cyclically controlled main rotor system, and thus heralding the emergence of the very first successful vertical lifting, single-main-rotor type helicopter, so did the XR-4 in 1942, unquestionably demonstrate the practicability of the helicopter, as yet another unique form of aerial transportation, albeit initially, for military purposes. We will now witness, in 1943, another year of significant events taking place.

This year began with VS-300 being rolled out for her first two-bladed-main-rotor-powered 'run-up', (Fig 112) sporting an attractive new front cockpit fairing by Alex Krapish and the added passenger 'cockpit' behind the pilot, consisting of two horizontal pieces of plywood. The upper one to sit on, the lower one for two feet. There was also a new Collective Pitch Lever (CPL) that Alex had cleverly devised, closely resembling the old car driver's ratcheted handbrake but located in a more horizontal position, as XR-4 and -5.

It was a bright sunny morning with little wind,

with a few inches of snow on the ground. VS-300, looking very trim without a front landing wheel and the tailskid moved forward, its new two-bladed main rotor was tracked for the first time with the 'flag' as she sat on the concrete apron in front of the VS-44 hangar.

After the necessary adjustments were made, Les gradually applied power. It was evident that further fine-tuning was necessary, but Les felt that the vibration was acceptable for a first lift-off. He was just as anxious as we were to see VS-300H airborne, which she became with little effort, much to Igor's delight. Incidentally, both three- and two-bladed rotors, when horizontally disposed to the airstream, have the same basic aerodynamic imbalance periods of two-per-revolution (Fig 113).

After cautiously checking out lateral and rear-wards flight, Les began the now-familiar routine of gradually increasing forward speed through the transition period, and found that VS-300H was just as responsive and manageable as -300G, with the transition period being slightly more evident.

This was remedied by a series of test flights, after adjusting the external Buivid adjustable orifices

'HEELICOPTER' – PIONEERING WITH IGOR SIKORSKY

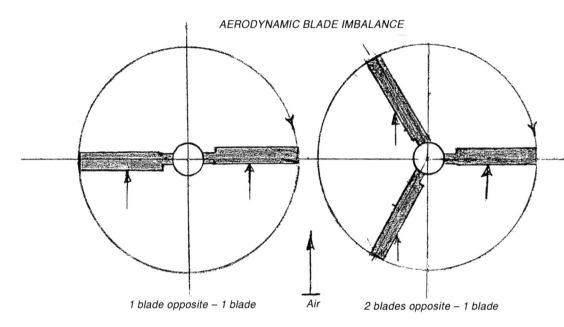

AERODYNAMIC BLADE IMBALANCE

1 blade opposite – 1 blade   Air   2 blades opposite – 1 blade

Fig 113

provided on each of the two borrowed 'G' horizontal hydraulic lead-lag dampers. Since each blade was of greater area and weight than on the 'G', the blade forces would also be greater on the 'H'. This took up almost the rest of the morning, so it was decided to postpone further testing until after lunch. Nevertheless, Igor, Michael, Serge and Les were greatly relieved and pleased by the initial results, not to mention my own similar feelings as the perpetrator of yet another significant change.

However, the real challenge took place after lunch, when Les enthusiastically had put the 'H' through her paces. In his own words: 'We found that the twin blades were able to do everything the three-bladed rotor could do - PLUS'.

The plus, of course, was the *raison d'être* for this whole effort; remodeling -300H as a two-seater. So who was to be the first passenger? The lot fell to Michael Gluhareff, who happily lowered himself into the 'passenger cockpit' buckled himself on to the cushion-covered plywood seat and gave us a cheery wave as Les gradually increased power. Slowly 'H' began to lift-off to about 5ft, accompanied by our cheers as Les nudged her forward. Slowly at first, then with increasing speed Les made

a sweeping circuit of the meadow at about 10ft and at 25/30 mph before making a large figure eight, ending up with a precise vertical landing in front of a very pleased Igor, and receiving our congratulations. Obviously the -300H was in the hands of a master pilot.

However, while he was very pleased with the way -300H handled, Les cautioned Igor that taking up any passenger weighing more than Michael should not be attempted especially in cold winter weather, as the engine could no longer develop its original power. Igor totally agreed, especially since the original goal had been achieved. Furthermore, -300H would be able to furnish us with important two-bladed performance information.

This did not prevent Igor from flying 'H' solo, which he did with his usual aplomb. In his book *Pioneering the Helicopter*, Les wrote: 'Some of our best flying was recorded with this installation . . .' of which more later, as we return to 1 January and XR-5.

The beginning of the year saw the addition of three more members to the XR-5 project, all eager to help but with no previous aircraft experience (par for the course), which meant that our 'engineering school' had acquired three additional scholars. Nevertheless, we were steadily increasing the output of engineering information to the shop.

A new section was being added to engineering in the form of an additional balcony that would pro-

Fig 114
(1) Pilot's control stick
(2) Observer's control stick
(3) Rudder pedal link
(4) Control cable quadrants
(5) Control cables to screw-jacks
(6) Collective pitch lever
(7) Rotor brake handle
(8) Rudder pedal
(9) Over-centre linkage disengages rudder pedals
(10) Vertical clear vision panel

vide room for producing an information manual for each production model, plus accompanying drawings depicting isometric views of the various subassemblies and 'exploded' views of the same, to help the shop understand the correct sequence for proper assembly. Two typical subassembly drawings (Fig 114) depict the cabin flight controls that fit on to the lower cabin structure.

So it came to pass that three accredited artists were attracted to this section, where they could answer the call to help in the 'war effort'. They were apparently well aware of each others' accomplishments, but each one considered himself quite capable of producing comparable, if not better results. During lunch hour this situation was

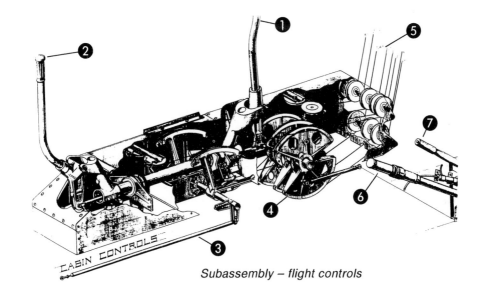

Subassembly – flight controls

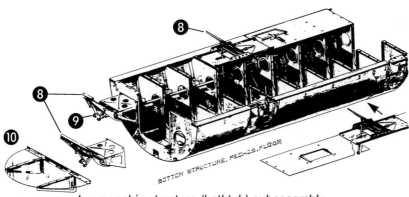

Lower cabin structure (bathtub) subassembly

highlighted by audible personal reviews of the absent one's efforts. Of course these reviews were promptly relayed to the absent party, eventually resulting in some rather heated, if not spectacular, exchanges.

This recalls another amusing incident, when Igor stopped by my desk regarding some matter he had in mind. At that moment I was designing the cabin section, and just before he left he looked intently at the lower structural area. Then, with his little habit of 'chewing his moustache' when somewhat agitated, he turned and, eyeing me quizzically, gently asked: 'Why do you show two venturi tubes?' (air suction tubes similar to the type connected to an airspeed indicator). I was momentarily baffled, then realisation dawned and with a chuckle I replied: 'Those are the suction tubes attached to the observer's and pilot's "relief tubes"'. It amused Igor no end.

Returning to more serious matters, one of the last major components I designed on the XR-5 was the main landing gear. In Chapter 5 there was an illustration showing Igor's sketch of a cantilever undercarriage, along with my remark regarding Igor finally having his way on the XR-5, as was indeed the case (Fig 89). The photograph of the mock-up (Fig 105) shows the main landing gear leg as being a cantilever unit with a faired elliptical shape to reduce air resistance. Furthermore, the structural assembly drawing of the centre section shows identical three-point attachment fittings to allow either (Fig 109) a forward main cantilever undercarriage with rear wheel, or a rear main undercarriage with nosewheel. At first, the former was fitted on XR-5, but my intention was to provide a built-in option.

Igor also agreed to a symmetrically faired cantilever leg section with a D-shaped front load-carrying spar section, at the outer end of which would be attached the vertical-acting hydraulic shock absorbers. The third single-point attachment would take the horizontal loads, while the D-spar would take both the vertical and torsional loads. The rear portion would be a lightweight fairing, but at the attachment end a mounting step would permit the maintenance crew to climb up to the hub service platform.

The hydraulic shock absorbers incorporated a variable-size orifice metering system that I copied from British designer Harold Bolas's first ever deck-landing aircraft shock-absorbers of the early 1920s. In these the initial abrupt vertical shock could be restrained, and then relieved at any pre-determined rate. As previously described, a helicopter attempting a vertical landing with a 'soft' landing gear could easily generate severe lateral bouncing, from side-to-side.

Once again a design change was made in my absence, with Serge's approval. The cantilever leg was changed to a circular section, tapering in diameter outwards, which would considerably increase air resistance. Apparently both Igor and Michael were initially unaware of the change. The schedule was so tight that there was no redress this time. After talking it over with Michael, who was quite upset, I took his advice and said nothing. It turned out to be sound advice. Igor never said a word, nor did his attitude change towards me.

One more member in February brought the XR-5 project team up to 42. Fortunately, this last member did have some aircraft draughting experience. Also, we were now 'over the hump' regarding the necessary shop information for the manufacture and assembly of the various parts. The outstanding information required had to do mainly with installation layouts such as flight controls, powerplant controls and lubrication, furnishings, etc. The estimated engineering time required to complete the necessary engineering information for the first XR-5 for the US Army, was between one and two months.

Although there were four XR-5s on order, two for the USA and two for Britain, the major effort was concentrated on the first American machine in order to ascertain, as soon as possible, any major revisions or changes that would need to be incorporated in the remaining three aircraft. This was especially true regarding the earliest possible date for initial roll-out and run-ups of No.1 before its crucial first lift-off and subsequent flight testing could take place.

XR-5 would be the largest ever single-main-rotor Sikorsky 'heelicopter' to become airborne. The stakes were high, but we now knew that we had a good grasp of the basic knowledge and confidence required to produce such a 'Heeli'.

On 26 January 1943 The Institute of Aeronautical Sciences (IAS), at its annual Honours Night Dinner at the Waldorf-Astoria Hotel in New York City, were honouring Igor Sikorsky's helicopter achievements by seating him at the head table as a featured speaker. At that time only a few of us 'Heeli-ites' were members of IAS. We were grouped together just in front of the head table dais, at its left-hand end, almost directly below where Igor was sitting, next to his friend Prof Jerome Hunsaker. What made this meeting so memorable for me was as he ended his talk, a brief history of the recent successes of his helicopters delivered in his usual delightfully enthusiastic and affirmative manner, he turned and directed his closing remark obviously at us, saying: 'Furthermore, all of the foregoing would not have been possible but for the valuable help I was given'. Later that year the American Helicopter Association came into being, largely due to the diligent efforts of A. Petroff, which were never properly acknowledged nor appreciated.

Apparently the US Navy finally decided to take notice of the XR-5 activities, for one day in February Serge advised me, a little piqued, that formerly Commander, now Capt Fleming, USN had arrived on the scene specifically to see me regarding the XR-5 project. This was the same officer that Frank Gregory had persuaded to buy XR-6s instead of YR-4s.

Fleming was particularly interested in the XR-5 mock-up, which we went over in some detail. He was pleasantly surprised at the completeness of the mock-up, and became less formal during his inspection. He next turned his interest to the estimated and actual weights of the finished parts, commenting that, when he was attached to Carrier Based Aircraft Command, he had familiarised himself with the exact weights of each of the aircraft types then being designed and built, including their structural and equipment components.

I introduced the captain to Ed Starzick, who was in charge of the Weights Department and Ed showed him the daily monitored charts that kept a continuous tally of actual against estimated weights. This apparently satisfied the captain. He then departed as unceremoniously as he had arrived, with a cordial handshake. It was only some time later that I happened to find out the real reason for his visit.   .

It appeared that a well-known and respected US Navy aeronautical engineer was convinced that helicopters were completely incapable of becoming a practical aircraft, mainly due to the excessive weight penalties involved, especially with regard to the main rotor blades and hub mechanism of a heli-

copter the size of XR-5. This had raised a number of top-brass eyebrows, so Capt Fleming had been asked to ascertain just how far 'off the mark' we were.

February 1943 was also, and will always be, a very special month for me, as the 23rd marked the birth of our daughter, our first and only beloved child. It was a special birthday surprise for my mother, who was then celebrating her 64th year.

With the advent of the follow-on 'Y' contracts for XR-4 from both the USA and Britain, it had been decided to subcontract their welded tubular truss-type fuselage structures to allow for a final assembly area in our limited factory floor space. Bob Labensky asked me to assist him in the choice of a YR-4 production supplier, and it turned out to be the Luscombe Company in North Wales, Pennsylvania. Donald Luscombe had been responsible for producing one of the first successful all-metal (except for fabric-covered wings) two-seat, single-engine light aeroplanes for the private aircraft market. He was thus well qualified and a reliable source to help the military in meeting their heavily burdened aircraft procurement programme. This turned out to be a fortuitous choice for me, as we soon formed a friendly working relationship.

As another sign of the times, some of the members of our machine shop found that evening and/or night overtime shifts were not initially as well supervised as the daytime shifts, and that personal so-called 'government jobs' could be surreptitiously phased in. This was highlighted when a machinist who had somehow managed to rebore the cylinder block of his Ford Model A was caught sneaking it out of the plant at the end of his shift by the same manner by which he had brought it in, which was ingenious to say the least. It was winter, and the culprit, being fairly tall but of stocky build, wore a long, heavy overcoat, under which he was able to carry the engine block by a rope slung round the back of his neck. All went well until, just as he was checking out, there was a resounding clang as the rope was severed by the sharp edge of the rebored cylinder block through which it passed and the block hit the floor.

Increasingly, pressure was being brought to bear regarding the estimation of the roll-out date for the first XR-5. One of the control items still to be incorporated was the fore-and-aft trim control system. This particular system allowed the pilot to adjust

Operating in and out of a small boat anchorage.

Tidal mud flats.

Fig 115 *Back-yard landing.*

the fore-and-aft tilt of the main rotor independently, without disturbing the existing main rotor cyclic pitch setting and/or the pilot's control stick setting, since, in effect, the main rotor did not sense it was being tilted. This was the case when the single horizontal tail rotor on -300 governed the fore-and-aft tilt of the main rotor, non-cyclically.

It was therefore suggested that this feature be temporarily deleted, presumably on No. 1 only, and this was generally agreed, including Col Gregory. For some reason or other it was not incorporated on the remaining three XR-5s and its absence was eventually spotted by a scrupulous Government auditor. As it was still listed equipment, he announced that he was holding up payment until it was installed! Unfortunately it never was installed; neither has a similar system ever been tested.

As mentioned earlier, I customarily stopped in the machine shop and assembly areas in the morning, before going up to my office area, thus keeping daily contact with Carboni and his shop personnel regarding any questions they might have. This particular morning I was a little bit late, and I was hailed by the welding foreman (this being the first area encountered) where they were welding together the circular tube member and fittings that attached the undercarriage leg to the fuselage structure. The welder had questioned a certain angle relative to a fitting, as shown on the drawing, and Carboni had told him to wait for me. Serge came by and asked the welder how the job was proceeding, and the welder explained his problem to Serge, who examined the print and approved the angle shown. However, the welder, as instructed, loyally waited for me and advised me of the foregoing. He had indeed spotted a mistake, but I said nothing about it.

With spring in the offing, the major pressures concerning the necessity of trials and their attendant errors, while urgently endeavouring to solve basic control problems with -300H, were now no longer the order of the day. Instead, Igor and Les found themselves in the relaxing position of enjoying the pastime of experimenting with negotiating all manner of restricted areas and operating from various types of surfaces, as only a helicopter could. Some of these are depicted on Fig 115.

Igor's main intention was to demonstrate the unique capability of a helicopter (power-on) to alight safely almost anywhere in an emergency, a rescue operation, or a direct hospital delivery. In other words it greatly improved the possibility of saving lives, whether its role be civil or military.

In addition, should a power failure occur, the helicopter's rotating wings would automatically continue to rotate, making a safe soft landing possible and allowing a far greater probability of human survival than with a fixed-wing aircraft.

Surprisingly, it proved quite easy to manoeuvre -300H on slimy or sticky mud when equipped with inflated floats. If the mud was exceptionally sticky the helicopter would easily free itself if rocked gently sideways. Similarly, snow or break-through thin ice presented no problems. In each case, however, as expected, more power than usual was needed. Flat roof-top landings and take-offs were also practised easily. Several years later, however, such landings atop tall buildings, where high or gusty winds could occur, did not prove to be entirely satisfactory unless there was a considerable area available, to avoid the wind turbulence created at the edge of the roof.

The most enjoyable restricted landing area demonstration for Les occurred when he used his own backyard (Fig 115). This was really done in response to Igor's often ebullient portrayal of his vision of the 'heeli' of the future. Mrs Morris was not quite so keen on such a vision when she saw her flower beds after the VS-300H's rotor down-wash had hit them.

At that time, the main mental obstacle to overcome when landing a tail-rotored helicopter in any restricted landing area was 'How near is that tail rotor to hitting something?' It might be recalled that this had prompted one of Igor's earliest suggestions; a fan in a vertical fin. There is now a single-main-rotor helicopter being produced that has the tail rotor replaced by compressed-air jets.

For its final configuration, Igor decided to have -300H returned to his favourite, original, three-bladed main rotor version, -300G, as he said he felt more comfortable with the 'feel' produced by the three blades. During this period Alex Krapish continued to be responsible for maintaining -300, also incorporating such changes as the foregoing and any other minor improvements requested by Igor.

Project Engineers were responsible for turning in a progress report each week. This was appreciatively well maintained by Ed Katzenberger, and we reviewed each report together before Ed personally handed it over to Serge Gluhareff, usually to be reviewed with him. Thankfully this was also diplomatically handled by Ed, who, with his calm manner, would satisfactorily answer Serge's queries. On one particular occasion, Serge was not in his office when Ed handed in the report. A while later Serge suddenly appeared in front of my desk, and in full view declared in a loud voice: 'This is just a lot of "Blah – Blah – Blah"!', simultaneously chucking the report on to my desk. He then turned and went back to his office. Both Ed and Edith Framson (the secretary), were left speechless, and so was I.

After a few moments I said I would attend to the matter. Ed, bless him, urged me several times to let him handle the situation, but I decided to do otherwise. As I have already mentioned, from time to time Serge had seen fit to interfere directly and/or disregard the limits of his authority. While this was very upsetting, I had been counselled not to make a fuss about it. However, this open, unwarranted and humiliating attack did not help matters. The meeting ended with my refusing to accept Serge's unreasonable criticisms and assertions. I decided to tick him off in no uncertain terms. I had finally 'lost my cool'. Not that I was above criticism, but I had learned from Igor to accept and respect constructive criticism.

It was not long before there was a noticeable reduction of the usual department noise level, as word spread that Serge had posted my dismissal as Project Engineer on the XR-5 project, and Ed was taking my place. Then, to my utter amazement, almost the entire XR-5 engineering team quietly walked down to the front of Serge's office to protest to him personally and request that he rescind his decision. It was to no avail. I could only later thank them individually (to me inadequately) for their courageous gesture. I told Ed he would, of course, have my full support at any time, if needed.

Curiously, I found myself becoming more and more relaxed as the remainder of that momentous day passed, without any feeling of resentment. After all, other than comparatively minor decisions, the whole project was now making good progress. Also, the estimated roll-out date of June for XR-5 No 1, looked more promising. The project would be in good hands, as Ed was both well liked and well informed. I was granted the next day off.

When I returned, earlier than usual, I found that my desk and belongings had been moved to an office next to Michael's, which included a telephone. It was also closer to Igor's office, which was on the other side of Michael's. This was a meaningful gesture.

As soon as Michael came in he asked me to see him. His first words were: 'It was my brother again, wasn't it, Beel?' I nodded affirmatively. He then went on to say how very sorry he was about what had happened. On the other hand, he had arranged to have me join him as his assistant. He then added, rather wistfully, I thought: 'You see, Beel, I am very glad we are together again, as I know so little about what is going on with the heelicopters now'.

My new assignment was to work with Michael on the design of a small four-seat, enclosed-cabin helicopter embodying all the latest knowledge, plus possible improvements, starting with the rotor hub, its controls, and then the blades; the heart of a helicopter. It was now late March 1943. I was still in charge of the VS-300.

While I very much appreciated being in more frequent contact with Igor and Michael, I felt I needed to breathe fresh air, as it were. It so happened that Don Luscombe was up on one of his visits regarding the YR-4 fuselages he was producing. On the spur of the moment I asked him if he might consider my joining his firm and he said he would give it very serious thought. Several days later he rang me up at home and invited me and my wife to be his guests at his home that coming weekend. It resulted in my accepting his offer of the position of Chief of Design.

Actually, the decision was predicated upon a visit I had made to offer my services to Capt Kossler, Commanding Officer of the newly formed US Coast Guard Helicopter Unit, established at Floyd Bennett Airfield on Long Island, NY. The visit had been arranged by Cdr Frank Erickson, his second-in-command, whom I had first approached because we had established a firm friendship, and who thought well of the idea.

Upon introducing me to his CO he inadvertently chose to remark that I had made my offer because Serge had 'swung at him a couple of times'. I noticed a change in Capt Kossler's expression. He concluded the meeting by saying that, while he admitted I was indeed well qualified to assist them, he felt that I would be of more value if I managed to stay where I was. Poor Frank realised he had made a mistake, and that it was too late to make amends.

Before making the final move (to which my wife agreed), I had a long chat with Michael Buivid and Bob Labensky. Both agreed that my reasoning was justified, and I then approached Michael Gluhareff with my decision. Apparently he had wondered for some time if and when I might reach such a decision.

The next day, after talking to Igor, he suggested I take a 'leave of absence', thus assuring my return. While I greatly appreciated the privilege that this gesture offered, especially as it came from both him and Igor, I preferred to make a clean break, so that, should I return, it would be because I was both wanted and needed. They both understood this, and appreciated it.

I contacted Luscombe, and he agreed to my joining his firm the following month, it being May. I was given a farewell dinner. Then Michael Gluhareff, entirely on his own, presented me with a letter of recommendation ending with: 'His work was always very satisfactory and inventive, and showed his great interest in the subject. Mr Hunt is leaving the employment of Sikorsky Aircraft at his own request, and I am very glad to recommend him as a design engineer of great merit.

Very truly yours,
SIKORSKY AIRCRAFT
(signed) Michael E. Gluhareff
Chief of Design and Research'
A true and trusted friend indeed.

Interlude

I have decided to include the following months with Luscombe since they were closely related with Sikorsky helicopter construction and my continual endeavour to find methods or means of improving and/or simplifying helicopter flight control. In addition, because I was continually kept informed of what was transpiring regarding the XR-5 and -6, I shall include timely news of same.

The town of North Wales, in Montgomery County, State of Pennsylvania, where Luscombe's manufacturing plant was located, was a small rural community, set in fertile farmland some 15 miles north of the state's capital city of Philadelphia. At first I had 'digs' in a famous local old Dutch Colonial inn, before renting a charming farm residence of the same style so that the family could be together.

Before I joined Don Luscombe he had agreed to my suggestion that I start investigating the practicability of a directly controlled, tilting helicopter main rotor hub, eliminating the need for all of the continuously moving parts associated with cyclic control. This was basically demonstrated with the Buivid-Labensky non-cyclic system.

Since my main objective was simplification, I chose to start out with the well established automotive-type universal mechanical joint as the means whereby the main rotor hub could be tilted in any desired direction. Furthermore, this was readily available in various sizes, and functionally designed, both as to type of service demanded and life expectancy. After consulting with several suppliers and users, a heavy duty, truck-type rear-end driving joint was chosen. Like all such joints it was designed to operate under severe weather and road conditions, and was thus well suited to helicopter operation. Regard Figs 116 and 117, and simplicity becomes immediately apparent.

With non-cyclic control, of course, only collective blade pitch changing is necessary (VS-300C). In this case there was to be a further simplification so far as flight control was concerned. An engine-driven governor would monitor increased engine speed/power and automatically increase rotor thrust, exactly as in an automatic variable-pitch aeroplane propeller, and also automatically return it to low pitch in the event of a power failure. (Fig 117)

A further feature was a rotating engine throttle monitoring knob that would enable the pilot, before lift-off, to preset the rotor collective blade angle to allow for variable atmospheric preflight conditions. He could also fine-tune the power output at any time. Also, should a 'jump lift-off' be required, pushing the knob inwards and then downwards automatically called for full power/pitch. The power/pitch synchronisation would be set to allow for necessary power increase before pitch increase.

To carry the throttle management a step further, I proposed to abolish the collective-pitch-throttle lever and replace it with the very familiar automobile foot-operated throttle. It is a well accepted fact that foot-throttle control is both remarkably easy and precise to operate, particularly during lift-off or landing conditions, thus freeing one hand entirely.

There was yet another possible simplification; elimination of the pilot's control stick by placing a similar but much shorter control lever at the front

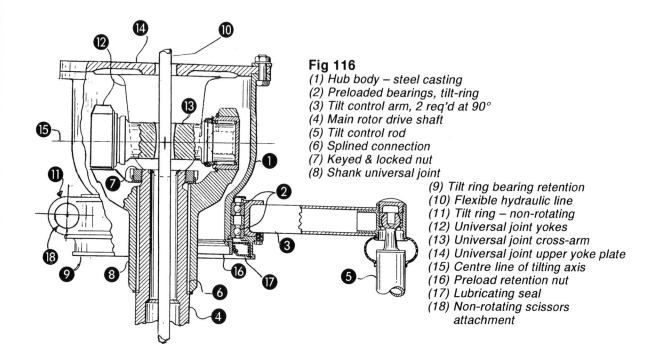

Fig 116
(1) Hub body – steel casting
(2) Preloaded bearings, tilt-ring
(3) Tilt control arm, 2 req'd at 90°
(4) Main rotor drive shaft
(5) Tilt control rod
(6) Splined connection
(7) Keyed & locked nut
(8) Shank universal joint

(9) Tilt ring bearing retention
(10) Flexible hydraulic line
(11) Tilt ring – non-rotating
(12) Universal joint yokes
(13) Universal joint cross-arm
(14) Universal joint upper yoke plate
(15) Centre line of tilting axis
(16) Preload retention nut
(17) Lubricating seal
(18) Non-rotating scissors
attachment

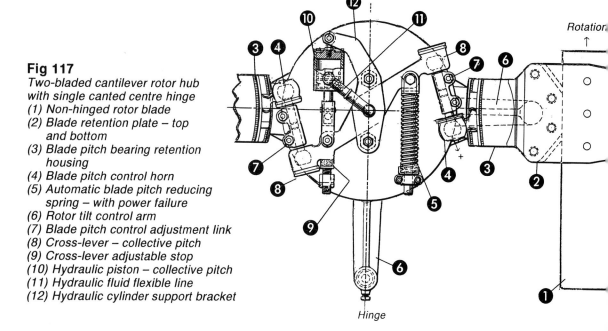

Fig 117
Two-bladed cantilever rotor hub
with single canted centre hinge
(1) Non-hinged rotor blade
(2) Blade retention plate – top
and bottom
(3) Blade pitch bearing retention
housing
(4) Blade pitch control horn
(5) Automatic blade pitch reducing
spring – with power failure
(6) Rotor tilt control arm
(7) Blade pitch control adjustment link
(8) Cross-lever – collective pitch
(9) Cross-lever adjustable stop
(10) Hydraulic piston – collective pitch
(11) Hydraulic fluid flexible line
(12) Hydraulic cylinder support bracket

Rotation

Hinge

end of a right-hand arm rest. That idea was, in fact, Peter de Havilland's. He had proudly showed it to me when I visited England in 1936, as the latest innovation on the company's D.H.87 Hornet Moth. I could now eliminate the two rudder pedals and just twist the flight control lever to the left or right to change direction by changing the pitch of the tail rotor. The new setting would remain locked-in until it was again changed, minimising pilot fatigue.

To make this control comfortably easy to move, a simple reliable hydraulic booster system would be incorporated, manufactured by the Vickers Company. It employed what the company called a follow-up-valve system. As soon as any movement of the control lever was initiated, it moved a sliding valve that allowed oil under pressure to enter a booster cylinder and move its piston and rod, attached to a primary control link, in the desired direction. However, should the booster oil pressure fail, pushing down on a thumb-button on top of the control lever permitted it to be lengthened sufficiently to maintain proper flight control. The hydraulic pressure necessary to activate the follow-up-valve system was powered by a rotor-shaft-driven system so it was not affected by engine failure.

The foregoing was the outline of my proposed new assignment, and would, of course keep me busy for quite some time. As a matter of fact it was exactly what I had planned to do with Michael before I left Sikorsky.

It might be wondered what my work had to do with Luscombe's Sikorsky R-4 war contract. It so happened that, in semi-retirement, he had set up a small private research and development engineering company on his own property, primarily to investigate ways of improving light civil aircraft manufacture. These included a unique approach to producing a simpler method of constructing a stressed-skin metal fuselage, a type that was becoming increasingly popular. It comprised dividing the total skin area into a series of practical rectangular sizes. Each piece had a peripheral narrow flat band, like a frame. Within this bounded flat area, a sheet metal forming press formed a very shallow, domed depression, so shallow that it would only be noticed if seen at certain angles of light. However the depression so measurably increased the stiffness of the rectangular metal sheet that the extra support normally

required with flat sheets could be greatly reduced.

In order to use this method practically and advantageously, the cross-section of the fuselage had to be rectangular, with rounded corners, which provided the most efficient area for maximum useful internal usage. It also allowed the rounded corners to be used as longitudinal stiffening members to which to attach the flat edges of the metal sheets. Another important feature was that, by marking identification information on the inside of each panel, a damaged portion of the fuselage could be quickly replaced. A complete fuselage had been built, as a four-seater, when Pearl Harbor was attacked.

As a result of this work, Luscombe had been sponsoring a militarily oriented project that was the brainchild of a young radio engineer of Polish descent. It was somewhat ahead of its time, and little interest was being shown in it by the military. The device was a bomb remotely controlled by an airborne bombardier, by means of radio signals. A model of the proposed control system had been produced, and was demonstrated by having its rear-mounted external control surfaces moved by an unseen radio operator located a considerable distance away.

With the advent of the Sikorsky work, all engineering activities were consolidated at the new main plant. The bomb project failed to materialise.

At about the same time as my arrival at Luscombe's, on 6 and 7 May 1943, an historic demonstration took place on Long Island Sound, within clear view of the Vought-Sikorsky plant on the Stratford shoreline. Colonel Frank Gregory had arranged, with the collaboration of the US Army Air Force, the Maritime Commission and the War Shipping Administration, to have their respective representatives witness the first ever helicopter landings and lift-offs from a small designated deck area on a sea-going merchant oil tanker. The purpose was to demonstrate the practicability of helicopters as aerial convoy escorts to guard against the devastating German U-boat attacks then taking place, even within a few miles of the US coast.

The seemingly indestructible XR-4 had recently been updated and refurbished with a new, more powerful, 225 hp Warner engine. The rotor blades had been extended another foot (38 ft diameter), increasing load-carrying potential, and a new strengthened gearbox had been fitted. The heli-

Fig 118
Historic first ever helicopter landing on ocean-going vessel. Colonel Gregory precisely lands VS-XR-4 in centre of Bullseye on S.S. Bunker Hill.

copter was mounted on a new set of inflated floats, and had already been thoroughly flight tested by Les Morris by the time Gregory arrived to acquaint himself with a rejuvenated XR-4(b).

During Les's initial landing tests with the new floats, XR-4(b) had exhibited her apparent joy of landing by bouncing around too bumptiously for comfort before settling down to a gently quivering, timed to her main rotor's slight two-per-revs. To reduce the landing bounce, a standard 2x4 in timber crossmember, had been lashed on to each end of the floats (Fig 121). Upon seeing this some-what bizarre 'fix' (it was such a contrast to XR-4's otherwise smart appearance) Frank could not refrain from remarking: 'It made the ship look as though she was wearing a pair of old work shoes'.

The demonstrations were to comprise two distinct phases. On the first day Frank would prac-tise landings and lift-offs from the stationary

anchored tanker *Bunker Hill*, to determine the best side for approach or departure. He would then go through the same procedure with the tanker under way, at ever increasing speeds up to normal cruising speed.

As Frank and Les viewed the *Bunker Hill*, lying close off shore, Les directed Frank's attention to the pilot's house amidships and the space between it and the foremasts. 'Well,' said Les, 'in between those two you are going to land the XR-4.' Frank replied: 'Are you kidding?' The next day, as he approached for the first time, the white 78 x 60 ft framed rectangle that delineated the deck landing area, with a large white circular bullseye at its centre, appeared to be even smaller than he had imagined when he first viewed the tanker from the shore. After hovering over the tanker a few moments, carefully inspecting the cluttered area beneath him, Frank slowly circled the tanker before choosing the port side to cautiously begin his final historic approach, at a downward angle of 45 degrees. Keeping the bullseye centred in the lower front cabin window, he demonstrated his outstanding piloting ability by maintaining both a constant rate of descent and an unwavering flight path to accomplish a truly 'spot-on' landing, XR-4 (b) gently touching down on the bullseye (Fig 118). 'A helicopter, for the first time ever, has landed on the deck of a freighter!' Frank wrote proudly in his book *Anything a Horse Can Do; The Story of the Helicopter.*

Almost immediately *Bunker Hill* got underway, escorted by two small Coast Guard cutters, and a series of 12 lift-offs and landings were successfully accomplished from both sides of the tanker. It was a remarkable feat of piloting, especially as, at the higher speeds, it became increasingly difficult for Frank to cope with the air turbulence set up by the ship's superstructure, mast, and rigging.

Up to about 9 mph tanker speed Frank did not encounter any particular trouble while lifting off or alighting on either side of the ship. However, as speed increased above 10 mph the turbulence created by the superstructure, masts and rigging in the landing area became increasingly hazardous. By the time *Bunker Hill* had reached its top speed of over 20 mph, XR-4 not only began bouncing around while hovering just before landing, but also after landing.

The necessity of placing the operational area at the stern became only too obvious. Only Frank's remarkably steady nerves and hands made such a demonstration possible. Igor was, of course, in attendance, and was very conscious of what Frank was having to overcome. He was unconsciously moving his arms, as though he was actually handling XR-4's controls, during every lift-off and landing.

The next day, 7 May, heralded another historic benchmark for Igor Sikorsky and his 'heelicopters'; the first full dress demonstration before top government, and military officials, gathered to witness and then decide the practicability of convoy escort by helicopter. The witnesses included Richard W. Seabury of the War Shipping Administration; Brig-Gen John W. Franklin of the Army Transportation Corps; Col R.C. Wilson, Chief of Staff of the Army Development Branch; Admiral Stanley Parker of the US Coast Guard; and a valued and greatly respected aviation consultant, Mr Grover Loening. Also in attendance, of course, were Igor and Les.

A low, dense, spring fog had settled over Long Island Sound by the next morning, and *Bunker Hill* was not visible to Frank Gregory as he lifted off XR-4(b) and headed slowly, as only a helicopter is able, in her general direction. In the stillness of that fog-bound morning the assembled officials eagerly awaiting XR-4's appearance could finally hear the unmistakable throbbing of a 'chopper' approaching. Then dramatically XR-4 emerged, its rotor causing the fog to swirl violently in its wake. The gradual appearance of a now familiar grey outline of the tanker was a welcome sight for Frank. He made a slow circuit around her as the onlookers waved their greetings to him. It occurred to him that as the water was so calm, and since nearly all of the assemblage had never seen an amphibious helicopter before, he would demonstrate, as a show opener, a water descent and lift-off, both of which he executed perfectly. Then he once again circled *Bunker Hill* before making a smooth, slow landing in the middle of the bullseye.

As on the day before, *Bunker Hill* immediately got underway and was soon ploughing the Sound at 15 kts (17.3 mph). By now the wind was freshening, coming in about 20 degrees off her port (left) side. This meant that Frank could demonstrate the helicopter's unique ability by lifting itself vertically a few feet above the deck, hovering, and at the same time turning around so that it headed directly into the combined winds. Tilting the rotor gently forward, Frank had XR-4 off and running in a perfectly executed manoeuvre, just as he had performed the day before.

As Frank made further descents and lift-offs (some 22 more), his expertise and daring dramatically increased as the tanker kept changing course and speed, which varied by as much as 18 mph. He demonstrated backwards and sideways departures from both sides (Fig 121) of the tanker, as well as straight-up vertical lift-offs beyond the height of the masts and superstructure. All agreed that the excellent demonstration left no doubt as to the possibility of developing a proper method of using the helicopter for convoy escort.

Soon after the demonstration was over, Col Wilson announced that he had to return immediately to his office in Washington, DC on urgent business. His aeroplane was ready and waiting for him at Bridgeport/Stratford Airport, so Col Gregory quickly had him aboard XR-4 and on his way to the airport, where he was landed right next to the administration building. Thus initiating the first ship-to-shore taxi service, as Frank ferried other members of the official party back to the 'meadow' next to the VS-44 hangar.

'HEELICOPTER' – PIONEERING WITH IGOR SIKORSKY

The demonstration had been indeed a success, and several days later the following statement was issued by Rear-Admiral Howard L. Vickery, Vice-Chairman of the Maritime Commission and Deputy of the War Shipping Administrator:

Under the circumstances existing at the time of the demonstration, of a helicopter's ability to take off and land on the deck of tankers, the United States Marine Commission and the War Shipping Administration believe that the feasibility of the operation had been sufficiently proved. These agencies are now preparing a plan for a small deck to be installed on Liberty Ships without interfering with the cargo arrangement, which will permit helicopters to be used at sea, thus giving the ships added protection against submarines.

Fig 119 *First ever helicopter lift-off with vessel underway. XR-4 has turned 180° hovering over Bullseye, leaving ship from same side on which she landed. 6 May 1943.*

Fig 120 *7 May 1943*
The show-opener. First amphibious military helicopter.

Fig 121
Colonel Gregory makes first ever ship-borne backwards lift-off from Bunker Hill *platform – note 2x4 spreaders (X).*

Thus assured, the next step of acquiring a suitable ship and having an operational platform installed was soon underway. The next series of tests would soon be carried out in the open ocean, when both the updated XR-4 and a preproduction YR-4 were to be used. The X would operate with wheels and the Y with air floats, to establish comparative results.

By the middle of July, when I had made good progress on my assignment, Don Luscombe and I were rewarded by a surprise call from Wright Field. Colonel Gregory suggested that we contact the General Motors (GM) research and development laboratory in Detroit, Michigan, regarding a new one-cycle, liquid-cooled 225 hp aircraft engine they were developing. Apparently interest had been generated in the possible advantages that might be gained by using a liquid-cooled aircraft engine having a simple radiator, which could be enclosed within a smaller area in a helicopter fuselage than would be the case with an aircooled engine, which

had to be fan-cooled and thus required air ducting. Moreover, the GM engine, being a one-cycle type (fuel ignition every one crankshaft rotation), its throttle response would be quicker than that of a two-cycle engine (ignition every two rotations).

So off I went to Detroit. I was to meet a Mr Rippengill, the Chief Engineer in charge of the programme, and before I left I was to have a meeting with Mr Kettering, the General Manager of Research and Development, who was greatly respected internationally for his outstanding contributions to the automotive industry. Evidently it was he who had generated the interest in the engine.

This turned out to be a most interesting and rewarding contact. In the first place the engine was quite unique in concept. It had been dubbed the 'X' engine because its eight cylinders were cast in four individual pairs, one in front of the other, and when spaced radially 90 degrees apart, they took the form of an X. Furthermore, each pair had but a single, domed, cylinder head, for the following reasons.

Usually, with a one-cycle engine, each piston on its downstroke compresses the air, now mixed with fuel, below the piston, into an individually divided (per cylinder) airtight crankcase compartment. The mixture is then allowed to flow up into the cylinder area above the piston. At that point the piston would begin its up-stroke, further compressing the air-fuel mixture. At the top of its up-stroke, a spark plug ignites the fuel-air mixture, which immediately starts the piston on its down-stroke to repeat the cycle all over again. This eliminates timing camshafts, valves, springs, etc.

However, the Rippengill system, with its paired cylinders having a common domed head for fuel ignition, not only eliminated the need for a separate timing system, but also the necessity for a pressurised, compartmented crankcase. This was ingeniously accomplished by having a single, double-acting crankshaft.

In other words, the rear cylinder piston's up-and-down crankshaft strokes were delayed or advanced by having its portion of the crankshaft offset with respect to that portion of the crankshaft actuating the movement of the front cylinder piston. This was arranged so that both pistons would arrive precisely together at the top of their strokes. At that point the spark plug would ignite the compressed fuel-air mixture. The rear piston then descended faster than the front piston, and towards the bottom of its stroke it uncovered the exhaust port and let the exhaust gases escape. Finally, shortly after the front piston had begun its up-stroke, the front cylinder intake port was momentarily opened to allow entry of the compressed air-fuel mixture. Both pistons then began to compress the mixture simultaneously, arriving together at the top and thus completing one revolution or cycle.

There was just one more requirement; delivering the correct amount of compressed air-fuel mixture. That was accomplished by means of a centrifugal blower attached to the rear end of the crankshaft. At first, even mixture flow at various shaft speeds was not attained, causing rough engine performance. The problem was solved by making an almost 4 in-diameter hole through the outer surface of the blower casing and covering it with a rubberised flexible diaphragm. From the centre of the diaphragm, a light tubular control rod was attached. The other end of the rod went to a valve that controlled air-fuel flow to the cylinders. Thus any change in air pressure was immediately sensed, and the air-fuel flow monitored.

All of this was carefully explained to me by Mr Rippengill as he conducted me on a tour of the completely self-contained facilities, including an engineering department, machine shop and engine test cells. As we left for lunch in a company Chevrolet four-door sedan, he casually remarked that the car was a trial test vehicle that was used as often as possible to test reliability and throttle response. He demonstrated this several times on the journeys to and from lunch. The car had an exceptionally smooth and rapid acceleration. Upon arrival back at the plant he asked me if I would like to see the 'special set-up' under the hood. There, down in the middle of the space normally taken up by the engine, etc, was an 'X' engine half the size of its aircraft counterpart, yet producing 110 hp.

We then concentrated on the operational requirements of GM's 225 hp aircraft engine when installed in a helicopter, which were obviously close to those required in automobiles. This was the reason for Mr Kettering's interest in the first place. Fuel consumption was a major concern, and I was shown test results which compared favourably with comparable two-cycle aircraft engines. All told, I was greatly impressed, and said I would so report to Don Luscombe. We would then contact Mr Kettering regarding possible collaboration for a militarily-sponsored R & D programme.

My meeting with Mr Kettering was most cordial and enlightening. He enthusiastically sought answers to questions covering aspects of engine adaptation, field maintenance, etc, and also the attainable reliability of such a mechanical bird as the helicopter, with respect to possible future peacetime commercial market acceptance. The meeting ended with my expressing similar comments to those I had made to Mr Rippengill, which obviously pleased him, as he hoped he would have the pleasure of collaborating with us.

As a result of the foregoing, Don asked me to come up with an initial general outline of what might be an acceptable programme to the military. In subsequent talks we agreed upon a programme that would include implementing some of my proposed simplification ideas, mainly to the rotor hub. This outline was sent to Mr Kettering, to which he also agreed.

Not long after my visit to GM, Don was chatting with a neighbourly acquaintance, a Mr Robert Bowse, concerning the foregoing. It so happened that Mr Bowse had a close friend, Mr Ditter, who was a long-standing and respected member of

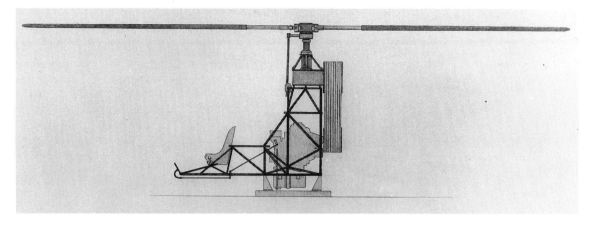

First stage

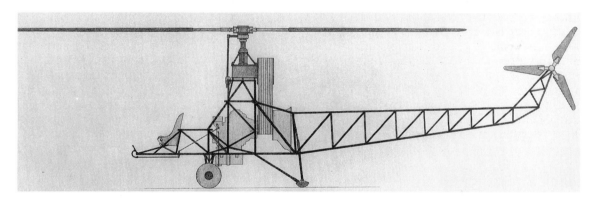

Second stage

Final stage

Fig 122 *Proposed Luscombe-Hunt experimental helicopter.*

Possible post-war model with retractable undercarriage

Amphibious safety feature

Fig 123

Congress, and Mr Bowse asked him what he might suggest as to the next step that should be taken, he said he would give it some thought.

In the meantime I got busy on the details of the engineering required for the proposal, which was basically to include three stages (Fig 122). The first stage would be a static test period, embodying the welded tubular forward and centre fuselage structural sections that would support the powerplant and its controls, the driving system, the main and tail rotor transmissions, and the main rotor hub, blades (R-4) and controls. This complete assembly would be mounted on a base, the attachment points to it having gauges on them to monitor loads generated by the various elements involved.

The second stage would have the necessary additional components added so that it could be used as a basic flight-test vehicle. Finally stage three would test the acceptability of the aerodynamic shape. All of this was obviously taken from both pre-and-VS-300 experience. (Fig 123)

We shall now catch up with a bit of late news, that I should have reported, that took place in mid-May 1943 when the first YR-4 had achieved another historic first, celebrating the 25th anniversary of the first civilian airmail route, started on 15 May 1918, by becoming the first helicopter to deliver official mail directly from the USA's Capitol terrace in Washington, DC, to a waiting commercial airliner at the capital's Airport, on 16 May 1943.

This accomplishment followed another first, when, several days earlier, both XR-4 with Maj Cooper piloting, and Col Gregory, piloting the YR-4 with Adolph Plenefisch, the official mechanic, as a passenger, flew in 'formation' from Stratford, Connecticut, to Fort Monmouth, New Jersey, to run special mission tests for the US Army Signal Corps. After a flight lasting 1½ hrs they made an unplanned spur-of-the-moment cheeky landing 'right at the base of the flag pole, a few feet away from the front door of headquarters'. All of the tests were successfully accomplished.

The preparations for the next series of tests to establish the feasibility of helicopter convoy duty, were finalised on USA's Independence Day, 4 July 1943. They had suffered a slight delay. It could have been more involved, not to say embarrassing, had Col Gregory not stopped by, purely by chance, to inspect the almost completed operational platform. The forward end of it had obviously been

placed too close to the two huge kingposts for the two rear cranes. This was quickly remedied by extending the platform further to the rear, but it was an example of the usual bureaucratic 'expert's' unwillingness to consult with the user first.

The particular ship chosen for the demonstration was a former transatlantic luxury liner, renamed the *James Parker*, which had been converted into a non-luxury troop transport. She would depend a great deal upon her speed and manoeuvrability to thwart the increasing danger of U-boat attack.

Now upgraded, Lt-Col Cooper was piloting the XR-4, and Lt Peterson the YR-4, on which he had just completed his pilot training at the Sikorsky plant. They arrived and hovered over the *James Parker*, still at dockside, right on schedule. Cooper landed first, Peterson following as soon as the XR-4 had been moved aside to make room for him. This was the first ever landing of two helicopters on such a restricted shipboard operational area.

At noon the next day, 5 July 1943, the *James Parker* cast off from her berth and several tugs moved her downstream past the Statue of Liberty in order to drop anchor in open water at the mouth of the Hudson River, and at the same time both pilots took advantage of the opportunity to make practice landings and lift-offs while the ship was in motion. Both pilots then spent the remainder of the afternoon practising while at anchor, along with Les Morris.

That evening a small flotilla of motor launches ferried the official spectators out to the *James Parker* in readiness for the next day's open-sea trials. Prominent among them were Brigadier-Generals B.W. Chidlaw and J.W. Franklin; Colonels E.E. Aldin (1st Sea-Search Attack Group) and E.H. Nelson (HQ Army Air Forces); Cdr J.S. Russel (representing the US Navy); and Wg Cdr R.A.C. Brie of the British Air Commission, who, it will be recalled, had been the first to land a rotating-wing aircraft on a ship, 20 years earlier. Government officials included R.W. Seabury (War Shipping Administration); Doctors E.L. Bowles and D.T. Griggs (Secretary of War's Office); and L. Hagemayer (official photographer from the War Department). Of course, Igor Sikorsky and Les Morris were also on board. Only one US Navy observer was aboard, and he actually had no direct contact with the helicopter programme, whereas Capt Kossler and Cdr

Fig 124
Colonel Gregory is first to land YR-4 on S.S. James Parker while underway, 5 July 1943.

Erickson of the US Coast Guard (under US Navy control), who were directly involved, were not present! Official US Navy interest was initially slow in recognising the helicopter's potential.

The first day was almost a repeat of the *Bunker Hill* trials, beginning with the *James Parker* anchored, and then underway as she proceeded out to sea, which produced only a small amount of roll with which the helicopter pilots had to contend. This was an ideal start for the *ab initio* pilots Cooper, Hermes and Peterson. The question of wheel gear versus air-floats remained unresolved, except that the wheel gear was far easier to handle on deck, but the float gear did not slip or roll after

landing. In any case, the stern location of the operations deck was obviously the correct location for it. (Fig 124)

The second day was more like that which the observers had come to witness. The ship was blanketed in an early-morning fog, and there was a freshening breeze. The pilots were soon having to contend with pitching and rolling conditions that, as the sea became rougher, finally built up to 10 degrees of roll, with 40 mph winds. Both pilots and aircraft were able to cope with these conditions without incurring any particular difficulties.

There was one anxious moment when Lt Hermes attempted a landing which was witnessed by Miller Wacks. Since YR-4 was mounted on inflated floats, Col Gregory would make his final approach by coming in well above the platform. He would then come to a hovering stop directly above his intended landing spot, and make a vertical landing.

Lt Hermes, on the other hand, having a wheel-type undercarriage, would make his approach more as though he was piloting a fixed-wing aircraft, making a power-on downward glide, starting well above and away from the edge of the platform, until wheel contact was made.

This time the main forward wheels touched down very close to the edge of the platform, leaving all the rest of the helicopter protruding out over the turbulent water. At that point (as Hermes later related) he pulled up on the CPL as quickly and as far as he could to get maximum vertical lift, but nothing happened. Turbulent air over the edge of the platform was pinning YR-4 down.

With great presence of mind he managed to turn YR-4 some 90 degrees so that it finally slid off over the side of the platform, with the CPL still calling for maximum lift. It took hold at the very last moment, only a few feet above the water, but high enough for Hermes to regain control. Undaunted, he then made a successful normal landing. It was a very close call, but was handled with prompt and level-headed judgement.

While the sea and wind conditions did not get worse, further flights had to be abandoned when driving rain set in. The one key factor at that time was the lack of adequate abrasive protection for the leading edge of the outer portion of the rotor blade, because the rate of rotation of the outer portion of the blade exceeds 250–300 mph.

The ship was manoeuvred through all points to the wind so that all types of wind turbulence were created over the platform throughout the entire test period, which totalled some 20 hrs. During that period, 162 combined lift-offs and landings were successfully made, and the helicopters were flown both with and without passengers. Their gross weight varied from 2,250 to 2,500 lb, with corresponding disc loadings (gross weight/total rotor area) varying from 1.92-to-2.2 lb/sq ft, and power loading (gross weight/horsepower) from 10.2 to 11.4 lb/horsepower. The latter was considered a safe maximum at that time, owing to the relatively light disc loading.

The entire exercise was acclaimed as being most encouraging, and definitely worth pursuing further. In the afternoon of the second day the shoreline of Long Island became close enough for Col Cooper, piloting XR-4 (his 245 lb ruled out a passenger), along with Lts Peterson and Hermes in YR-4 to lift off from the flight deck of the *James Parker* for the last time and head for the meadow next to the VS-44 hangar at the Sikorsky plant. It was a proud moment for all concerned, especially Frank Gregory, Igor Sikorsky and Les Morris.

Soon after this historic event the first XR-5 was rolled out for her first run-up, to check all the mechanical drives, lubricating systems, power-plant, controls, etc., before attaching and running up the main rotor blades. Enough adjustments were needed to keep her in the shop, including further run-ups, until mid-August, when she made her maiden lift-off with Les Morris at the controls.

In the meantime, through Mr Bowse's friend, Congressman Ditter, it had been arranged for me to see a Cdr Klopp at the Navy Bureau of Aeronautics in Washington, DC. The purpose of the meeting was to ascertain the Navy's possible interest in the proposed programme I was preparing. While he could not speak for other than himself, he encouraged us to continue with our present approach, and to keep him informed of its progress. At that point I was doing all the preliminary design work, just as I had done previously for Igor. There will be more news relating to this before long.

You may recall that the reason for the Army considering an additional experimental helicopter programme to that of the first major Government helicopter investment (in nearly 20 years) in the Platt-Le Page XR-1, was two-fold. Firstly, it was to be a basic helicopter trainer. Secondly, the XR-1 was unfortunately taking a great deal longer than expected to overcome its initial flight problems. In the meantime the original, cumbersome, non-cyclic XR-4 control system was discarded as -300G finally overcame the basic problems connected with full cyclic control. So the Army then decided to use the XR-4, incorporating the much-desired full cyclic control system, as a back-up to the XR-1. Finally, as the XR-1 programme became further delayed and the XR-4 successfully demonstrated its potential, it was upgraded as the XR-4A, with more power and an increased rotor diameter. That led to the awarding of the pre-production YR-4 contract, soon to be followed by further upgrading to the YR-4A, and ending up with the production contracts for R-4s.

The above resumé provides a reminder of how fortunate it was that Col Frank Gregory had the courage to follow his long-shot premonition of the need for some sort of additional back-up to the

XR-1 contract by initiating the XR-5 project, a year ahead, on 8 May 1942. For it was not until June 1943 that XR-1, piloted by Gregory, was able to fly a full closed-circuit course for the first time, and only then at reduced speed. XR-5 made its first lift-off only two months later, in August.

It was somewhere around this time that I heard that Nik Nikolsky had also decided to part company with Sikorsky. Apparently he was not too happy with the circumstances then prevailing. At any rate, he found a much more congenial atmosphere at Princeton University in New Jersey, where he took up residence as a professor in the Mathematics Department. It was not long before he was lecturing, in early 1944, on the 'Theory of Helicopter Design' before groups of engineers representing the US Army Air Forces, the US Navy Bureau of Aeronautics and a number of representatives from various aircraft manufacturers. He later published these lectures in book form, via the Princeton University Press.

Nik was one of the younger members of the Russian post-revolution immigrants, who ended up with Igor Sikorsky. He had been an officer in the Imperial Russian Navy, and had escaped to France and then come to the USA. He was a nephew of Prince Yusupoff, one of those chiefly responsible for disposing of the notorious monk Rasputin. Nik was a most engaging person with whom to engage in conversation and had a delightful sense of humour once the ice was broken. Sadly he succumbed to cancer while still relatively young. He was also a graduate of the Massachusetts Institute of Technology in Boston.

Evidently it was not uncommon for Nik to dine with the Sikorskys from time to time, as he related the following domestic vignette. On one such occasion the staff was on holiday, and while Mrs Sikorsky was quite willing to prepare light meals, she drew the line when it came to coping with the dirty dishes. So when Nik helped to clear the dining table, he was confronted in the kitchen by a considerable mound of dishes and cutlery, carefully covered by a sheet, under which the settings just used were also placed. In the past this had apparently occasioned an acute shortage of dinnerware, requiring the immediate purchase of additional items. It would also result in some rather bizarre utensil arrangements.

It is now 18 August 1943 and another historic day for XR-5 No1, the latest offspring of Igor Sikorsky's burgeoning family of helicopters. She was the largest direct-lifting single-main-rotor helicopter so far, and was destined to be a distinct step forwards and upwards, towards creating larger, more useful helicopters. This was possible now that the basic functional helicopter design requirements were better understood and sufficiently tested.

After several weeks of run-ups and adjustments, she was now ready to attempt her first lift-off in the experienced hands of Les Morris. It would be the third time that Les had piloted an experimental helicopter on its very first lift-off. Closely watching him, Igor will, in spirit, also have his hands on those same controls.

Les told me later that he wondered just how different XR-5 would be from VS-300 and XR-4, and how much of what he already knew was going to be of help to him, as he settled into the pilot's seat, behind the observer's seat. His first reaction as he looked around him was the feeling that he was sitting inside a huge fishbowl, because there was such a tremendous supply of external vision. He had sat inside the cabin several times before, but always when the aircraft was in a closely restricted area.

Next he reacquainted himself with all the instrumentation, and moved all the controls, before calling out 'Clear?' to Adolf Plenefisch. Upon receiving his answering call of 'Clear', Les turned on the ignition switch and engaged the starter. There were several revolutions before the deep throated throbbing of the 450 hp Wasp Junior took hold.

Les waited for the engine gauges to indicate the required operational temperatures before releasing the main rotor brake and gradually revved up the engine, so that the centrifugal clutch would automatically engage the driveshaft and start slowly turning the main and tail rotors. At the same time, with the directional foot pedals, he adjusted the thrust on the tail rotor to counteract the main rotor torque, which was steadily building up as the rotor turned faster.

Gradually, with his left hand, Les began to raise the main rotor pitch control lever (which automatically also increased power) so as to detect any movement that required inordinate control stick adjustment from its normal neutral position. This was soon experienced, just as XR-5 finally broke free of the ground and immediately started to drift to the left. Instantaneously Les moved the stick to his right, noting the degree of movement, and immediately landed. Like VS-300, it had been a very fleeting first lift-off.

As mentioned earlier, the vertical location of the centre of thrust of the tail rotor, relative to its distance above the CG of the helicopter, determined how much influence it had on tilting the aircraft to one side. That was the cause for the control stick adjustment. With the control stick duly adjusted, Les repeated similar lift-offs three more times before he became acquainted with the XR-5's initial erratic and rough behaviour. On his fourth try, however, with a very concentrated effort, Les managed to keep the helicopter just above ground, as she 'swayed elephant-like' for a first flight of 1 min 25 sec. It was a demonstration of the pilot's exceptional co-ordination.

The initial roughness of those first flight efforts was directly associated with the first all-wood main rotor blades and the non-adjusted lead-lag hydraulic blade dampers. Apparently the outermost portion of the blade was bending upwards too far. This was remedied by adding additional spanwise weight to the outer portion of the blades. With the dampers and blades readjusted, XR-5 was back in the air 12 days later, on 30 August 1943. The following message was wired to Wright Field:

Aircraft flown for a total of 33 minutes 25 seconds. longest flight approximately 9 minutes. Following revisions had been made subsequent to test flight August 18: blades recovered, redoped, repainted, rebalanced, approximately five pounds of Woods Metal added to taper section of blade at leading edge to decrease excessive bending noted in previous tests . . . general behavior of ship smoother than at any time previous . . . flights included backward and forward flight at approximately 12 to 15 miles per hour. Sideways flights made indicated adequate control.

The first XR-5 had made a remarkably promising beginning.

On 13 September XR-5 lifted ten persons and hovered a few feet above the ground; pilot and passenger, plus four each side astride the main cantilever undercarriage legs. This was possible because the vertical lift of the rotor was being greatly augmented by the rotor wash, which was rebounding from the ground back up under the rotor, thus forming an air cushion (ground effect)

under the rotor. Nevertheless, psychologically it was an encouraging demonstration, for it meant that XR-5 was capable of gaining sufficient forward speed to transport a similar useful load at normal cruising altitudes, prompting this wire to Wright Field:

[XR-5-No1] TOOK OFF TODAY WITH TEN PERSONS ON BOARD AND STILL SOME RESERVE POWER. USEFUL LOAD WAS 600 POUNDS ABOVE CONTRACT.

A little less than a month later, on 11 October, Les was able to boost this encouraging news when he demonstrated before Col Gregory the considerable additional progress that had been made. He made a smooth, rapid vertical lift-off to about 15 ft (out of ground effect) hovered there for several moments, then suddenly made another rapid vertical climb at 800 ft/min for an additional 100 ft. After pausing there a few moments, he smoothly accelerated rapidly up to an indicated 75 mph. Obviously very pleased, Gregory eagerly climbed aboard and buckled himself into the observer's seat in front of Les, who repeated the manoeuvres, much to Frank Gregory's delight. Frank remarked several times about the extraordinary feeling he had, sitting there in front, with nothing between him and the ground. It was just as he imagined a bird would feel, with such a complete range of clear vision.

Having carefully noted the movements of the flight controls as Les performed the demonstration, Frank then took over the dual controls. At first XR-5 was so very different from the YR-4 that it took him a little time before he had mastered his new mount and was able to duplicate Les's routine.

Upon landing they changed positions, and Frank then proceeded to skilfully put -5 through all the various flight manoeuvres unique to the helicopter, including its present high-speed limit of 75 mph. Upon landing he expressed his satisfaction with -5's excellent performance and ample power reserve.

The very next day, Igor's nephew Jimmy Viner, who had been training on XR-4 and YR-4 and had recently started to fly XR-5, had just lifted-off with a passenger to run some additional tests. As he reached about 75 ft altitude there was a sudden loud bang, as about 4 ft of the tail cone, just forward of the tail rotor, was smashed off, and left dangling by its control cables, together with the tail rotor.

Immediately, the whole aircraft began to revolve in the same direction as the main rotor, (there being no anti-torque from the tail rotor). But Jimmy did not panic, as he skilfully made a relatively soft landing in spite of the revolving fuselage. However, as the left main undercarriage wheel struck the ground the leg buckled back against the fuselage, causing XR-5 to tilt over and permitting the still turning rotor blades to slam into the ground. Miraculously, both occupants escaped uninjured. Total damage to the aircraft was assessed at 25%. Luckily, XR-5 No2 already had started her initial test flying, on Thanksgiving Day 1943, with Les at the controls.

Subsequent inspection revealed that one of the tail rotor blades suffered a failure of its pitch changing axle, because it had not been manufactured according to the required specifications.

Only three days after the shocking temporary loss of the first XR-5, Ralph Alex's XR-6 was made ready for its first lift-off on 15 October 1943, with Les Morris piloting her. Like VS-300, XR-4 and XR-5 No1, she was reluctant to commit herself to no more than one foot of altitude for a few brief seconds. Three problems needed immediate attention. The pilot's control stick wobbled around in a circular path so vigorously that it was all Les could do to use it; the rudder pedals were uncomfortably stiff to operate, and the CPL had a continuously heavy download.

During the next 40 days XR-6 tried its best to make things difficult for Alex and Plumb. The transmission overheated at forward flight up to 70 mph (maximum), and there was still excessive vibration. The total accumulated flying time during those 40 days, amounted to only 1 hr 25 min. Consequently, Col Gregory paid a visit on 27 November, determined to see for himself just what was still bothering XR-6. It took both him and Les, simultaneously handling their flight control sticks, to fly her, she was shaking too much. Finally, before he left, a load lifting test was made. She managed to hover in ground effect, à la XR-5, with six persons aboard, but it was still not to be 'her day'.

Meanwhile, on 15 October at Luscombe's, we had finished our informal research and development proposal for the US Navy and had submitted it to Capt Klopp. Mr Bowse had also been very

busy in Washington, DC, and advised us that he had arranged another meeting, again through Congressman Ditter, this time with the Chairman of the Appropriations Committee regarding the possibility of allocating funds for the necessary manufacturing facilities, should our R & D contract proposal be awarded. By now I was beginning to see and understand the meaning of 'whom you know'.

The meeting took place in a small office so as not to attract attention, as apparently a new appropriation Bill was in the process of being written, and, as usual, a number of special requests were being asked of the chairman. In our case, however, the increasing interest of the military in the helicopter, not to mention the recent successful demonstrations on the *James Parker*, had helped considerably to generate sufficient interest for Chairman Powers to listen to my brief presentation of our proposal. He agreed to take the matter up with certain other members.

Then Robert Bowse, who was very interested in doing all he could to help further our cause, mentioned our R & D proposal to another friend. That friend, it turned out, was a special assistant to Mr Pugh, President of the Sun Oil Company. It appeared that Mr Pugh, like other industrialists, was beginning to consider the extent to which this war-based machinery could be used to advantage in a peacetime economy. The idea had been suggested to him of entering the new potential helicopter market, perhaps by manufacturing a main rotor hub system such as I was proposing. So a meeting was arranged, which Bob Anderson, Don Luscombe's consulting engineer, and I would attend.

It was a very private boardroom meeting with Mr Pugh, his son Howard, Bob and myself. Mr Pugh was of medium height, thin and energetic, while his son was tall, heavy and methodical. First they showed us photos of the fully equipped facilities they had in mind and would employ a workforce of several hundred. They then asked our views regarding the possible future helicopter market potential.

Before specifically answering their question, I asked if they would first consider developing a helicopter hub such as I was proposing, that would encompass several sizes. Yes, they replied, they had that in mind. My next question was how long a development period would they be willing to consider. A year; possibly two? I could tell by their expressions that they were beginning to reassess their original thoughts. I then went on to explain how very new operational helicopter requirements were, especially regarding reliability and functional life expectancy, for a helicopter was far more of a mechanical bird than a fixed-wing aircraft. While present operational performance gave promise of a possible, practical commercial market, I added, it should be tempered by realising that, even at that time, fewer than 100 helicopters had been produced, almost all of them for the military. Anderson concurred.

The Pughs looked at us very intently for quite a few moments. Then Mr Pugh quietly said how very much he appreciated truly honest, experienced opinion, and that we had indeed given them much about which to think and assess. Not too long after that meeting, Don Luscombe received a very cordial letter thanking us for our time and wisdom, which had brought the Pughs to the timely decision

Fig 125
Her last curtain call 7 October 1943.
Igor and -300 deliver the ultimate package.

not to pursue the matter further. At first Don had mixed feelings, but he soon agreed it would be too much of a gamble for both parties.

I have kept one item until last in this chapter, because it marked the end of VS-300's four years of unique and historic life. Igor parted with his beloved VS-300 with great reluctance, mixed with pride and fond memories, on 7 October 1943. As indeed, I too would also miss her.

It was fitting that, on the previous day, it was Alex Krapish, one of Igor's 1923 team, with Jim Maxwell his assistant, who for the last time made the final adjustments to his charge, the VS-300Ha. He had inherited her from Adolf Plenefisch, and had been in charge of incorporating all the subsequent changes, including some of his own, that finally made -300 look so trim and attractive.

On the morning of the 7th, VS-300Ha was reactivated for her final performance. Les lifted her off from Ford Airport at Dearborn, Michigan, to land her in the centre of the uniquely helicopter type airport designated as the demonstration area, a roped-off section located on the front lawn of the Ford Museum and measuring 100 x 300 ft, which was in fact, barely 300 yards from the airport. The

area was bounded on one side by the Museum, and on the other three sides by standing room for the spectators, including a grandstand for the invited guests.

By 1.30 p.m. several thousand spectators had arrived, as well as Henry Ford Senior with Mrs Ford, their son Henry Junior, top executives of the Ford Motor Company, and honoured guests Igor I. Sikorsky and Mr and Mrs Charles A. Lindbergh.

At this point, the start of the show was announced, as Les climbed into -300's cockpit for his final demonstration. In her final version, as VS-300-Ha, she had a wire basket on the front with a direction wind vane attached to it, and a probe sticking out beyond the basket (see Fig 125).

The show started with Les, Alex Krapish and Jim Maxwell going through the engine starting and warm-up routine. Then the 300 lifted off vertically to about 10 ft, moved slowly forward – hovered, bowed respectfully to the occupants of the grandstand, flew backwards to the starting point, hovered a few moments, and then proceeded to make a figure eight.

To demonstrate the precision of which she was capable, Les had Alex and Jim stand some 50 ft apart, each holding an outstretched hand straight up, with the palm facing forward. VS-300 then proceeded slowly to approach Alex first, and gently placed its probe in the centre of his palm. She then moved backwards slowly a few feet at the same height, then moved sideways slowly until she was directly in front of Jim, where she performed the same manoeuvre with him, maintaining a constant height. This was repeated several times, each time a little faster, and was followed by another figure eight in the opposite direction.

Next, Alex had placed a one-foot square of white cloth in front of the grandstand. VS-300 promptly hovered above it, then slowly descended and gently placed her left main undercarriage wheel in its centre.

For Les's finale, he dutifully plucked a 12 in ring from the top of a pole and delivered it to Alex, followed by another precise landing on the cloth square, this time with the right wheel, to the accompaniment of much applause.

Then, for the grand finale, Igor climbed aboard his faithful -300 for their last flight together. A cheer went up as she rose smoothly on her last lift-off, hovered a few moments, then slowly turned and circled over to where Alex was waiting with a large package of souvenir postcards. With the familiar precision that he and -300 had so patiently achieved together over the past four years, Igor precisely placed the basket directly under the package while hovering, so Alex only had to drop it in. He then made a short delivery flight over to the grandstand – hovered a few moments – then slowly descended vertically to make a soft, perfectly executed landing.

Igor reached down and switched off the engine, unbuckled his seat belt and waited for the rotors to stop turning, seemingly oblivious to the loud applause, for what was running through his mind (he told me much later) was the realisation that time had finally caught up with him.

His first attempt to master the art of direct vertical flight had ended in failure. Now, 33 years later, he had reluctantly turned -300's engine ignition switch off for the last time. For it was she that had so faithfully endured the rough passage of his search for the final successful solution, which had made possible her faultless behaviour that afternoon. It was indeed an historic ending for the first ever practical, single-main-rotor, direct-lift type helicopter.

After climbing down from the cockpit, Igor reached out and, as a parting gesture, fondly patted -300, remarking to Les, the first to join him: 'She was a good ship, a sweet little ship'.

This brings us to the end of 1943, and our first Christmas away from home, this time in beautiful rural Pennsylvania in a picturesque, centuries old, large, warm, stone farmhouse with an 8 ft-wide fireplace, 6 ft Yule logs aglow, and three stockings, also for the first time, hanging above it.

Before I go any further, it is my intention to keep an even flow of up-to-date Sikorsky activities interspersed between current Luscombe events.

Chapter Seven
1944

YR-4 Errand of Mercy – Luscombe Activity – XR-5 No 2 Test Flight – XR-6 No 1 March Flight – U.S. Army Briefing – Return to Sikorsky – Renewed Status and New Assignments

On the third day of the New Year of 1944 an errand of mercy was performed that brought national attention to the helicopter, exactly in a manner Igor Sikorsky had predicted as being one of its keynotes. It also highlighted the little-known helicopter activity of the US Coast Guard Air Unit stationed at Floyd Bennett Field, Long Island, under Cdr Frank A. Erickson.

Without any warning, a terrible explosion blew apart a US Navy destroyer in the Atlantic Ocean, just off the New Jersey coast, opposite Sandy Hook. Many members of its crew were killed instantly, and many others, including the wounded, were hurled into the icy waters. Prompt Coast Guard action had saved almost all of them, and emergency hospitals were set up on the beaches. A critical message immediately went out; 'Send us blood plasma – urgent'.

To make matters even worse, there was considerable wind and snow plus mist with which to contend, but not sufficient to ground a helicopter. Within minutes, Cdr Erickson had warmed up a Sikorsky YR-4 and was on his way to the little lawn at historic Battery Park, at the mouth of the Hudson River, where cases of plasma were quickly loaded aboard. Within a few minutes he was able to fly directly to the emergency hospitals on the beach at Sandy Hook and land beside them. This effort made possible the saving of lives that otherwise would have been lost due to delayed ground travel. Considerably more will be said about Cdr Erickson in this chapter.

About mid-December 1943 at Luscombe's I had started to look into the feasibility of a scaled-down version of the Sikorsky R-5 as a lighter, purely light scout/observation two-seat helicopter that could be used by either the Army or the Navy. The main idea was to reduce maintenance and increase reliability by using the direct-tilting hub and the General Motors engine, or an equivalent aircooled aircraft engine.

It was now almost the end of January 1944, and preliminary enquiries at Wright Field had resulted in our receiving encouraging responses. In the meantime, our tireless advocate Robert Bowse had also started making similar enquiries in Washington, DC, and had found similar interest. A briefing was possible in several weeks.

To that end, on 26 January Igor was able to inform Col Gregory at Wright Field that both XR-5 No2, and XR-6 No1, were showing signs of improvement, especially the former, which now had 8½ hours of flight time to its credit. During that time an important improvement had been made by noticeably reducing the flight control stick forces. Igor reported: 'This aircraft is performing exceedingly well, and demonstrating good flight characteristics'.

The main problem, from the outset, had been the considerable frictional forces associated with the double-acting screwjacks. It transpired that the original manufacturer had never before had occasion to produce such an item, though at that time the company had not evidenced any concern as to

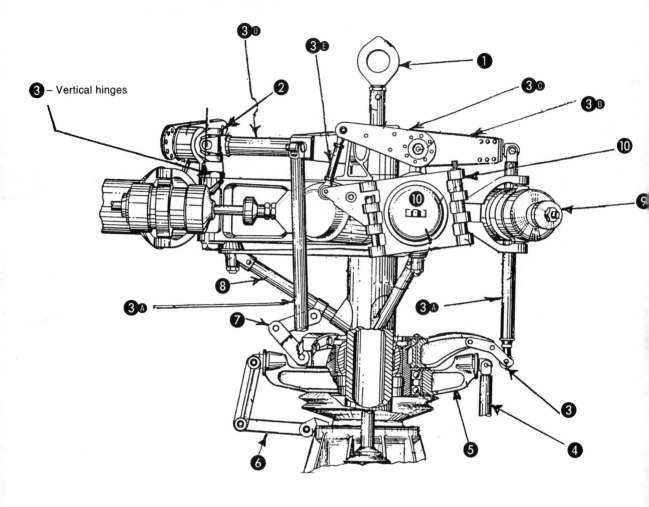

3 – Vertical hinges

Fig 126
XR-5 Main rotor hub
(1) Lifting eye
(2) Universal joints at vertical hinges
(3) Rotating-tilting cyclic blade pitch control arm
(3A) Blade pitch control link – outer
(3B) Blade pitch control inner crank arm
(3C) Blade pitch control outer crank arm
(3D) Blade pitch control torque tube
(3E) Blade pitch control – inner
(4) Tilt control – static
(5) Tilting cyclic blade pitch control arm – static
(6) Static scissors
(7) Rotating scissors
(8) Blade support
(9) Lead-lag blade damper
(10) Blade root attachment

its ability so to do. As a result, insufficient time was devoted to developing accurate tooling and proper machining methods. However, by the time the US Army production order was in hand, much of the problem had been solved.

The immediate problem had been solved by introducing a gimbal-mounted, three-pronged star, on top of the hub, just below the LIFTING EYE (1) Fig. 126. That had three tension springs linked to the three similarly rotating upper swash-plate, cyclic blade pitch control arms (3). The springs provided sufficient downward load relief on the screwjacks as to make the control stick forces manageable. Later, blade pitch reducing forces, coupled with corrected production methods, produced acceptable control forces.

Fig. 126, correctly depicts the XR-5 control system, as finalised for shop production. Which also prompts me to include two photos. The rotor hub cyclic control system (Fig. 127), and the view

(VertiFlite)

Fig 127
*Russian Mil Mi-10 transport helicopter main rotor
hub. This rotor hub is a direct copy of the hub I
used on the Sikorsky R-5 and S-51 helicopters
1941–1960 (compare with Fig. 126) only difference in number of blades, ie: 6 instead of 3 (R-5)*

(C. A. Davenport)

Fig 128
*Mil Mi-10 helicopter – main rotor diameter 114 ft.
10 in. Normal gross weight (STOL) 96,010 lbs,
VTOL 83,775 lbs. Maximum speed 127 mph.*

of the Russian giant Sikorsky-type helicopter, the Mil Mi-10 as depicted in the October 1969 issue of *VERTIFLIGHT*, some 25 years later. Compare (Fig. 126 with Fig. 127 and notice the exact copying (imitation is the sincerest form of flattery).

By the end of January 1944 the XR-6 had decided to co-operate, and began to behave as she was supposed to do. Both Les Morris and Jim Viner (pronounced Veener) were now quite enthusiastic about the way she handled; in fact, she was rapidly becoming a pleasure to fly. This was proved on 2 March 1944, when Col Frank Gregory, accompanied by XR-6 Project Engineer Ralph Alex, flew a record non-stop flight from the airport at Washington, DC, to the US Army Wright-Patterson Field in Ohio, a distance of some 378 miles, in 4 hr and 55 min, thus averaging a ground speed of some 77 mph with reported headwinds ranging at times from 10 to 30 mph, but of what duration is not noted. This indicates that, at certain periods, airspeeds up to possibly 100 mph were attained, certainly a splendid performace all round. In any case, it was a record flight for both speed and endurance.

Another outstanding feature, remarked upon by Gregory, was the comparatively low level of noise in the cabin, which greatly reduced flight fatigue by permitting normal conversational voice levels. This delivery flight, however, was almost as unique as Les Morris's 'first ever' in XR-4. On the other hand, no less a person than the CO of the Rotary Wing Section was the sole pilot, while the contractor's representative went along as a passenger.

In mid-February at Luscombe's, we received word from Bob Bowse that a briefing had been set up for us with representatives of the US Army in Washington, D.C., for the last week in the month. Bob Anderson would be accompanying me, as he did when I met with the Sun Oil Co.

On the morning of the day Bob and I were about to depart for Washington, Don Luscombe advised us that he had decided to accompany us, as well as his Chief Engineer, because, he said, 'the last thing I want right now is another Government contract'. I exchanged glances with Bob (he was, by the way, some years senior to me and knew Don well), who gave me a slight positive nod, so I made no comment. But I sensed something was brewing, as I tried to appear casually surprised.

Little else was mentioned on the subject as we paired-off on the railway trip to Washington, but I gathered from Bob that something was bothering Don. As our appointment was in the early afternoon, we had lunch together, and as a form of bait on the way to the restaurant I remarked that a bit of stimulant always helped me overcome self-consciousness before a briefing (which was not true). However, when we were seated at our table, Don announced that there would be no cocktails ordered.

At the meeting the Army was represented by a full Colonel, a Lieutenant-Colonel and a Civil Service Engineer. Don was careful to place himself next to the Colonel, so I ended up at the other end of the table. I passed out copies of the proposal and gave a general outline of its main features. I then started at the beginning and went over each item in detail, noting and answering their questions. They were genuinely interested in the proposed design, with its simplified control system, but apparently were divided as to the use of the liquid-cooled GM engine versus the aircooled Fairchild engine.

Don had little to offer, but was careful not to be too affirmative. The meeting concluded with Don saying how much he appreciated the Colonel and his staff's timely comments and suggestions, and that he would like to reconsider some of their suggestions. He would then contact the Colonel. Needless to say, I was becoming more and more curious as to what sort of game Don was playing. In fact, once or twice I saw the Colonel giving his second-in-command a quick glance with a questioning look.

Next morning I rang up Bob Bowse and said I would like to drop by and see him that evening. Bob was as puzzled as I was regarding Don's performance, so he started making enquiries. In the meantime I had a call from Don's accountant, but since we were on friendly terms I did not attach much importance to his asking me if I could perhaps help him with a certain matter the next day. It so happened that Don and his Chief Engineer would be away on a business trip.

During the noonday break he confided in me that he had received a call from some government bureau regarding company overhead charges that appeared in his last report. He then showed me a copy of a billing whereon the word 'steers' had been rather clumsily reworked to read 'stairs'. Don had allegedly bought the equivalent of two steers, a year's supply in frozen cuts, that filled his rented freezer lockers at a local butcher at a considerable price saving. The accountant said he had questioned Don about the entry, but had been told not to worry about it. What would I suggest he should do? I suggested he just tell Don the truth about the call, and ask him what to do. The poor fellow was really worried.

The next information I received from Bob Bowse was that the Luscombe Company was being investigated by the FBI. That weekend I rang Michael Buivid first and then Bob Labensky, and asked them what sort of reception I might receive regarding the possibility of my returning, having advised them that matters had not turned out to be quite as I had expected them. Bob said he would speak to Michael Gluhareff about it. Several days later Bob advised me that Michael had spoken to Igor, and that he was agreeable to it. The chain of command was still important.

Two matters now remained to be settled. I had to hand in my resignation to Luscombe, and advise Cdr Klopp not to proceed with the GM engine and rotor hub proposal. Several years later, as Capt Klopp, he told me he had received the final OK signature for the proposed programme on the day my signal arrived!

Just before the mid-March weekend I handed Don Luscombe my resignation, wherein I had made it clear that I was leaving with considerable regret, but found there were certain circumstances prevailing with which I did not care to continue my association. He did not take it lightly, but realised there was nothing he could do about it. Before the end of the month my family and I were back home in Brooklyn, Connecticut. In leaving North Wales we reluctantly left behind newly acquired friendships that we would truly miss, especially Bob Bowse and his family, who had tried so hard to help me. However, we did keep in touch.

My return to the Sikorsky fold was to a now reinstated, separate Sikorsky Division of United Aircraft, much to Igor's satisfaction. He was now Engineering Manager, and Ben Whelan was General Manager. The plant had been relocated near the Bridgeport Harbour, only a few miles from the old base at Stratford and the Bridgeport Airport, owing to the rapid expansion of Vought's manufacturing space requirements, as well as Sikorsky's. We all missed the more idyllic, rural waterside, and quieter setting of yore.

The warm and friendly reception by Bob Labensky, Misha Buivid and Michael Gluhareff was most heartening. Michael first showed me my new quarters, then took me on a tour of the new facilities. When showing me the new production version of the R-5 he pointed out her new landing gear and remarked, in his usual gentle manner: 'You see, Beel, we have changed her only a little bit'.

Later, after the day's work was ended, Michael accompanied me to Igor's office, where I received an equally warm reception from him. There were also other friendly greetings from the old XR-5 team, both in engineering and shop, especially when Ed Katzenberger remarked that, should I be asked to take over the XR-5 programme again, he would gladly step aside and work with me again. An unforgettable moment.

My first assignment, curiously enough, made it seem as though I had never been away. Because, before I left Sikorsky, I had suggested to Michael that, since it was a new design, we investigate the simplification of both the main rotor hub and the flight control system, which I did at Luscombe's (Chapter 6) and possibly replace the present XR-5 system, as depicted in Chapter 6 (Fig. 116). While patents were granted for these and subsequent ideas, I realised that the possibility of their ever being adopted on an already accepted system was somewhat remote, unless they were applied to an entirely new model at some time in the future.

These last two chapters will have a different tone to them than the preceding ones. This is because the Sikorsky helicopter was now entering the usual phase of 'fine tuning' the now 'accepted' basic arrangements of the various mechanical devices, peculiar to helicopters. In other words, the more exciting phase of experimentation and development was now over for the XR-4, -5 and -6. Improving performance, safety and reliability were now the order of the day. This did not mean new concepts would be 'pigeon-holed', for advanced thinking is the very essence of a continuing successful future.

With that in mind, I shall now turn to the all-too-seldom mentioned contributions from the little-known US Coast Guard Helicopter Rescue Unit at Floyd Bennett Field, Long Island, New York (under war-time Navy control). It was the far-sighted judgement of Capt Kossler, who backed his CO, Cdr Frank Erickson of the

Fig 129
Commander Frank Erickson, U.S.C.G., coming aboard with new floats on R-4B.

Helicopter Rescue Unit, who was responsible for the continuous search for methods, that improved the helicopter's role in air-sea-rescue operations.

The first helicopter issued to Cdr Erickson's Unit was an R-4 with wheeled undercarriage and/or air-floats. The latter, it will be recalled, had a tendency to bounce around when landing on the ship's platform under windy conditions. Frank's immediate improvement was an inflated keel on the bottom of each float that would initially engage between two padded rails on the operational platform.(Fig 129)

While I believe it was Ralph Alex who designed the first rescue hoist on the XR-4, it was Cdr

Erickson's crew who came up with a more sophisticated hoist, located further back to allow easier access to the cabin entrance. (Fig 130) The photograph was taken when Cdr Erickson flew up from his base on Long Island in their Navy designated HNS-1 (R-4) to demonstrate the new hoist. He 'rescued' several of us 'stranded' on top of a huge packing case. He was also a superb pilot.

With the advent of shipboard helicopter operation, Frank instigated the erection of a land-based practice roll-platform that would simulate the combined pitching and rolling movement of a ship underway at sea at various rates of motion. It proved to be of great help to the training programme.

Then there was the 'hands-on' basic flight control simulator. This ingenious basic trainer was attached to a hangar wall. It consisted of the complete forward structural section of an R-4, minus powerplant and rotor drive system, but included a complete standard R-4 control cabin. This unit was capable of simulating all helicopter movements, including lift-offs, landings and initiating flight in any direction. It even included the natural-frequency vibrations normally associated with various modes of flight. These capabilities were attained by using a combination of pantographic, parallel linkages that were attached to a gimballed mounting above the cabin. This permitted the cabin to correctly assume any of the desired attitudes of flight by means of actuators that responded to the trainee pilot's movement of the various flight and power controls.

Fig 130

Commander Erickson "rescues" Igor with new Coast Guard hoist HNS-1 (R-4).

As noted, the first R-4s/HNS-1s delivered to the Coast Guard Helicopter Rescue Unit had wheeled undercarriages. While that was quite suitable for land operations, especially ground manoeuvring, Cdr Erickson reasoned that, other than the last mentioned advantage, the wheeled gear served little purpose with regard to offshore operations, and it certainly retarded the speed of the helicopter. So, why not fit a simple, light, minimum air drag pair of tubular steel skid-like runners? For ground handling, all that was needed was a small, castor mounted landing platform. Furthermore, for the first time an R-4 could be flown at considerably over 80 mph.

I believe it is only fair to remind the reader that the original basic role conceived for the R-4 was that of a rugged, reliable, easily maintained and

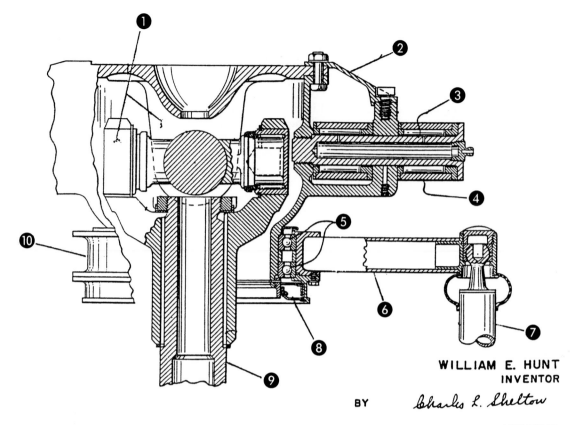

WILLIAM E. HUNT
INVENTOR

BY   *Charles L. Shelton*

ATTORNEY

Fig 131
(1) Universal joint yokes
(2) Flapping link support
(3) Flapping hinge bearings
(4) Flapping hinge link
(5) Tilt ring bearings
(6) Tilt control arm – 2 at 90°
(7) Tilt control rod, – 2 at 90°
(8) Lubrication seal
(9) Main rotor drive shaft
(10) Static tilt ring

controlled flight trainer, in which speed, range and load carrying ability were not the prime requirements. The entirely unexpected and unfortunate delays suffered by the prime helicopter contractor, Platt-Le Page with its XR-1, and similarly with the succeeding XR-1A, suddenly thrust the Sikorsky XR-4, YR-4, R-4 into the entirely unplanned limelight. That it was able to meet the challenge, speaks for itself.

There were of course, other areas of air-rescue that Cdr Erickson and his able crew covered, such as: rescue harnesses; remotely controlled, quick-release cable hooks; and single-point, vertically-lifted litters, etc.

Let us now return to my assignment, the adaptation of my simplified, non-cyclic, direct-tilting main rotor control system to a normally cyclically controlled R-5 helicopter, (Fig 131) and I am calling this portion 'Variations on a theme', by Paganini-Hunt, for there were actually two distinct variations covered in my proposed application of methods which would simplify the control of a single-main-rotor helicopter.

Item One was to eliminate the necessity of a collective pitch control lever and its interconnection with the engine throttle, together with the over-riding twist-grip handle used to independently adjust the engine throttle.

Instead of using an engine-run speed-sensing governor that would monitor the speed increase of the engine power first before increasing the collective pitch of the main rotor blades, as I had proposed in the Luscombe approach, I now proposed that, since the vertically root-hinged R-5 rotor blades would automatically react as engine power was either increased or decreased by pivoting horizontally backwards or forwards about their vertical hinge pin, they could, by so

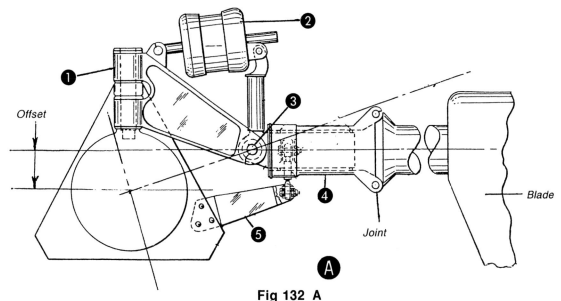

Fig 132 A
Plan view R-5 – non-tilting hub with automatic pitch control

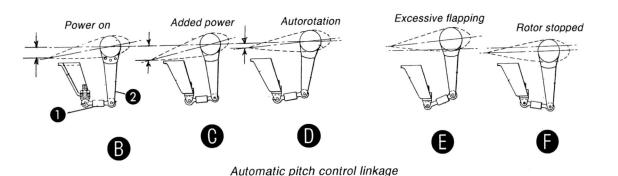

Automatic pitch control linkage

doing, be made to increase or decrease their blade pitch angles automatically, by the introduction of a simple linkage system (Fig 132-B). (Two years later I had a similar scaled-down hub-rotor test version built, driven by a 5 hp variable-speed electric motor, and it worked perfectly.) In other words, a standard engine throttle lever is all that was now required.

Item Two was to eliminate the tilting cyclic blade pitch control mechanism (Fig132-A), by using a simple mechanical universal joint, as already described and depicted in Chapter 6 (Fig 117) when a similar approach was adapted to a direct-tilting-type hub to replace the existing cyclic R-5 hub. Regarding Fig 132, you will notice that the top plate on the hub **(1)** is completely free of any other mechanism. That is because the previous modification eliminated the need for a pilot-operated

collective-pitch power lever, by using a linkage system (Fig 132-B).

Figure 132-A is a top view of the proposed linkage system, using the identical geometric positioning of the flapping hinge (132A*(1)*) and the vertical lead-lag hinge (132A*(3)*) as used on the R-5. The only additional member is the static link-supporting unit (132A*(5)*), which never changes its relative position on the hub. It thus permits the connecting link (132B*(1)*) between arm (132A*(5)*) and the rotor blade pitch control arm (132B*(2)*) to regulate the rotor blade pitch angle. Thus, as the blade root attachment arm (132A*(4)*) moves back (Fig 132C) in response to added power, it automatically increases the blade angle, and vice versa when power is reduced, or fails, when the forward movement of arm (132A*(4)*) reduces pitch, as per Fig. 132D.

195

By the same token, should a sudden local air disturbance cause excessive vertical blade movement (flapping) (Fig 132E), then link 132B*(1)* will automatically decrease the blade angle. This link is provided with self-aligning, pivoting end connections to arms 132A*(5)* and 132B*(2)*. Fig 132F depicts static rotor zero lift.

Referring to Fig 134, the two hub-tilting control rods 134**(1)** and 134**(2)** are actuated by means of a control arm moved by an irreversible spiral gear system similar to a car front wheel steering arm system where, in this case, the spiral pinion **(1)** is turned by means of a chain operated sprocket **(3)**, connected by cable to a quadrant Fig 133-**(6)** that is moved by the pilot's control stick 133**(5)** through link 133**(7)**.

I also worked out a relatively simple adaptation of the foregoing for R-5, but could not generate sufficient interest to try it out. Even to this day, I believe I am correct in so stating, that neither has anyone else. Strangely enough, a Cierva autogyro of the mid-1930s (the origin of my foregoing ideas) successfully flew a direct control tilting rotor embodying the ultimate in control simplicity, wherein a simple 'drop-stick' (pilot's control lever) directly connected to the rotor hub was all that was needed!

On the other hand, efforts were being made to better understand the behaviour of a helicopter main rotor blade during a normal complete flight sequence; during lift-off, climbing, level flight, manoeuvring and landing. This investigation was undertaken by Ralph Lightfoot, one of the early members of the XR-4 team and an excellent aerodynamicist who has not received the attention he rightfully deserves. He became involved, I believe, with the aerodynamic loads that were imposed upon the flight control system.

At any rate, it ended up with a movie camera being mounted on the hub of an R-4. I shall never forget the first time the results were shown to a small gathering of those of us directly associated with rotor problems. There was the usual amount of chatter as the room was darkened and the camera started, but it soon died out, for the gyrations that the rotor blade was going through were almost unbelievable. Especially when sudden applications of control inputs occurred, when the blade would act like a flexing fishing rod with a lively 40 lb fish on the end of the line. There was also the concertina effect on the rear two-thirds of the fabric covering of the blade as it passed through its advancing and retreating cycles. However, when steady forward flight was being maintained the blade acted as though it was performing to the rhythm of a beautiful waltz, only to be wrenched aside without mercy when made to perform like a 'whirling Dervish' as it suddenly changed course. When the film came to its abrupt ending there was total silence; then unmistakably, there burst forth from Michael Gluhareff: 'MUH-MUH-MUH-My-i-iiii!'

Main rotor blade aerodynamic, downward pitching forces were very much in evidence, and these produced very tiresome control loads with which the pilot had to contend. Blade root counterbalancing weights helped, but also added weight. As with aeroplane wings, until the right structural metal material became available, to withstand the constant bending, fatigue-producing loads, the familiar methods prevailed.

Thus, even after four years of rotor blade experience, there was still no truly 'substantial and reliable' (as Igor would have put it) basic, production type, metal helicopter main rotor blade.

An attempt was also made to introduce some form of additional flight stability by adding gyroscopic-producing forces, using hinged flyweights attached to the outer rim of the tilting cyclic pitch control plate. Adequate weights, however, would become prohibitive.

The reason I have gone into considerable detail concerning both the collective pitch lever and the direct tilting main rotor hub is to draw attention to the age-old problem of decision-making when the pressures of limited time and/or resources are involved. Under such circumstances, in retrospect, certain simple improvements that could have been made were not. On the other hand, certain other 'improvements' that were made only succeeded in introducing still other problems. What remains so baffling to me is how consistently, when both time and resources are available, the stubborn resistance to change prevails.

Alex Krapish, like the rest of us who were directly involved with VS-300, missed her very much, but he is now contentedly heading up a small but busy experimental test shop that works closely with the flight test department. One such example was when I suggested to Igor and Michael that main rotor 'stalling', due to insufficient rotational speed or power, could be forestalled (no pun

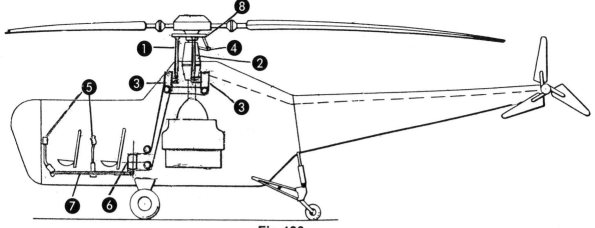

Fig 133

Proposed direct tilting hub*

(1) Fore/aft tilt control (2) Lateral tilt control (3) Irreversible spiral gears (4) Static scissors (5) Flight control stick (6) Cable quadrant (7) Flight control link (8) Hub tilt ring
* (compare with Fig. 3B)

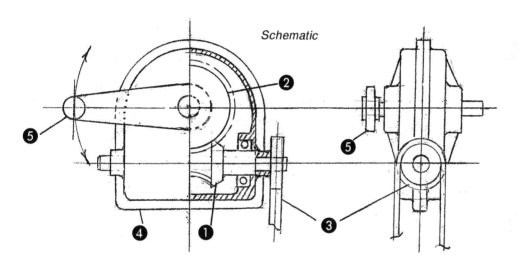

Schematic

Fig 134

Proposed irreversible spiral gear system for tilting main lifting rotor hub

(1) Spiral pinion
(2) Gear
(3) Operating chain and sprocket
(4) Gear casing
(5) Hub tilting control arm
N.B.: Both (3) and (5) can be mounted on either side of gearbox.

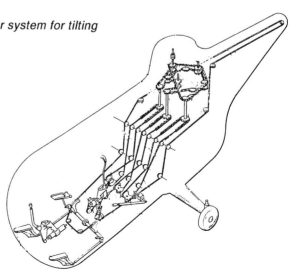

Fig 135
*XR-5 cyclic blade control system
compare with Fig. 3*

intended) by means of a standard propeller constant-speed governor. In this case, since it did not involve any production or engineering personnel, they agreed to try it out. Since the speed sensitive governor was produced by the Hamilton Standard Propeller Division of United Aircraft, there was no problem in acquiring one. It was to be belt-driven off of the tail rotor driveshaft, at the juncture where the tailcone is attached to the central fuselage section and the tail shaft mates with the angled section that is driven off of the main transmission.

At a predetermined, minimum safe main rotor revolutions the governor would automatically activate a sliding valve which transferred oil under pressure to an hydraulic actuator. Attached to its piston-rod was a cable that in turn was fastened to the underside of the pilot's collective pitch control lever. It thus immediately pulled down the lever, and by so doing simultaneously reduced the rotor blades to their minimum pitch angle at any engine throttle setting.

That action causes the helicopter to pitch downwards and initiate autorotation, and would be the crucial moment in the whole exercise. For, as earlier, the time it took for the helicopter to attain sufficient forward speed to allow the rotor blades to keep rotating automatically, also meant a simultaneous rapid loss of altitude and that predetermined the safe hovering altitude above ground (dead man's curve).

The day arrived to test this arrangement, and I was granted permission to act as observer. It would be the first time I was to be airborne in the offspring of my XR-5. I was also honoured by having Jim Viner, now Chief Test Pilot, at the controls. Sitting up in front of Jim as we steadily climbed out and away from our little Heeli flight test area, with nothing but clear plastic surrounding me, was absolutely astounding and thrilling. Jim kindly gave me a few moments to enjoy the clear near and distant sunlit views, deliberately making a wide sweep while slowly gaining the desired test altitude of 1,200 ft. We then headed back towards the plant, and as we approached the test area Jim began to throttle back slowly while maintaining altitude.

Both of us intently watched the combined engine/tachometer needles. Then, as they approached the red line, Jim suddenly exclaimed 'OH!' as the CPL jerked his arm down with it. The governor had automatically asserted itself spot-on.

I quickly turned and glanced at Jim. He was registering a broad satisfied grin, as the R-5 pitched downwards. I then found myself looking almost straight down at *terra firma* coming up at us at an alarming rate for what seemed like minutes, rather than seconds, before Jim gently pulled out of the forward dive as soon as the rotor tachometer needle was again well inside the safe operating margins. But we had lost more than half of our original altitude.

Jim repeated the test several more times from different directions, to take into account the effect when heading other than straight into the prevailing wind, and I tabulated the results. We were quite pleased with the results, as were Igor, Michael and Ed Katzenberger, but for the life of me I cannot recall whether or not the system was ever installed in a production helicopter.

As mentioned earlier, Igor's office was no longer directly connected with the main engineering draughting department, but was now located in the front, as part of the Executive Offices. These also included Marketing under Mr Bighley and Field Services under Mr Ellsworth, etc. Igor was thus more involved with Engineering Management activities, and my contacts with him were less frequent. Michael Gluhareff still conferred with Igor, but not on the daily scale of a year ago. By the same token, I was generally involved with Michael in design matters, at times relating to maintenance problems.

It was becoming more evident, however, as more areas of helicopter usefulness became apparent, that additional interior cabin space was needed, together with greater useful loads, power and operational rage. In other words, a larger version of R-5, with all-weather rotor blades, was required.

The US Navy was anxious to improve upon existing anti-submarine warfare tactics, using detecting methods on board helicopters. This involved relatively bulky equipment that demanded more precise control and greater stability to detect a submerged submarine. I suggested using a horizontal tail rotor control, with its long leverage control advantages. Igor immediately agreed, as he had been so enthusiastic about the excellent manner in which VS-300 had responded so smoothly and accurately with that type of control. In fact, he had been very loath to abandon it in favour of the military insistence on an all-cyclic main rotor control system. It made

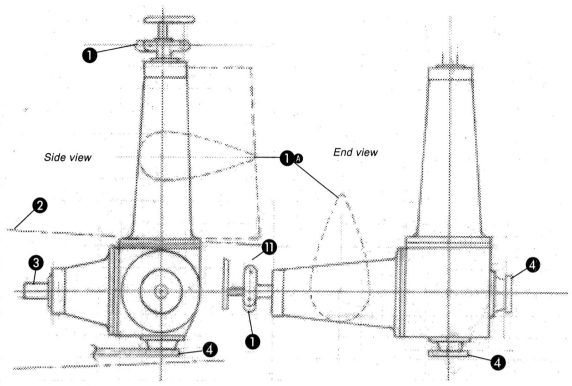

Side view   End view

Fig 136   *Combined vertical and horizontal tail rotor gearbox.*

(1a) Optional fairing   (1) Same hubs – R5   (2) Tail cone   (3) Tail rotor drive shaft   (4) Pitch control sprocket   (5) Thrust bearing   (6) Driving gears   (7) Pitch control screw   (8) Pitch control shaft nut moves control shaft up, or down (flat sided) inside of slotted anti-torque control pitch control shaft (9) (10) All housings are cast aluminium   (11) Blade pitch control link

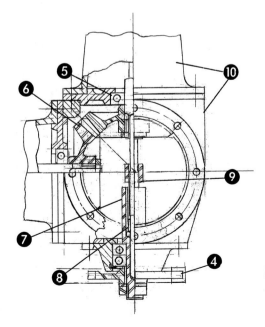

Fig 137   *Cross section of gearbox.*

(Drawings are not to scale)

longitudinal control far more precise by avoiding the need to mix longitudinal control signals with the lateral signals. Furthermore, since this would be a new model, there would be no question of making changes on an existing production aircraft. While I realised it would be a long shot, I still hoped that, with the possibility of an upgraded R-5, Igor might relent and simplify the main rotor flight control system. (Figs 133, 134 & 135)

As we had found out two years previously, it was necessary to keep the horizontal tail rotor well out of the downwash from the main rotor. With that in mind, I set about designing a combined vertical (directional control) and horizontal (longitudinal control) tail rotor gearbox. (Figs 136 & 137)

Fig 138
The first ever, single-main-rotor Sikorsky type helicopters, the R-4s, are shown being produced in the Bridgeport plant in a dual assembly line. Beginning on the left, with final on right.

I would be able to use an R-5 vertical tail rotor as the horizontal tail rotor, since the thrust required to raise and/or lower the tail (to tilt the main rotor fore or aft) was actually considerably less than that required to counteract the torque generated by the main rotor. Similarly, only additional R-5 gears and bearings would be needed. This made the proposed design possible with a minimum of expenditure.

At about this time George Lubben 'joined the colours' and went to Cdr Frank Erickson's Helicopter Air Rescue Unit at Floyd Bennett Field, Long Island, where he became a Petty Officer, taking with him his valuable field and shop experience with VS-300 and XR-4. Our main shop was busy producing R-4; the first XR-5 was repaired and flying again, and the third and fourth XR-5s were almost completed. Adolf continued to be in charge of the XR-5 shop programme.

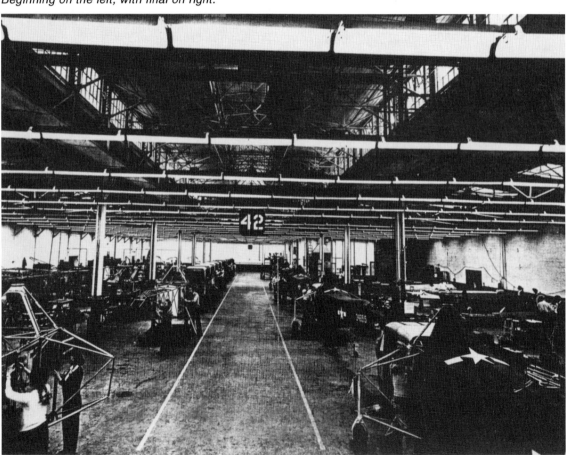

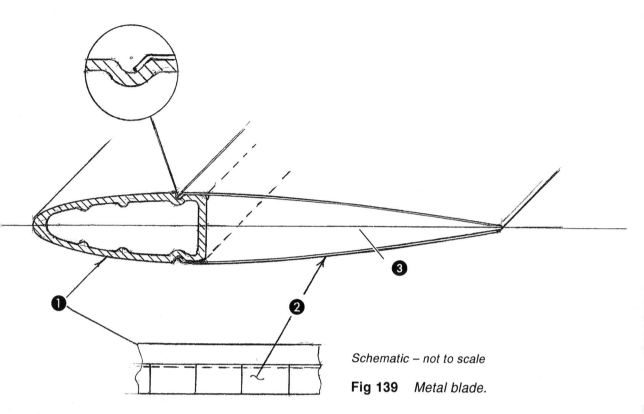

Schematic – not to scale

Fig 139 *Metal blade.*

George 'Red' Lubben, bless him, possessed a Puckish sense of humour which never failed to help brighten an otherwise dull meeting, or break prevailing tension. Before he left for Coast Guard duty, there was a certain individual who apparently never failed to find several complaints to voice at weekly shop meetings. Finally, one day, Red brought with him a large paper bag. When it was time for the aforementioned chap to speak, and he had got well into one of his tales of woe, Red quietly removed from the paper bag a little toy violin and bow. He then proceeded to rasp out some ghastly discords. After a momentary abrupt silence there was loud laughter, to which the speaker finally succumbed by permitting himself a wry smile.

Not long after Red had joined the Coast Guard there was a similar meeting at Sikorsky's, this time regarding matters pertaining to Coast Guard maintenance procedures for the newly acquired R-6 at their base on Long Island. Red explained several of the difficulties encountered when servicing certain items under the top decking of the central aluminium sheet, stressed-skin central fuselage structure. However, completely 'dead pan', he said that fortunately they had been able to come up with a very simple solution. So saying, he took out of his pocket a large can opener.

The next most important phase was the all-metal main rotor blade. A helicopter designer can use either a cantilevered rotor blade, such as is normally associated with an aeroplane propeller, or one that is horizontally hinged from its hub at its root end, so that it can move vertically (cone) upwards upon any increase in the blade's lift, which mostly occurs at the outer third of the blade (speed/radius ratio). In addition he can add a vertical hinge that allows the blade to move horizontally back and forth to compensate for any increase or decrease in the blade's air resistance. In both cases the main object is to reduce the bending stresses in the blade.

Then there are the outward (centrifugal) tension stresses, caused by the weight of the whirling blade trying to tear itself away from its hub. That, of course, is also true with the cantilever blade. In both cases the tension-producing forces help to stabilise the bending stresses, and can be used to advantage by adding properly distributed weights to the outer third of the blade.

Finally, there are the twisting (torsional) stresses generated by the aerodynamic forces as the centre of pressure moves back and forth between the leading and trailing edges of the blade owing to blade pitch changes. If the designer only needed to take each individual stress-producing moment and meet its requirements, that would be ideal, but it would mean neglecting the basic design problem, which is that all these stress-producing moments are occurring at the same time and thus completely interrelated, yet at varying frequencies as well. Not to mention the fact that the blade is made up of numerous separate pieces fastened together, all having different characteristic reaction movements. Then, to top it all, there is fatigue, in other words, life expectancy. How many cycles can these interrelated materials endure before failing? The answer is determined, of course, by vigorous testing under all weather conditions, but before that the designer, as a final precaution, multiplies all his calculations by a recommended safety factor, or one based on personal experience.

Having carefully considered and calculated all of the foregoing, the final design was as depicted in (Fig 139). The basic load-carrying element 1, is an aluminium alloy extrusion which maintains constant characteristics throughout its entire required length. Similarly, a series of individually attached elements 2, are rear-mounted to 1, and consist of thin aluminium alloy formed sheets called 'pockets'. In this manner both the desired centre of balance, as well as the overall flexibility of the blade, is maintained. These light and thin aluminium pockets by themselves would have been too flimsy but for the durable, light, preformed foam-type filler to which the outer skin was bonded. In fact it was the method of bonding the two major elements together that completely eliminated the need for hundreds of drilled holes, rivets and a multitude of small parts, not to mention expensive jigs and fixtures, plus labour. This metal-to-metal bonding system had been developed by the Chrysler Corporation. Wherein a synthetic rubber-like substance developed, under simultaneous heat and pressure, an extraordinary ability to adhere to the opposing metal surface areas, especially when subjected to repetitive load vari-

ations that would normally induce fatigue problems for both the metal elements and the bonding material. It was called Cycowelding.

Of course, close collaboration was needed with the supplier as to the correct bonding areas required, as well as their prebonding surface treatment. A considerable amount of specimen testing was also required. The resulting successful acceptance of the Sikorsky-type all-metal helicopter blade speaks for itself. The first helicopter with all-metal blades was the Sikorsky S-52, in February, 1947.

An interesting consequence of the move from Stratford to Bridgeport was the change in the nature of the ground supporting the buildings we occupied. For when excavations were made under the floor area of the main manufacturing building to provide foundations for very heavy machinery, it was discovered to be almost entirely sand. Due to tidal effects much of it was damp, if not wet, and about 12 ft down puddles began forming, not of water, but of clear golden oil. Since our buildings were fairly near to Bridgeport Harbour, where oil tankers had for years delivered crude oil to an oil refinery, enough spillage had occurred to create sand-filtered oil pools. It was being recovered by the bucketful by hopeful shop personnel for possible home usage.

This reminds me of the enterprising maintenance worker who, for a short time, was making extra pocketmoney by occasionally selling slightly used wheelbarrows. Some shop materials were delivered packed in sawdust and, in addition, considerable sawdust would accumulate at the maintenance shop. All this chap had to do was to take a wheelbarrow load through the guard gate into the car park, where the waste dump was located. There, behind the dump, he had parked his pick-up truck. He would then substitute his own similar wheelbarrow and return to the shop. The next time he visited the dump, he would retrieve his own barrow.

On 27 March 1944, Jim Viner put on an excellent flight demonstration of the XR-5 for the top executives and personnel of United Aircraft at East Hartford, Connecticut. It included all directions of flight, precision lift-offs and landings, autorotation landings, speed runs and 'pull-outs' and ended with short scenic rides for those officials who wished to participate. (Fig 140) Igor, of course, received many well deserved congratulatory comments, but

Fig 140 *XR-5 Demonstration flight at Hartford, 27 March 1944.*

what to me was most interesting, judging from the tone of those comments, was their evident lack of knowledge regarding the extent of our progress at Bridgeport (in spite of our secondhand facilities), less than 60 miles from Hartford. It would be quite a few years before Sikorsky Aircraft would finally be rewarded with a modern new plant near Stratford.

An historic Sikorsky helicopter milestone was reached during March, when the Western Allies fielded their very first military helicopters. These comprised a small team of four Sikorsky R-4Bs under the command of Col Philip Cochran of the US Army Air Forces First Air Commandos, in the Burma jungle campaign. Their primary mission was the rescue of the wounded jungle fighters (the Chindits), under command of the legendary British General Orde Wingate and transport them back to Col Cochran's secret base of operations, where they would be given immediate field hospital care.

The pilot allotted to carry out the first rescue mission was Lt Carter Harman, who successfully retrieved a downed US Army pilot, along with three British Commandos, from a small jungle-surrounded rice paddy deep inside a Japanese occupied area. In another daring rescue, Lt Harman was able to lift out two badly wounded jungle fighters from a small jungle clearing some 3,000 ft up on a steep mountainside. The R-4 rescue helicopters had provision for a single external canvas-covered litter (Fig 141). The more severely wounded Commando was placed in the litter, and the other in the cabin. However, at that altitude it took all of Harman's skill to coax every last ounce of power out of the engine to lift off, clear the surrounding trees and dive downwards towards the valley below in order to gain sufficient forward speed. In all, some 18 other wounded were rescued from behind enemy lines by the same R-4 rescue team. Twenty-seven R-4Bs were produced, and some were still operating in 1948.

We had an interesting visitor when William Stout, the Chief Engineer and Manager of the Ford Aircraft Division, came to see Mr Sikorsky, through Henry Ford, Senior.

The main purpose of his visit was to ascertain the feasibility of converting his latest creation, an attractive four-seat all-metal aeroplane with a rear mounted engine and propeller, into a Sikorsky-type helicopter. In addition, he wondered whether the Sikorsky Division might be willing to collaborate with him in such a venture.

At the start of the meeting it included Igor, Michael and Serge Gluhareff, Boris Labensky and myself. We went over Mr Stout's design layouts

Fig 141
Canvas litter capsule on side of YR-4.
Shown operating in Canadian winter conditions.

with him at some length, and Igor congratulated him upon his proposed 'heeli' version, especially his design ideas for an all-metal main rotor blade. However, Igor told Mr Stout that for the duration of the war the United Aircraft Sikorsky Division would be unable to offer him anything, other than to encourage him to continue his present efforts.

As this meeting was being held in a conference room, first Igor and then the others were called away, thus affording the two of us the chance to have an interesting personal chat before I escorted him back to Igor's office. In a way, he was very much like Igor in his conceptual thinking, but he was also a mechanical design engineer. Mr Stout's original rise to fame came when he had the idea of extending the life and utility of Anthony Fokker's famous 12–14-passenger tri-motor transport by adopting Dr Hugo Junker's successful method of using thin corrugated aluminium sheets as an external structural skin. The Ford-Stout all-metal Tri-motor was an instant success.

My design layouts regarding the proposed adap-

tation of the horizontal tail rotor for more exact longitudinal control of the anti-submarine helicopter were translated into a full-scale mock-up on an XR-5 tailcone, and approved by Igor and Michael Gluhareff. However, even though the reintroduction of the single horizontal tail rotor was actually included on the mock-up of the proposed US Navy anti-submarine warfare version of an up-dated R-5 to enhance longitudinal stability and precise control, it was finally turned down by the Navy. Igor was quite disappointed.

This was the initial effort towards creating what was to eventually become, in 1948, the HJRS, a still further updating based on the original XR-5. It perpetuated the seemingly undying usefulness (with increased power) of the organic centre-of-energy of the original XR-5; its 'centre section'.

The first updating was, of course, the S-51, which was to be the world's very first commercial single-main-rotor Sikorsky-type helicopter. Begun towards the end of this account year of 1944, under the overall supervision of Ed Katzenberger, this model was also to be the first to test successfully an automatic helicopter flight control system, in the very capable hands of Chief Test Pilot Jimmy Viner.

It was also at about this time that Michael Gluhareff's son, Eugene, joined the Division's design office. One of his first assignments was the enlarging of the cabin section of the existing R-5 to accommodate three or four passengers plus the pilot (S-51). He contacted me concerning the layout of the control system. He was a pleasant young fellow with only slight resemblance to his father, being blond and not as tall.

While 1944 was not as diversified in content for me as the previous three years, especially since the retirement of VS-300, there was, instead, a calmer, less tense atmosphere that allowed me more time to think, which was actually quite welcome. For one thing, my contacts with Serge were far fewer, and of much less consequence than before, and therefore cordial. While the meetings with Igor, as already mentioned, were less frequent, they were nonetheless warm, refreshing and more relaxed. The same could be said of Michael, with whom I had frequent contact and still met socially. I saw Misha Buivid and Bob Labensky less frequently during office hours, but often socially as neighbours. Misha was now well entrenched, involved with main rotor hub development.

As I write these words we have been celebrating the 50th anniversary of the 6 June 1944 Allied landings on the beaches of Normandy, known as D-Day. At that time, for us safe and secure in the USA it was a distant occurrence, and we had little comprehension or appreciation of what it meant to those who had endured over four years of ghastly uncertainty. I shall never forget receiving my father's next letter, in which he wrote: 'At long last – WE ARE ON OUR WAY BACK'.

Igor Sikorsky could now finally realise his earliest dream, a practical 'heelicopter', for barely four years since VS-300 had made her first timid attempts to become airborne, no fewer than three different models of his single-main-rotor helicopters were simultaneously being produced; another unique world record to his credit.

Before closing this chapter I must pay a special tribute to Les Morris, whose presence has vanished from this account. Shortly after Igor's nephew, Jimmy Viner, became Les's assistant, he realised that his tenure was being challenged. Although this was a bitter pill to swallow, he left us without rancour, as he recorded in the preface to his book *Pioneering the Helicopter*. He wrote: 'D.D. "Jimmie" Viner . . . joined the piloting staff early in 1943, and in one brief year was able to assume the duties of Chief Test Pilot'.

No one, other than Igor, could have done what Les did to help bring Igor's Dream to reality, nor so enthusiastically enter into every phase of the flight development that finally brought forth the eighth version, VS-300H. The first successful single-main-rotor helicopter. Les joined the Bendix Helicopter Corporation next door to us near Bridgeport, and was much to their benefit in the successful development of their co-axial helicopter. Happily our paths crossed many times in the subsequent helicopter years. I shall always treasure his friendship.

The next, and final Chapter, of this account is noticeably brief, due to both the ending of hostilities in Europe and my final departure (with mixed feelings) from Igor and company during August 1945.

Feb. 28, 1950   W.E. HUNT   2,499,314

TWO-BLADED TAIL ROTOR ON COMMON HINGE

Filed Sept. 12, 1947   2 Sheets-Sheet 1

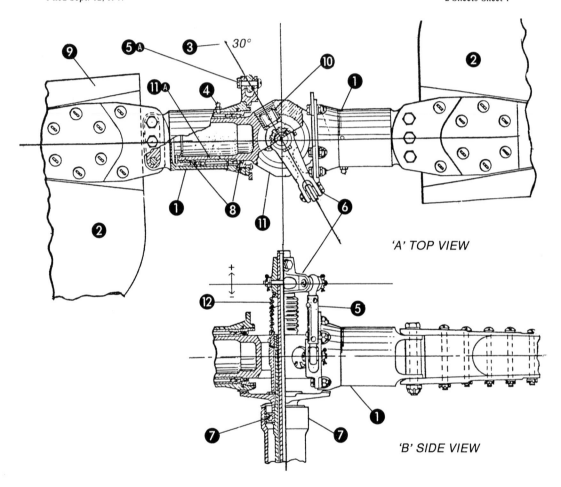

'A' TOP VIEW

'B' SIDE VIEW

Fig 142

(1) Hub bearing housing & blade retention 'A'
(2) Tail rotor blade similar to R-5 'A'
(3) Skewed common flapping hinge angle 'A'
(4) Bearing lube nipple – 2 'A'
(5) Blade pitch control link 'A'
(6) Blade pitch control crossarm 'A'
(7) Gearcase outer rotor support bearing 7 'B' housing 7A 'B'

(8) Blade pitch & thrust bearings 'A'
(9) Blade leading edge 'A'
(10) Flapping hinge bearings – 2 'A'
(11) One-piece hub with single hinge & spindles 'A'
(11A) Integral spindles 'A'
(12) Blade pitch control shaft. 'B'

Chapter Eight
1945

**Two-bladed Tail Rotor – Simplified Main Rotor and Control –
V-E Day – Flight to England – Engineering Department Changes
– Ed Katzenberger's Contributions – Post Departure Events –
Igor Sikorsky**

This final chapter is a protracted one, but my account would not be complete if I failed to include the end results of matters in which I was involved, and initiated before my final departure from Igor's fold. I have also included some retrospective comments, in the context of the times, that have reactivated memories of various personalities or events.

The year 1945 opened with an in-house pride of achievement at having attained the status of number one helicopter producer. There was also a general feeling that the tide of battle in Europe had definitely turned towards a victorious ending (though at a terrible sacrifice of human life on both sides) for the Allies. At the same time, we, and our Allies in the far Pacific Ocean area in the struggle against Japan, had also turned the war in our favour, to the extent that our thoughts were beginning to turn towards post-war industrial products incorporating the benefits and experience derived from producing wartime materiel for the armed forces.

It was on such an occasion, during a meeting with Igor and Michael Gluhareff regarding the updating of the R-5, that the question of reducing overall aircraft costs and/or complexity arose. I suggested a relatively easy beginning by replacing the present three-bladed anti-torque tail rotor with a much simplified two-bladed rotor, based on the original single-bladed VS-300 tail rotor. That produced smiles from both Igor and Michael as they agreed that I should proceed to do whatever I had in mind.

In addition to the simplicity of a two-bladed rotor, with but a single teeter (flapping) hinge, there was the added advantage of skewing the single hinge line, such that any tendency for a blade to flap too much is being automatically governed by the amount of skew-angle used. For as the blade flaps upwards it automatically reduces pitch until it becomes balanced between the forces produced by the power required versus the rotational speed to produce the amount of thrust required. It was counterbalanced in exactly the same manner by the opposit blade as it flaps downward. (Fig 142)

The simplicity of this arrangement becomes quite apparent when one notes that there are only three major components to the basic hub, visible in the top view; item **11** which provides the single central hinge **10** plus the two opposing integral spindles **11a**, on which rotate two of item **1**. The bearings **8** upon which the two bearing housings **1** rotate are (pre-loaded) thrust bearings that retain the housings against the outward centrifugal forces created by the whirling rotor blades. These bearings are to be periodically lubricated through the lube nipples **4**. The bearing housings are rotated by means of the pitch control crossarm **6** connected to the blade pitch control links **5** (side view) that are in turn attached to control arms **5a** on the housings. Blade pitch change is initiated by the outward/inward movement (+/-) of the pitch control shaft **12**, on which the crossarm **6** is mounted.

There was also the advantage of using two instead of three blades (as per R-4 and -5) when considering the reintroduction of a horizontal tail rotor for longitudinal control, where they would be intermeshing with the vertical anti-torque rotor and would thus cause less aerodynamic interference between the two rotors. (Fig 136)

It was actually a considerable concession on the part of Igor to agree to go back to a two-blader, for he had an undying belief that three blades were better (smoother) than two blades, even though both three- and two-bladed rotors have the same natural frequency of two-per-revolution.

My original thought was to use a constant-chord metal extrusion for the rotor blade, or an all-metal structure. While the former was agreed to at first, it was rejected for the immediate future on the grounds that it would require considerable testing, as against the known qualities of the existing laminated wood/veneer blades. Eventually a similar two-bladed tail rotor was used on no fewer than ten Sikorsky models derived from the R-5 and R-6. Tail rotors then went to four and five blades as the size of the aircraft increased. You may notice my design was not filed until two years after I had left Sikorsky.

Some time during 1946, according to Michael Buivid, a single-bladed rotor was tried out quietly, and never made public, on a production R-4. This was, of course, the very original concept of Igor's, as being the optimum form of simplicity possible for a helicopter main lifting rotor. You may recall that this was the configuration that Michael and Boris Labensky had used on the little rig they had secretly made for Igor back in 1938, while he was visiting the helicopter firms in Europe. The R-4 tests were both disappointing and inconclusive,

and were therefore quietly forgotten. Actually, as Michael said, trying to match a single-bladed rotor against a three-bladed rotor, using the same total blade areas at the same rotational speeds, was like comparing apples with oranges. As might be expected, vibration was the outstanding problem associated with trying to design an appropriate counterbalance to the single blade, both aerodynamically and centrifugally.

I meant to mention earlier, even though the reintroduction of the single horizontal tail rotor was actually included on the mock-up of the proposed U.S. Navy anti-submarine warfare version, of an up-dated R-5 (in order to enhance longitudinal stability and precise control) it was finally turned down by the Navy. Igor was quite disappointed.

Les Morris was now Chief of Flight Testing for the Bendix Helicopter Corporation. Quite near the Sikorsky Division, close to the Electric Power Station near the Housatonic River Bridge. He was once again enthusiastically engaged in flight testing, and was enthralled by the responsive behaviour of the little Bendix experimental coaxial (one rotor counter-rotating above the other) single-seater, as it was considerably nippier than VS-300.

We saw each other fairly frequently, and when he was going to do some flight testing during one weekend, involving improved directional control, he asked me if I would like to watch him. It was fascinating to see how Les had so quickly mastered the art of coaxial rotors, as he deftly, smoothly and precisely manoeuvred his new mount. His favourite finale, was to make a complete circuit of the demonstration area while continuously and slowly revolving through 360° turns; a real show stopper. His ability to manoeuvre so rapidly reminded me of a hummingbird darting from flower to flower, endlessly twisting and turning, momentarily hovering, seemingly without effort.

Vincent Bendix was a remarkable entrepreneur. I believe he started his career of fortune making by inventing an electrical automatic car engine starter where an electric motor engaged a gear that initially cranked over the car's engine, but immediately backed away as soon as the engine began to run. He also developed the Bendix-Weiss constant-speed universal joint and the Bendix washing machine, etc.

As Igor's success with his helicopters became more lucrative, it became increasingly evident that both the Pratt & Whitney Division and the Hamilton Standard Propeller Division, but more particularly the latter, had decided to pay more attention to what was going on at the Sikorsky Division. It was a certain Mr Oswalt, a very likable and knowledgeable young engineer, who was genuinely interested in the problems that had become apparent with helicopter main rotor aerodynamics as they related similarly to aeroplane propellers. This generally concerned their overall shape, but more particularly the shaping of the rotor tip. Oswalt felt because of his studies and knowledge of propellers, that there was still much to be understood regarding the airflow over and around the advancing/retreating tip of a helicopter rotor blade, both during hovering and in advancing flight. He was certain that the shape of the tip of the rotor would be directly related to the most important goal yet to be attained by helicopters, namely increasing their present maximum and/or cruising speeds. For as the rotor tip speed necessary to lift-off a helicopter vertically had to be such that, when added to the desired top speed of the 'heeli', the advancing rotor blade tip would not exceed the speed of sound at sea level, which amounts to some 1,130 ft/sec, or 770 mph at 60°F in dry air.

Oswalt thus initiated what was to become a major research and development (R & D) effort that has culminated in the quite unexpected, or possibly unimagined, rotor tip shapes now used on Sikorsky helicopters. Not to mention the years of effort spent in designing, constructing and wind-tunnel testing, even devising rotors that could actually be stopped while in flight, also the full-scale co-axial flight testing of the Advancing Blade Concept (ABC) helicopter.

To me this area of rotor performance became increasingly more important, as I had by then decided to part company with the Sikorsky Division. I felt certain that Igor's ultimate goal, and that of United Aircraft, was to enter the larger commercial-passenger, or military-troop-carrying helicopter market. Whereas it was the high-volume production of light helicopters that really interested me.

In this respect I also had the opportunity of being able to consult with Oswalt on the desirable aerodynamic features for a two-bladed, cantilever helicopter main rotor, having but a single hinge, basically because of its inherent simplicity, especially when considering a light helicopter, as I knew

Igor was still thinking of a possible VS-300 follow-on. Also, I had begun to finalise my concept of a post-war light helicopter, incorporating the simplified control features described previously, both in this Chapter and Chapter 6.

A fascinating characteristic of Oswalt's was his facile ambidexterity. For instance, as he drew a graph he would start with one hand and finish with the other. In fact, when sketching an example his ability to switch deftly from one hand to the other, as a matter of course, was quite remarkable.

Yet another visitor from Hamilton Standard was Charles Kaman, another young engineer who had been bitten by the helicopter bug. Referring back to Igor's early ideas described earlier, his early ideas of cyclic control of the main rotor blade he had devised fixed-wing type ailerons on the outer portion of each blade (Chap. 2). Kaman had similar ideas, as earlier conceived by both Curtiss-Bleeker and D'Ascanio in Italy. It comprised a separate small aerofoil located to the rear of the outer end of the rotor blade. Actually, this arrangement was more complicated than the cyclic blade system finally used on VS-300 and subsequent Sikorsky models.

However, Kaman's first helicopters were an adaptation of the German, Dr Flettner's, outward-canted biaxial intermeshing main rotor configuration, as also used by the Kellet company in Philadelphia, which was the first successfully to fly a ten-passenger commercial transport version. When this configuration failed to gain public acceptance, Kaman shifted to the Sikorsky configuration, incorporating his described cyclic control system on his US Navy carrier support aircraft. It never evolved into a commercial transport type.

Ralph Alex's R-6 was the first helicopter to receive a production order for some 500 aircraft. In the event, it actually turned out that closer to 250 were actually produced, but it was nevertheless, a milestone in helicopter history. The Nash-Kelvinator (refrigerator) Company won the contract, and their representative at the Sikorsky Division was a Mr Moore. Earlier he had made the wise choice of marrying Mr Nash's daughter, and eventually became a vice-president of the firm.

Naturally Mr Moore knew nothing technical about helicopters, but evidently he had learned to 'always keep a tidy work bench', because whenever I passed by his office, en route to Igor's, all I could see on his desk was a blotter pad, a pen, a telephone

'HEELICOPTER' – PIONEERING WITH IGOR SIKORSKY

and an empty letter basket. However, my lasting mental image of him occurred one day when, just visible over the glass top of his desk were a periscopical lighted cigar, with smoke rising lazily therefrom, and two protruding shoe toecaps. War? What war?

Wing Commander Reginald Brie was still very much alive and actively engaged in keeping in touch with the goings-on at Bridgeport, Washington, and elsewhere. He was mainly concerned with the status of both the R-4 and R-5, which were, you may recall, co-sponsored by the British through Reggie. He had finally won his helicopter pilot's ticket, through Les Morris, and had been granted permission to fly a British R-4 solo, for the first time, when commuting between New York and the Sikorsky Division at Bridgeport, Connecticut, as he had become quite familiar with the intervening landmarks during flights as a passenger.

His arrival at the Sikorsky 'Heeliport', as scheduled, was triumphantly acclaimed as he duly circled and made an excellent landing. He promptly enquired about refuelling, and was pointed out the pumps that had been moved to the other end of the landing area. Rather than bothering the ground crew to move the aircraft, Reggie decided to hop over to the pumps. All went well until he was directed to move sideways before landing, which he did. Unfortunately, upon stopping at the desired spot he overcontrolled, losing height and control. He immediately switched off the engine, but an undercarriage wheel contacted the ground, tilting R-4 too far over, and a blade hit the ground. There was momentary silence as a shaken, mortified Reggie emerged unhurt.

Soon after the war ended, Reggie joined Westland, the UK helicopter manufacturer as its top consultant on helicopters. He lived out an active retirement, during which period we maintained happy personal contacts, when I visited England fairly frequently. He lived a long and fruitful 93-year life, much of it devoted to aviation, particularly with regard to his pioneering efforts with rotating-wing type aircraft and their successful inventor, Juan de la Cierva.

During this 1945 period I had occasion to meet Mr Teicher, mentioned earlier, in regard to his company supplying specially formed parts for XR-4 and XR-5. This he had continued to do, along with personal contacts. It was on several such

occasions that we struck up a mutually agreeable acquaintanceship over luncheons, and ended up with our confiding in each other; his desire to enter the post-war helicopter market, and mine too, by designing a simplified light helicopter. This resulted in our agreeing to join forces at the appropriate time.

V-E Day, 6 June 1945, was unlike the fateful suddenness of Pearl Harbor on 7 December 1941, a 'ceasefire' in Europe had been expected for several days. However, eventually the victory news was announced over the company speaker system by our General Manager, Benjamin Whelan, in his customary matter-of-fact, flat nasal Yankee tone of voice, directly followed, in the same manner, by 'And na-a-a-ow, back-to-work'. It seemed so devoid of any emotion that I looked around outside my office to observe the effect it had upon others. There were a few scattered voices raised in hurrays, and some raised chatter that was soon reduced to the usual normal murmur. It seemed to me that the general consensus was perhaps: 'So that is finally finished', for only those who had lost loved ones 'over there' could really begin to understand the utter senseless horrors of modern war. Not to mention the German extermination centres.

A week earlier I had been advised, via cable, by his doctor in Cambridge, England, that my father was terminally ill with tuberculosis. He advised that I should come over as soon as possible. Now, with V-E Day declared, I dared think it might just be possible for me to book passage on one of the Sikorsky (Fig. 2) VS-44s of American Export Airlines, fly out of New York La Guardia Airport to Foynes, Ireland, then go by DC-3 to Croydon Airport, London. I immediately contacted Mr Lewis, the American Export representative at Sikorsky, with whom I shared a mutual friendship. He promptly made enquiries at top level, and advised me that if I could get permission from Igor, I could leave on the *Excalibur* out of La Guardia on the 15th. If permission was granted, I immediately had to contact a Mrs Shipley, head of the passport department in Washington, D.C., for an appointment.

Upon explaining the foregoing to Igor and Michael Gluhareff, Igor quietly and without hesitating, said: 'Take whatever time is necessary, Beel'. They both wished me, with a warm handshake, God speed and a safe journey.

The following account of my voyage I am

Fig 143
One of American Export Airlines 'Flying Aces' La Guardia Field.

including because it signalled the ending of transatlantic, commercial passenger-carrying flying boats. It was an adventure that is no longer available to the travelling public.

I shall never forget, just six days after VE Day 1945, boarding the huge, four-engined flying boat *Excalibur* of American Export Transatlantic Airlines, lying majestically at their dock next to La Guardia Airport, New York, at 2.00 pm, and being welcomed aboard, along with the other 28 passengers, by the Steward, and taking our seats for take-off in the comfortably roomy, attractively appointed forward compartments, for best take-off hull balance.

The flying boat taxied out into the East River, and when just under the great suspension bridge there came the dull roar from the four engines as the pilot called for full take-off power. The take-off run, with the water swiftly surging past halfway up the window panes, within inches of my eyes, the water level decreasing as *Excalibur* gained speed and rose up on to her forward hull step the water suddenly disappearing as she was smoothly and

deftly lifted off the surface of the water by long-experienced hands, to the deep humming of the engines.

Soon Long Island and its Sound were well below us, then her port wing gently dipped as she banked and turned northwards towards our first port of call, Botwood Bay, Newfoundland, Nova Scotia. Then levelling-up on course and steadily climbing to the allotted cruising altitude, levelling off and cruising at some 190 mph over the green Connecticut countryside. Soon after we got to our cruising altitude, those whose assigned seats were further aft moved back to them. It was a fine clear day and I was able to spot my home village of Brooklyn. We then followed the east coast, with the lakes and mountains of Maine and New Hampshire spread out inland to our left.

On approaching the southernmost islands of Newfoundland, I was struck by their high, smooth, light golden-brown rock shorelines, almost devoid of safe or sheltered inlets or bays, with only scraggy, weatherbeaten green growth sparsely covering their interiors. It was hardly a spot where one would expect to find human habitation, yet there they were. Tiny clusters of fishermen's huts, just above a cleft in the solid rock shore that permitted a tiny beaching for several boats hauled up above the high-tide mark, reached by long ladders. Such detail being made possible only by the low altitude at which we were cruising.

The island of Newfoundland was also sparsely populated, as was the green vegetation around Botwood Bay, as we experienced our first water alighting, just as smooth as the take-off had been four hours earlier. We docked, stepped ashore shortly after 6.00 pm and relaxed at the hotel before having a leisurely dinner, and reboarding a little after 8.00 pm. I found out that my dinner partners, by chance, were top executives of Standard Oil, apparently wasting no time regarding postwar business.

The final, spectacular take-off from Botwood Bay at about 8.30 pm, for the transatlantic crossing, was longer than our first take-off owing to the much greater fuel load, as was the 'aquarium' effect of the water rushing past the cabin windows as we smoothly lifted off into the twilight.

The huge dull red disc of a sun was just starting to set behind slate-grey mountainous clouds, against a glowing mixture of pale gold and the steely-blue of the northern sky. It cast an eerie light upon the flat, calm, leaden waters below us, dotted with small offshore islands topped with green shrubbery. Among them drifted great, stark, towering white icebergs, their shallow sub-surfaces often reflecting a startling pale shade of green. At the same time, late homeward-bound fishing craft carved arrow-like paths in the grey, calm ocean waters.

Later that evening, I was happily surprised when the Steward brought me the message that the Captain would like me to visit him on the flight deck. This unexpected privilege was evidently prearranged by our mutual friend Mr Lewis. By then, a full moon was shining down upon the scattered white fleecy clouds over which we were skimming, as I was warmly greeted by the Captain and his flight crew. After exchanging friendly comments with the Captain about our mutual friend, and my unexpected pleasure and privilege at visiting his 'bridge', I was given a 'guided tour' of the flight instrumentation. Of course, as we were flying at low altitude, the aircraft was completely unpressurised.

The steady droning of the engines was now more noticeable, and I could look up and backwards through the cabin windows to see the shimmering discs made by the propellers as they pulled us along over the ocean at over 200 mph, due to a friendly jet stream. Below us the patchwork of dark shadows and sparkling ocean slipped by under the bright moonlight. A ship was spotted, and contacted to check our position. I was allowed to stay there for a while, just drinking in the atmosphere of the calm, assuring flight chatter of the Captain and his flight crew in the dark red glow reflected from the instrument panels, and the endless panorama of the black, star-studded sky and cotton-wool cloud carpet accompanied by the steady engine beat.

I had been allocated an upper berth that folded down railway Pullman fashion. The reason given was that these mattresses, not being used during the daytime, were in far better condition than the compartment seat cushions below, and there was also a little window. I slept rather well, only being awakened once when we passed through a bumpy stretch.

By daybreak we were up and having a light repast. Soon landfall was made, and not long afterwards we were alighting at the mouth of the River Shannon, on the south-western coast of Ireland, next to the village of Foynes on its east bank. As the tide was on its rapid ebb, and due to the added flow of the river, it took several tries before a tie-up was made to the mooring buoy, there being no sheltered, non-tidal shore docking. To save weight, all of our meals were eaten ashore. The 'galley's' main purpose being for the single Steward to provide snacks for the passengers and crew.

A motor launch approached us, bringing the Customs Officer to inspect us before we were permitted to land. He was a tall, immaculately uniformed (à la 1914) Irish Army Officer. Customs inspection turned out to consist of a polite, perfunctory 'inspection' of our overnight necessities, plus passports and visas. Awaiting us ashore was a non-rationed breakfast of hot porridge topped with cream, followed by jam and toast, and then the choice of either sausage or bacon with scrambled eggs, plus coffee or tea.

Then we were off by bus to the military-controlled aerodrome at Reannah, on the west side of the River Shannon, via the nearest bridge at the famous old town of Limerick. That journey was made on a country dirt road full of potholes in a bus with exceptionally stiff springs. On the way through beautiful fertile farmland we passed a small encampment of gaily decorated horse-drawn gypsy caravans in the process of being moved to a new grazing ground for the horses; by the women, of course. 'I wish my wife could see this', remarked the person sitting next to me.

As we alighted from the noisy bus on the main street at Limerick, to transfer to the airport bus, the otherwise quiet traffic was dominated by an unfamiliar sound. It turned out to be coming from the hobnailed boots contacting the hard pavement worn by the large number of passing citizens.

The comfortable, smooth airport bus ride to Reannah was in marked contrast as we passed through the rich, well-kept farmlands, and by quaint thatched cottages, well-kept villages and towns. We next boarded a military, paratroop carrying, olive drab, American Douglas DC-3 Dakota, with its two parallel bench seats facing each other, one on each side of an otherwise empty interior. This would take us on our final leg of the journey, to the drab remains of London's famous old Croydon Aerodrome, with its grass-covered landing field with a dip in the middle of it that caused aeroplanes taking off or landing to suddenly disappear then reappear.

Our flight path over the south coast of England at low altitude still vividly revealed the intensive pre-invasion training that took place there, by virtue of the countless vehicle and tank tracks that led down to the beaches. Similarly, as the train passed through the bombed-out areas of London en route to the railway terminus I began to appreciate what it must have been like to have actually witnessed the terrible devastation. I then caught the next train to Cambridge, and to a most heart-warming reunion after a nine-year absence.

The foregoing trip account, was a last minute thought I had of sharing with you an experience, that was only available, at that time, to relatively few 'very important persons' (VIP) during the war. Also, since the long range, trans-ocean, non-pressurized, flying boat era, has long since passed away, so has the comforting thought of a safe emergency water landing, and no need for oxygen masks.

Several years later I saw the beautiful non-pressurised, 100-passenger Saunders-Roe Princess flying boats that had become redundant when transocean intercontinental passenger transport had been taken over by the pressurised, high-flying landplanes. The latter might be described as pressurised aluminium tubes stuffed with humans in a semi-foetal position, jammed up against each other, not only side-by-side but also fore-and-aft. From time-to-time they are fed queer concoctions on tiny trays, and try to manipulate this food from tray to mouth using small plastic utensils. *Quo vadis*?

This period of 1944–45 was one concerned primarily with engineering problems associated with consolidation and production, rather than experimentation. Thus, upon my return, I found that the departmentalisation of the engineering department had become more evident. This was one of the typical results of increasing the personnel required to keep up with the growing number of different aircraft models being, or in the process of being, produced, namely the R-4, R-5 and R-6.

Concurrently, specialisation was also being introduced. For instance, in the stress analysis department there were stress engineers specialising in structural stress analysis relating to fatigue caused by rotational vibration, in order to determine the 'inherent natural frequency' of any proposed supporting structure. Such that the Design Engineers when designing the supporting structures for any of the rotating elements, they would design them so that they did not have a similar inherent natural frequency of vibration to that generated by rotating elements such as the main and tail rotor blades or the power transmission systems.

Similarly, wherever possible, the isolation of any revolving element from its supporting structure was attained by the use of flexible mountings, which is the normal procedure when installing a powerplant. As helicopters increased in size, and the main rotor increased in diameter, its rotational speed decreased, thereby producing, at an ever-lower frequency, greatly increased vibratory loads on its supporting structure. This was somewhat relieved by increasing the number of rotor blades, but in so doing the designer's scope was limited, as rotor blade efficiency can be reduced by the airflow from one rotor blade interfering with the airflow over the following blade, if the blades are spaced too close together. While the helicopter has many components that produce or are subject to vibration, more recent models have attained, through careful pre-production engineering investigation, remarkably smoother operational levels of flight.

Thus every aspect of the various sections that

make up the complete aircraft becomes increasingly more independent of its originator and his overall concept of the complete design. This can carry through to the point where, if it is not carefully controlled, for the 'left hand not knowing what the right hand is doing', so to speak, and the flight control department finds it needs more room to bypass an electrical actuator that retracts the undercarriage, and so on *ad infinitum*.

That is why there soon emerged the Project Manager, in addition to the Project Engineer. Close collaboration between them was required to ensure a smoothly running operation. What actually developed later on has been described as 'design by committee', in which a consensus of inputs from all the top members of the various involved engineering departments (including production) concerned with any part or whole of either an ongoing or new project, had to act as a coherent collaborating team.

I have included the foregoing little treatise to try to bring the reader somewhat closer to visualising and appreciating the task that faced Russian engineers when they began designing the world's largest successful helicopters, such as the Mil Mi-10 (Chap. 7). Let alone a modern aeroplane manufacturing concern which contemplates designing and producing a 300-passenger commercial airliner that cruises at 550 mph at over 30,000 ft, and in addition has to satisfy both government and airline requirements.

Thus for those of us (in the context of the time of this account) with an innovative, conceptual and/or visionary turn of mind, who had enjoyed the great privilege of initiating a concept, the hands-on designing it, and being in complete charge of constructing the experimental model (also overseeing any subsequent changes or pre-production improvements as a result of flight testing), were experiencing the end of a unique era in aviation history.

Ed Katzenberger

It was with a great deal of both pride and pleasure for me, over the years, to learn of the continuing successful contributions Edward Katzenberger made, during his thirty-four years association with Igor Sikorsky. I am, therefore, including this résumé of his actitivies, which I feel, is a recognition that is long overdue.

After two years as a design engineer with the Brewster Aeronautical Co., on Long Island, New York, and as already related, Ed joined the Sikorsky Division engineering staff, in January 1942. Shortly after that he was the first to join me on the XR-5 project, and by November 1942, at my request, he was appointed my Assistant Project Engineer. A most fortunate choice for both me, and the project.

The basic concept of the XR-5 helicopter had already been well established, both mechanical (full scale) and structural, in the form of detailed design layouts. However, Ed was soon contributing significantly helpful suggestions, concerning both conceptual and engineering details, as well as helping in the supervision of the full scale 'mock-up' of the proposed XR-5 design.

Then, as of March 1943 he became Project Engineer, and assumed the complete responsibility of the XR-5 Project. Bringing the Project to a successful conclusion, which culminated in the acquisition of the contract to produce four experimental models.

In 1945 Ed supervised the preliminary design studies for the very first commercial Sikorsky helicopter. Basically, this was a revamped version of the R-5, in which the military R-5 forward control cabin was replaced by a completely new, enlarged four to five-seat cabin, with the pilot and a passenger side-by-side in front, and two or three passengers seated abreast behind, depending on whether its intended usage was civil or military. The civil version was designated S-51, and the Navy HO3S. In fact, the first versions merely had additional sheet metal panels attached to the existing centre-section R-5 firewall panels to fair-in the increased width of the new cabin. This first derivative of the original R-5 was also produced under licence by Westland in the United Kingdom.

In 1946 Ed was appointed Chief of Design, retaining that position (according to Ed) under a variety of titles until 1976. During that 21-year period he directly supervised the design of the numerous successful models, all of which were direct descendants of the first Sikorsky helicopter, the XR-5, to embody all the basic elements that had made the final version of the VS-300, the VS-300H, the truly first successful single-main-rotor helicopter.

The line began in 1946, with the already mentioned S-51 civil version. In 1947 came the US

Fig 144 *S-55*

Army version, and next, in 1948 came a sleeker, more powerful version, the HJS. A 'one-off' experimental model competing against a Piasecki tandem main rotor, which won the competition. The XHJS-1 had a 600 hp. 1340 Pratt & Whitney engine, (R-5,450hp), and an increased main rotor diameter from 48 to 53ft and an up-rated transmission by adding an input gear. The following year 1949, the H-5H became the first production amphibious model.

That same year, 1949, was to become a milestone for Sikorsky helicopters. For, earlier on, Ed had initiated an inspired follow-on version of the XHJS-1, by using its basic components rearranged. Wherein the most distinctive feature was placing the engine forward of the centre section, and the flight control cabin above it, thereby providing a roomy passenger/cargo area. A full scale mock-up was made. Its designated model number was S-55, or H-19.

Ed then presented the proposed S-55 model to the Helicopter Divisional Office of the U.S. Air Force, at Dayton, Ohio. Adding that, if the Air Force would be willing, in place of the last order in the H-5H series, the Sikorsky Division was prepared to supply them with half that number of S-55s (or H-19s) for the same price. They bought it.

The subsequent impact of the S-55 on international, and national usage, both commercial and military, was quite unimagined at the time of its introduction. This version marked the dawn of a new era, for the Sikorsky type single-main-lifting rotor helicopter, by demonstrating its reliability, versatility and adaptability to diverse require-ments. This resulted in an unprecidented demand for both varieties, totaling some 1,700 units, of which, 1,281 were produced in the USA.

The remaining foreign civil and military units of the S-55 were produced under licence in Britain, France and Japan. With Britain producing over 400 Westland 'Whirlwind' versions, of which many were sold throughout Europe. In France they were dubbed the 'Joyeux Elephant', by the manufac-turer SNCASE. Very soon a similar helicopter appeared in Russia.

Between 13 and 31 July 1952 the first crossing of the North Atlantic by helicopter, in this case from east to west, was accomplished by two S-55s in a series of over-water stages from pre-established land bases some 800 miles apart. On 1 September 1953, the Belgian Airline SABENA began the very

first international helicopter airline service, from Brussels to neighbouring cities in Holland and France.

Also within the same time frame as the S-55, yet another best seller appeared. Ed supervised the design of the S-58 which was used by the US Navy for anti-submarine warfare (ASW) detection and as a medium size transport helicopter. In fact, during its many years of service life, the S-58 proved to be the most successful, and cost-effective of any helicopter in its category. With worldwide sales totaling almost 2000 units. Then in the 1970s, twin-turbine powered versions were introduced into the assembly line.

It was also the S-58 that laid the engineering ground-work for the larger more powerful S-61 and its several variants. These were the 30-passenger, land-based S-61L and the amphibious 28-passenger S-61N. Two of the US Air Force Rescue and Recovery versions were the very first to fly the North Atlantic Ocean non-stop, by re-fuelling in flight, 31 May–June 1967.

1949 proved to be a banner year for initiating

Fig 145 *The same model in service with the US Marines, known as the HR25–1*

VS-300 first flown 14 Sept. 1939. Shown – Final VS-300-H July 1943

1942 R-4

1944 R-6

1945 R-5

1946 S-51 1947 HO35-1

1948 HJS

Fig 146

1949 H-5H

1950 S-55 HO45 Hrs H-19

*1951 S-52-2 HO55-1, H-18 First Sikorsky
helicopter with all-metal main rotor blades.*

Fig 147

new design concepts, for it also included the S-56.
The prototype flew successfully on its maiden flight
on 18 December 1953. It was in fact, the largest
helicopter in the world at that time, other than the
Soviet Russian Mil Mi-26.

The first production delivery was to the US
Marine Corps which began in 1956, designated the
HR2S-1, and to the US Army, as the H-37A. In
both cases, as either a heavy duty troop, stretcher,
or cargo carrier, with the ability to load, or off-
load directly through a large, self-contained
ramp-cum-front door. It established category
world records, by flying at 162.67 mph, fully
loaded, and lifting 2,727 lbs to an altitude of
7000 ft.

Ed's next helicopter was the S-62, which used the
same rotor system and power transmission system
as the S-55, but had an amphibious boat hull
similar to that of S-61. The first turbine-powered
Sikorsky helicopter, it was ordered by the US
Coast Guard. (Fig.148) In the 1960s the S-64 flying
crane appeared as the US Army CH-54 Tarhe
heavy-lift helicopter. This was an improved version
of the original prototype S-60, which had been
initiated by Ed, employing components of the S-56,
and had been evaluated by the US Army during
August and September 1959. It saw useful service
during the Vietnam war.

Similarly, Ed supervised the design of the S-65,
which entered service in 1964 as the S-65A,
powered by two General Electric 2,850 shaft-hp
turbines, and incorporating S-64 flight components. Ordered by the US Marine Corps, it was
designated the CH-53A 'Sea Stallion', as their
heavy assault transport. It was followed by more
powerful versions C and D. The E version in 1984,
the 'Super Stallion', incorporated three 3,696
shaft-hp General Electric turbine engines. The then
largest helicopter, other than Russian.

Finally, the last two production models, before
Ed's retirement, in which he continued to make
significant contributions, was first, the two S-70
versions. The US Army combat, assault version,
the UH-60A 'Blackhawk', capable of carrying up
to 10,000 lbs of external stores, and the US Navy
version, the SH-60B 'Seahawk' version, for both
anti-ship and submarine surveillance, and also
targeting.

A major break-through in helicopter main rotor
design was successfully accomplished when Ed was
able to put through the crucial decision to fabricate

Fig 148   *S-62*

Fig 149   *S-60 First Sikorsky flying crane*

Fig 150
The XH-59A/S-69 Advanced Blade Concept

Fig 150A   *S-76*

the Blackhawk rotor blades of a special light-weight, high-strength metal called titanium, in spite of its significant extra cost.

During the transitional period, prior to his retirement in 1976, Ed joined the model S-76 engineering team as overall supervisor of its design. Powered with twin Allison turbines, delivering 650 shaft-hp each, this 12-passenger version, with its exceptionally sleek lines included a fully retracting

undercarriage. It was the Sikorsky Division's formal, successful entry into the highly competative, well established, commercial-corporate helicopter market.

The foregoing resumée would not be complete without the following review of Ed's equally important engineering programmes. They started in the early 1950s, with a series of studies of numerous multi-rotor configurations, in order to

Fig 151

Fig 152

compare them with the Sikorsky type single-main-rotor-type helicopter. They included tandem rotor, sesqui-tandem, syncropter (two closely, lateraly spaced intermeshing rotors, having their driving shafts tilted outwards V fashion) and co-axial rotors, one above the other.

The net result clearly indicated the soundness of the decision to continue to concentrate on the single-main-rotor type configuration.

In the mid-fifties Ed established operations and systems analyses to improve the matching of engineering efforts with customer requirements, subsequently developing helicopter design principles; establishing methods of analysis; instituting new engineering techniques. Initiating and supervising major research programmes, aimed at improving and extending the technical basis of helicopter engineering. With the result that, Corporate Funded Research and Development, as well as, outside contracted Research and Development, were both substantially extended.

During the latter part of this period he initiated a complete study to assess a variety of approaches to the 'convertiplane', in which the lifting rotor(s) is used for take-off and landing, then stopped to act as a fixed lifting wing. He finally concentrated on the stopped/stowed-rotor configuration, and carried this concept through the windtunnel testing of scale models including both single-bladed and two-bladed configurations. This effort was not pursued any further owing to lack of interest by the Government. On the other hand, the stiff-bladed, hingeless, coaxial rotor system, also referred to as the Advancing Blade Concept (ABC), was carried through successfully to prototype construction and flight testing. During the transition period to retirement in 1976, Ed joined the S-76 project, as over-all design supervisor.

Such was Edward Katzenberger's contribution to Igor Sikorsky's equally remarkable lifelong dream of producing a 'substantial, reliable, controllable, direct-lifting, single-main-rotor-type heelicopter'.

Of course, the foregoing brief outline can in no way convey to the reader the great amount of patience and dedication required to arrive at a desired goal, unless it is in familiar territory, not to mention all the others involved who made this legacy possible.

Not long after my departure from Sikorsky the first true offshore helicopter rescue mission was successfully carried out by Jimmie Viner, using an R-5 specially equipped with a rescue hoist, on Friday 30 November 1945 (Figs 151 & 152). A barge broke loose and drifted on to a reef off Fairfield, Connecticut, during a severe storm. The system used had been developed by Cdr Frank Erickson of the US Coast Guard, Long Island, NY, and there was no room for anyone other than the hoist operator in the helicopter's cabin. Also, the rescued person had no more than a simple harness to hold him, and it required considerable courage on his part to be towed through the stormy winds to safety, gallantly clutching the hoisting cable. Fortunately all those aboard were safely airlifted ashore.

Soon after the war's end, Cdr Frank Erickson and his Helicopter Rescue Command were transferred from Long Island, to Elizabeth City, North Carolina, close to Albemarle Sound, with access to the Atlantic Ocean via the Barrier Islands, upon one of which is situated Kitty Hawk, where the famous first successful powered aeroplane flights by the Wright brothers took place in 1903.

George 'Red' Lubben was still with Frank, and they had been experimenting with a device invented by Frank and constructed by Red that would automatically maintain a longitudinal steadying control and/or restore a helicopter to horizontal level flight if it was suddenly disturbed from its normal desired flight path.

Frank had asked me to visit him the next time I was in the Washington, D.C. area, so that he could demonstrate his device to me. It was indeed a very simple and ingenious mechanism, consisting of a small inverted winglet that was rigidly attached, at a predetermined distance rearwards, on to the rear of the cyclic, main rotor blade pitch control swashplate, below the main rotor hub. If the helicopter suddenly pitched forwards and downwards into a nosedive, the negative lift-force on the winglet as the airspeed increased was sufficient to tilt the swashplate backwards. This automatically caused the main rotor gradually to tilt backwards and bring the helicopter smoothly out of the nosedive, restoring horizontal level flight.

I was sitting up front in an R-5 as Frank put her into a power-on, hands-off nosedive. I was gazing directly down at a rapidly approaching assortment of anchored and/or moving surface craft, then gently, as if by an unseen hand, disaster was avoided as we gradually and smoothly pulled out of the nosedive, and I turned round to catch Frank's reassuring smile. He then proceeded to repeat the same manoeuvre at an even lower altitude to make sure I was properly impressed with the safety of his device. Later, when Frank retired, he joined the Brantly Helicopter Company, and his device was incorporated in their helicopter.

* * *

It was not long after I had returned from that last visit that I was privileged to have with my father, having first discussed with Michael Buivid and Boris Labensky the reasons for my final departure, that I made known to Igor and Michael Gluhareff my decision to try my hand at creating a small

(hopefully popular) helicopter based on the important knowledge I had gained during my never-to-be-forgotten close association with them. I would be joining the Teicher Manufacturing Company on Long Island to design and produce the Teicher-Hunt two-place helicopter. Mr Teicher having produced first-class formed sheet metal parts for both the R-4 and R-5 models, was thus not unknown to them.

Both Igor and Michael were supportive of my decision, and warmly wished me success, hoping I would continue to keep in touch with them. It was not long before I was privileged to be joined by three of the R-5 engineers, Jerome Friedenberg, Bernard Engel and Chester Mayerson, who made

Taken 11 October 1972, during visit by members of the Young Russian Club, of greater N.Y. This is the last photo to be taken of Igor, before he died, fifteen days later, on the 26 October 1972.

a splendid, enthusiastic and loyal team. Their combined knowledge of the workings of the helicopter made it possible to produce all the necessary detailed design drawings as well as the strength and performance calculations.

The Three Chauffeurs

Igor had a parable he liked to tell, on occasion, that emphasised what he considered to be a necessary human asset.

It was about three chauffeurs who had answered an advertisement, and had individually presented themselves to their prospective employer. Each candidate was told en route where to go, which was to a well-known coastal cliff. He was then to drive to the edge of the cliff so that the employer could have a good view of the shoreline.

The first candidate drove up quickly to the very edge of the cliff. The second one drove up carefully, but too far away from the edge of the cliff, and suggested that the employer might like to walk over, as near to the cliff's edge as he desired, for a better view of the shoreline. The third driver drove slowly towards the edge, stopping at a comfortable distance from it and so placing the car so as to afford a good view of the shoreline. So he hired the third chauffeur, because of his *good judgement.*

One of the most lasting and endearing characteristics I have of Igor Sikorsky, other than his loyalty towards those who had helped him, including myself, was his remarkable resilience in the face of tremendous odds. Like the sudden ending nationally and internationally of the Sikorsky flying-boat era, especially his amphibious creations as already related, resulted in his sudden demotion from his front office as Chance-Vought moved in. Yet, undaunted, he started for the third time in his remarkable career 'back at square one', with the firm conviction that the great future potential of direct-lift aircraft had still to be proven. Furthermore, he believed that the helicopter with but a single main lifting rotor, cast aside by all the other pioneers as being impracticable was actually the correct answer, even though its inherent problems had still to be solved.

His refusal never to give up trying. His self-control, and his quiet, keen sense of humour. That calm, soft, educated voice, with such a buoyant, emphatic and precise way of expressing his thoughts. Every now and again, when I am reminded, I can still hear him saying: 'Perhaps gentlemen, vot vee need heer is a —. Furdermore . . .'

Index

The index is arranged alphabetically on a word-by-word basis, except for the entries under William Hunt and Igor Sikorsky, which are in chronological order. Page numbers in italics refer to subjects in illustrations.